Private International Law in Taiwan

Private International Law in Taiwan

Rong-Chwan Chen

This book was originally published as a monograph in the International Encyclopaedia of Laws/Private International Law.

Wolters Kluwer

Published by:
Kluwer Law International B.V.
PO Box 316
2400 AH Alphen aan den Rijn
The Netherlands
E-mail: international-sales@wolterskluwer.com
Website: lrus.wolterskluwer.com

Sold and distributed by:
Wolters Kluwer Legal & Regulatory U.S.
7201 McKinney Circle
Frederick, MD 21704
United States of America
E-mail: customer.service@wolterskluwer.com

ISBN 978-94-035-4222-5

e-Book: ISBN 978-94-035-4223-2
web-PDF: ISBN 978-94-035-4224-9

The Author

Rong-Chwan Chen is an associate member of the International Academy of Comparative Law, University Distinguished Professor of Law at National Taipei University (Taiwan), Vice President of Taiwan Society of Private International Law, and Secretary General of Taiwan Jurist Association. He got a PhD degree in Law from National Cheng-Chi University and was granted Fulbright Fellowship as a senior scholar in 1997. He is the author of about 200 academic articles and several books published in Chinese on civil law and private international law, such as *Selected Essays on Private International Law* (Wu-nan 1998), *Private International Law in Practice: Analytical Study on Civil Cases with Foreign Elements* (Wu-nan 2015), and *Liu and Chen on Private International Law* 6th edn. (San-min 2018). He contributed a lot in several English books on comparative private international law, including *Private International Law in Mainland China, Taiwan and Europe* (Mohr Siebeck 2014), *Encyclopedia of Private International Law* (Edward Elgar 2017) and *Optional Choice of Court Agreements in Private International Law* (Springer 2020). He was a commissioner of Taiwan's Fair Trade Commission, the head of Faculty of Law at National Taipei University, Professor of Law at Soochow University, Visiting Professor at City University of Hong Kong, Macau University and several prestigious universities in China. He was invited to stay at Harvard Law School, Max Planck Institute for Comparative and International Private Law, University of Maryland School of Law. He is a leading scholar who drafted the provisions and explanatory comments of the Choice-of-law Act 2010 and whose opinions are often sought by thc courts and government.

The Author

Table of Contents

List of Abbreviations

Act for Implementing Interpretation 748	Act for Implementation of J.Y. Interpretation No. 748 (Si-Fa-Yuan Shi-Zi Di Qi-Si-Ba-Hao Jie-Shi Shi-Xing Fa, 司法院釋字第七四八號解釋施行法), adopted in 2019.
Act Governing Relations with Hong Kong and Macau	Xiang-Gang Ao-Men Guan-Xi Tiao-Li (香港澳門關係條例), adopted in 1997 and last revised in 2017.
Act on Labour Matters	Lao-Dong-Shi-Jian-Fa (勞動事件法, aka Labour Incident Act), adopted in 2018.
Act on Liquidation of Consumers' Debts	Xiao-Fei-Zhe Zhai-Wu Qing-Li Tiao-Li (消費者債務清理條例), adopted in 2007 and last revised 2018.
Act on Non-contentious Matters	Fei-Song Shi-Jian Fa (非訟事件法), adopted in 1964 and last revised in 2018.
Act on Supporting Foreign Courts on Consigned Cases	Wai-Guo Fa-Yuan Wei-Tuo Shi-Jian Xie-Zhu Fa (外國法院委託事件協助法), adopted in 1963.
Act on the Taiwan Area and the Mainland Area	The Act on Relations between the People of the Taiwan Area and the Mainland Area (Tai-Wan Di-Qu Yu Da-Lu Di-Qu Ren-Min Guan-Xi Tiao-Li, 臺灣地區與大陸地區人民關係條例), adopted in 1992 and last revised in 2019.
AFM	The Act on Family Matters (Jia-Shi Shi-Jian Fa, 家事事件法), adopted in 2012 and last revised in 2019.
Arbitration Act	Zhong-Cai Fa (仲裁法), adopted in 1998 to replace the Commercial Arbitration Act of 1961, last revised in 2015.
Art.	Article
Assisted Reproduction Act	Ren-Gong Sheng-Zhi Fa (人工生殖法), adopted in 2007 and last revised in 2018.

List of Abbreviations

Banking Act	Yin-Hang Fa (銀行法), adopted in 1930 and last revised in 2019.
Bankruptcy Act	Po-Chan-Fa (破產法), adopted in 1935 and last revised in 2018.
Business Mergers and Acquisitions Act	Qi-Ye Bing-Gou Fa (企業併購法), adopted in 2002 and last revised in 2015.
CC	Taiwan's Civil Code (Min-Fa, 民法), adopted in 1930 and last revised in 2021.
CCP	The Code of Civil Procedure (Min-Shi Su-Song Fa,民事訴訟法), adopted in 1930 and last revised in 2021.
Choice-of-law Act 1953	The Act Governing the Choice of Law in Civil Matters Involving with Foreign Elements (She-Wai Min-Shi Fa-Lyu Shi-Yong Fa, 涉外民事法律適用法), adopted in 1953.
Choice-of-law Act 2010	The Act Governing the Choice of Law in Civil Matters Involving with Foreign Elements (She-Wai Min-Shi Fa-Lyu Shi-Yong Fa, 涉外民事法律適用法), revised in 2010.
Commercial Arbitration Act	Shang-Wu Zhong-Cai Tiao-Li (商務仲裁條例), adopted in 1961 and replaced by the Arbitration Act in 1998.
Company Act	Gong-Si Fa (公司法), adopted in 1929 and last revised in 2018.
Commercial Case Adjudication Act	Shang-Ye Shi-Jian Shen-Li Fa (商業事件審理法), adopted in 2020 and coming into effect from July 1st 2021.
Compulsory Enforcement Act	Qiang-Zhi Zhi-Xing Fa (強制執行法), adopted in 1940 and last revised in 2019.
Conflicts Rule	The Rule on Conflict of Laws
Consumer Protection Act	Xiao-Fei-Zhe Bao-Hu Fa (消費者保護法), adopted in 1994 and last revised in 2015.
Copyright Act	Zhu-Zuo-Quan Fa (著作權法), adopted in 1928 and last revised in 2019.
Cultural Heritage Preservation Act	Wen-Hua Zi-Chan Bao-Cun Fa (文化資產保存法), adopted in 1982 and last revised in 2016.
Employment Service Act	Jiu-Ye Fu-Wu Fa (就業服務法), adopted in 1992 and last revised in 2018.

Enforcement Act of the CCP	The Enforcement Act of the Code of Civil Procedure (Min-Shi Su-Song Fa Shi-Xing Fa, 民事訴訟法施行法), adopted in 1932 and last revised in 2018.
Enforcement Act of the Part of General Principles of the Civil Code	Min-Fa Zong-Ze Shi-Xing Fa (民法總則施行法), adopted in 1929 and last revised in 2021.
Fair Trade Act	Gong-Ping Jiao-Yi Fa (公平交易法), adopted in 1991 and last revised in 2017.
Insurance Act	Bao-Xian Fa (保險法), adopted in 1929 and last revised in 2021.
Integrated Circuit Layout Protection Act	Ji-Ti Dian-Lu Bu-Ju Bao-Hu Fa (積體電路電路布局保護法), adopted in 1995 and last revised in 2002.
Intellectual Property and Commercial Court Organization Act	Zhi-Hui Cai-Chan Ji Shang-Ye Fa-Yuan Zu-Zhi Fa (智慧財產及商業法院組織法), adopted in 2007 as the Intellectual Property Court Organization Act (Zhi-Hui Cai-Chan Fa-Yuan Zu-Zhi Fa, 智慧財產法院組織法), last revised and changed to the current name in 2020.
Intellectual Property Case Adjudication Act	Zhi-Hui Cai-ChanAn-Jian Shen-Li Fa (智慧財產案件審理法), adopted in 2007 and last revised in 2014.
IP	Intellectual Property
Labour Standards Act	Lao-Dong Ji-Zhun Fa (勞動基準法), adopted in 1984 and last revised in 2020.
Maritime Act	Hai-Shang-Fa (海商法), adopted in 1929 and last revised in 2009.
Name Act	Xing-Ming Tiao-Li (姓名條例), adopted in 1953 and last revised in 2015.
Negotiable Instruments Act	Piao-Ju Fa (票據法), adopted in 1929 and last revised in 1987.
Organization Act of the National Immigration Agency, Ministry of the Interior	Nei-Zheng-Bu Yi-Min-Shu Zu-Zhi Fa (內政部移民署組織法), adopted in 2005 and last revised in 2013
para.	paragraph
Patent Act	Zhuan-Li Fa (專利法), adopted in 1944 and last revised in 2019.
PIL	Private International Law

List of Abbreviations

PRC	The People's Republic of China (China), Zhong-Hua Ren-Min Gong-He-Guo (中華人民共和國)
Procedural Rules for Courts in Handling Family Matters	Jia-Shi-Shi-Jian-Shen-Li-Xi-Ze (家事事件審理細則), adopted in 2012 and last revised in 2020.
Regulation Governing the Detention of the Aliens	Wai-Guo-Ren Shou-Rong Guan-Li Gui-Ze, (外國人收容管理規則), promulgated in 2000 and last revised in 2015.
Regulations Governing the Detention of the People of the Mainland China Area and the Residents of Hong Kong and Macau	Da-Lu Di-Qu Ji Xiang-Gang Ao-Men Ju-Min Shou-Rong Guan-Li Ban-Fa (大陸地區人民及香港澳門居民收容管理辦法), adopted in 2000 and last revised in 2017.
Regulations Governing the Privileges and Immunities of the United Nations Missions and Their Personnel in the Republic of China	Lian-He-Guo Ge Zu-Zhi Ji Ren-Yuan Zai-Hua Ying-Xiang-Shou Zhi Te-Quan Ji Huo-Mian Ban-Fa (聯合國各組織及人員在華應享受之特權及豁免辦法), adopted in 1947.
ROC Constitution	Constitution of the Republic of China, Zhong-Hua Min-Guo Xian-Fa (中華民國憲法), adopted on 25 December 1946.
ROC	The Republic of China (Taiwan), Zhong-Hua Min-Guo (中華民國)
Statute Governing the Privileges and Immunities of Foreign Offices and their Personnel in the Republic of China	Zhu-Hua Wai-Guo Ji-Gou Ji Qi Ren-Yuan Te-Quan Ji Huo-Mian Tiao-Li (駐華外國機構及其人員特權暨豁免條例), adopted in 1982 and last revised in 1997.
Statute on Application of Laws	Fa-Lyu Shi-Yong Tiao-Li (法律適用條例), adopted in 1918.
Trade Secrets Act	Ying-Ye Mi-Mi Fa (營業秘密法), adopted in 1996 and last revised in 2020.
Trademark Act	Shang-Biao Fa (商標法), adopted in 1930 and last revised in 2016.
Trust Act	Xin-Tuo Fa (信託法), adopted in 1996 and last revised in 2009.
UN	The United Nations

General Introduction

§1. Historical Development

1. Taiwan bears the 'Republic of China' (the ROC) as its official name.[1] The ROC was established by the Constitution of the ROC and its Amendments. China was divided because of the civil war in the 1940s. The Chinese Communist Party abolished all the laws promulgated by the Nationalist government after it established the People's Republic of China (the PRC) on 1 October 1949.[2]

2. From then on, the ROC coexists with the PRC, while the territory that the ROC effectively controls has been limited to the 'Taiwan region' and the application of the ROC's laws is restricted to this jurisdiction. The original ROC state formed by the Constitution is now composed of four different legal territories. The 'original' ROC legal system was inherited and revised by its government on Taiwan. Mainland China, Hong Kong and Macau have, respectively, developed different legal systems for themselves.

3. The ROC promulgated in 1918 its first code of conflicts rules, the 'Statute on Application of Laws'.[3] Its main objective was to show the government's determination to recover the ROC's jurisdiction, which had been excluded by the unequal treaties signed by its predecessor, rather than to demonstrate its readiness to apply

1. In order to introduce and analyse the legislation and judicial practice of the ROC on Taiwan, this monograph utilizes geographical terms and political terms interchangeably. 'Taiwan', 'Mainland China', 'Hong Kong' and 'Macau' refer to the separate geographical regions that have been defined in the related statutes of the ROC. The ROC refers to the government that was established in 1912 by Dr Sun Yat-Sen and has been governing Taiwan effectively since 1949. Taiwan or the ROC currently has jurisdiction over the main island of Taiwan, Penghu, Kinmen and Matsu and the related island groups.
2. Art. 17 of the Common Programme of the People's Political Consultative Conference of China, adopted on 29 Sep. 1949 at the First People's Political Consultative Conference of China, calls for abolishing all laws and regulations and the whole judicial system established by the ROC (Nationalist) government. *See* Henry R. Zheng, *China's Civil and Commercial Law* 1, n. 1 (Lexis Pub 1988).
3. 'Statute on Application of Laws' (Fa-Lyu Shi-Yong Tiao-Li, 法律適用條例) was put into effect on 5 August 1918 when Taiwan was ruled by Japan. Its 26 articles were divided into six chapters: General Rules, The Disposing Capacity of Persons, Family Relations, Succession, Property Rights, and The Formality of Juridical Acts. For texts in German and French, *see* Aleksandr N. Makarov, *Quellen des internationalen Privatrechts*, Band I: Gesetzestexte, 10. China (2nd ed., Walter de Gruyter 1953).

foreign laws.[4] Needless to say, the legal effect of the statute was symbolic. The ROC enacted in 1953 the 'Act Governing the Choice of Law in Civil Matters Involving Foreign Elements'[5] (the 'Choice-of-law Act 1953') to replace the Statute of 1918.[6] This Act established the foundation for the new ROC to deal with the legal problems arising from international trade, multinational marriage, migrant workers, foreign tourists, etc.

4. In order to reflect the new trends in private international law in foreign countries and international conventions, a committee charged with revising the Choice-of-law Act 1953 was established in the Judicial Yuan in 1998. The proposed draft was passed by the legislature on 30 April 2010 and promulgated by the President on 26 May 2010.[7] According to its Article 63, the new Choice-of-law Act entered into force and replaced the Choice-of-law Act 1953 on 26 May 2011 (the 'Choice-of-law Act 2010').[8]

5. In addition to private international law, the legislation and the judicial practice in the area of a private interregional law are also noteworthy. They reflect the historical development of Taiwan's interaction with the outside world and its unique consideration of the relations across the Taiwan Strait. The legislative distinction between a foreign country and a sister region or area, namely Mainland China, Hong Kong or Macau, is demanded by the Constitution of the ROC.[9]

6. In terms of conflict of laws, an international conflicts problem involves elements of foreign countries (foreign elements), and the law applicable to it shall be decided according to private international law, mainly the Choice-of-law Act. An interregional conflicts problem involves elements of sister areas or regions within an un-unified and divided country rather than a foreign country. The law applicable

---

4. Herbert H.P. Ma, *General Part of Private International Law* (國際私法總論) 11 (11th ed., Taipei 1983).
5. The Act Governing the Choice of Law in Civil Matters Involving with Foreign Elements (She-Wai Min-Shi Fa-Lyu Shi-Yong Fa, 涉外民事法律適用法) was adopted in 1953 and last revised in 2010.
6. Promulgated on 6 June 1953, the Act is composed of thirty-one articles without grouping into chapters. For its text in German, *see* Aleksandr N. Makarov, *Quellen des internationalen Privatrechts* 272 et seq. (3d ed., Mohr 1978). For a comprehensive introduction of this Act, see Herbert H.P. Ma, *Private International Law of the Republic of China: Past, Present and Future*, in *Private Law in the International Arena - Liber Amicorum Kurt Siehr*, 413 *et seq.* (Jürgen Basedow et al. eds, T.M.C. Asser 2000).
7. For its texts in English, *see* Rong-Chwan Chen, *Taiwanese PIL Act 2010 (Translation)*, in *Private International Law in Mainland China, Taiwan and Europe* 453–465 (Jürgen Basedow & Knut B. Pissler eds, Mohr Siebeck 2014); Rong-Chwan Chen, *Taiwan (National Report)*, in 4 *Encyclopedia of Private International Law* 2559–2569 (Jürgen Basedow et al. eds, Edward Elgar 2017). *See also* the annex of this monograph.
8. Art. 63 of the Choice-of-law Act 2010 provides: 'This Revised Act enters into force one year after the date of its promulgation.'
9. In Judicial Yuan's Interpretation 328 of 1993, the Grand Justices declined to decide the boundaries of the national territory of the ROC after it was divided. The foundation was that 'the delimitation of national territory according to its history is a significant political question and thus it is beyond the reach of judicial review.' In Judicial Yuan's Interpretation 329 of 1993, it was mentioned that 'agreements concluded between Taiwan and the Mainland China are not international agreements.'

to such conflicts shall be decided in accordance with the relevant provisions of the Act on Relations between the People of the Taiwan Area and the Mainland Area of 1992 (hereinafter 'Act on Taiwan Area and the Mainland Area')[10] and the Act Governing Relations with Hong Kong and Macau of 1997.[11] This design reflects the fact that 'private Interregional law' or 'quasi private international law' coexists with 'private international law' in the present Taiwanese legal system.[12]

7. For cases which involve elements of the Mainland China, the applicable law shall be decided in accordance with the Act on Taiwan Area and the Mainland Area, of which Chapter 3 (Articles 41–74) includes rules for conflict of laws between the Taiwan Area and the Mainland Area. For cases which involve elements of Hong Kong or Macau, the Act Governing Relations with Hong Kong and Macau provides that the Choice-of-law Act shall apply *mutatis mutandis* to any question pertaining to conflict of laws between Taiwan and Hong Kong or Macau (Article 38).[13]

8. This book discusses mainly the problems of private international law, while the questions of private interregional law will only be touched upon when their comparison is necessary.

§2. International and Supranational Legal Framework

9. Due to its unique status in the international arena, Taiwan has hardly any participating role in the process of formulating international or supranational rules on private international law. Taiwan is not bound by any current system of supranational law. The multilateral international legal framework established by international organizations is as far as it cannot be directly applied by the Taiwanese courts. The bilateral international legal framework between Taiwan and a few states is binding due to the supremacy of international law over domestic legislation. The most remarkable example is the Treaty of Friendship, Commerce and Navigation between the United States of America and the Republic of China.[14] Although the United States diplomatically de-recognized the Republic of China in 1979, such treaty

10. The Act on Relations between the People of the Taiwan Area and the Mainland Area (Tai-Wan Di-Qu Yu Da-Lu Di-Qu Ren-Min Guan-Xi Tiao-Li, 臺灣地區與大陸地區人民關係條例) was adopted in 1992 and last revised in 2019.
11. The Act Governing Relations with Hong Kong and Macau (Xiang-Gang Ao-Men Guan-Xi Tiao-Li, 香港澳門關係條例) was adopted in 1997 and last revised in 2017.
12. Tieh-Cheng Liu & Rong-Chwan Chen, *Liu and Chen on Private International Law* (劉鐵錚、陳榮傳，國際私法論) 703v704 (6th ed., San-Min 2018); Rong-Chwan Chen, *A Boat on A Troubled Strait: The Interregional Private Law of the Republic of China on Taiwan*, 16 Wisconsin International Law Journal 559 (1998).
13. Rong-Chwan Chen, *The Current Situation and Practice of the Conflict of Laws across the Taiwan Straits* (兩岸法律衝突的現況與實務), 15 *et seq*. (Sharing 2003).
14. Treaty of Friendship, Commerce and Navigation, Nov. 4, 1946, U.S.-China (R.O.C.), 63 Stat. 1299. It was signed on November 4, 1946, and became effective on November 30, 1948.

remains in force till now on the ground that its Congress passed Taiwan Relations Act later on 15 April 1979, and stated it approves the continuation in force of such a treaty.[15]

§3. Nature and Scope

10. Private international law comes into play whenever domestic courts are faced with a civil matter that contains a foreign element. It is a separate and distinct unit in the Taiwanese legal system to deal with the questions that do not arise in purely domestic cases. The questions are grouped into three major categories, namely: (a) jurisdiction of the Taiwanese court, (b) the choice of law, and (c) recognition and enforcement of foreign judgments or arbitral awards.

11. Category (a) concerns the conditions under which a Taiwanese court is competent to exercise international jurisdiction over such a litigation or case. Category (b) regards the criteria to determine for each civil legal relationship at issue a particular legal system by reference. It is the domestic law or a foreign law to which is referred that can be relied on to determine the rights and duties of the parties. Category (c) includes the specifications by which a foreign judgment or arbitral award can be recognized as decisive of the question in dispute and can be enforced by a Taiwanese court. Categories (a) and (b) arise in a litigation or case initiated in the Taiwanese court for a judgment to ascertain the rights and duties of the parties. If such a court decides that it possesses jurisdiction, then a further question, as to the choice of law, must be considered; i.e., which system of law, Taiwanese or foreign, must govern the case? In each case the Taiwanese court shall determine what legal system governs the case in pursuance with Taiwan's private international law.

12. Rather than a specific topic of private law, private international law is combined of rules and principles that relate to the three questions above. It touches almost every branch of private law but only solves such questions that the domestic rules applicable to purely domestic cases may not be applicable due to the effects of foreign elements. The rules on jurisdiction and on recognition and enforcement of foreign judgments or arbitral awards need to be clearly formulated so that the domestic courts can follow and make definite decisions. The rules on choice of law provides only which legal system or law, Taiwanese or foreign, shall govern the legal relationship in question and says no more on the substantive effects when the applicable law applies.

13. Although private international law is a separate unity in Taiwanese law, its nature is diversified since the relevant rules deal with different types of questions.

15. 'For all purposes, including actions in any court in the United States, the Congress approves the continuation in force of all treaties and other international agreements, including multilateral conventions, entered into by the United States and the governing authorities on Taiwan recognized by the United States as the Republic of China prior to January 1, 1979, and in force between them on December 31, 1978, unless and until terminated in accordance with law.' Taiwan Relations Act, § 4(c), 22 U.S.C.A. § 3303(c); 17 U.S.C.A. § 104(b)(1).

The nature of rules on jurisdiction and rules for recognition and enforcement of foreign judgments is no doubt procedural. The rules for choosing the governing law are empowering the courts to apply domestic law or a foreign law to determine the substantive rights and duties of the parties. Such rules are no doubt only 'indirect' in resolving the parties' dispute since it is resolved directly by applying the applicable domestic or foreign law.

§4. Characteristics of National Private International Law (PIL)

14. The Choice-of-law Act 1953 follows the pattern set by the 1918 Statute and adopts the legislative mode of multilateral or 'all-sided' conflicts rules, which treat domestic and foreign laws with equal applicability. It was aimed at providing a modern code of private international law that fit the developing needs of the ROC (Taiwan) at that time. The description of the *lex fori* was silently changed from 'the law of China' in the 1918 Statute to 'the law of the ROC' in the Choice-of-law Act 1953.

15. As a unique country shaped by a remarkable history, the ROC (Taiwan) features a novel approach to conflict of laws codifications. The judicial practice of the Taiwanese courts with regard to the Choice-of-law Act 1953 was a reflection of its citizens' activities with foreign elements. It is beyond doubt that the provisions of the Choice-of-law Act 1953 played an important role in supporting the ties of international trade, cross-border tourism and transnational marriage. The disputes arising from such activities between the parties from various countries are resolved on the basis of such Act.

16. The spirit of international uniformity is widespread but courts cannot achieve the goal of international uniformity simply by following the rules provided in the Choice-of-law Act 1953. Mere judicial interpretation of the current provisions cannot narrow the gap between the domestic and international uniformity the public has come to expect. Given the fact that it is not a member of the influential conventions on private international law, the rules adopted in such conventions have very little direct influence on the development of the ROC's conflicts rules. Judicial practice and academic comments have continuously formed the ground on which Taiwan's private international law stands and develops. However, due to the tradition of the civil law system, the gap between the Choice-of-law Act 1953 and the international trend remained too great to be accepted. It was therefore necessary to launch a legislative reform to respond to the call from the public.[16]

---

16. In October 1998, the 'Committee for Revising the Act Governing the Choice of Law in Civil Matters Involving Foreign Elements' was organized as a preparatory legislative body within the Judicial Yuan. Five years later, the Committee announced a draft consisting of 60 articles on the Judicial Yuan's website. Although not yet finalized, the draft conveyed some fundamental ideas that are still guiding the legislative work. *See* Rong-Chwan Chen, *New Directions of Private International Law: A Bird View of the Revising Draft for the Act Governing the Choice of Law in Civil Matters Involving Foreign Elements*, 57 Taiwan Law Journal (台灣本土法學雜誌) 207 (2004).

17. The enactment of the Choice-of-law Act 2010 was a legislative response which incorporates the ideas and goals of international uniformity. In addition to the new policies embodied in the different provisions, the preparers kept some strategic plans in mind during the legislative process. They considered, *inter alia*, the social needs, practical predictability, hierarchical balance and legislative reality. The provisions were examined and amended to reflect the modern legal system of private international law. The renovated Choice-of-law Act transformed from its original 31-article version into a new 63-article statute. The provisions are, furthermore, grouped into 8 chapters, namely, Chapter 1 General Principles[17], Chapter 2 The Subject of Rights[18], Chapter 3 Formal Requisites of Juridical Acts; Agency[19], Chapter 4 Obligations[20], Chapter 5 Rights over Things ('Rights *in Rem*')[21], Chapter 6 Domestic Relations[22], Chapter 7 Succession[23] and Chapter 8 Final Provisions[24].

18. Some conflicts rules were added for legal relationships that had developed significantly since 1953. Products liability, torts via media, statutes of limitation, intellectual property rights and the right to securities held by an intermediary are just some of them. The revolution of conflicts theory has influenced basic thoughts on reforming the structure and changing the essence of conflicts rules for torts and contracts. Some erroneous designs in connecting factors, such as the factors to determine the law applicable to the internal affairs of a legal person, spousal relationships and maintenance obligations, were corrected in the revised provisions to meet the needs of 'conflicts justice.'[25] Some rules were added to correct the erroneous judicial interpretation of existing conflicts rules. Bills of lading and the formal requirements of a last will both fall into this group.

19. Many provisions in the Choice-of-law Act 1953 were revised to cope with the international trends in private international law.[26] Besides the rules for contracts and torts, the 'closest connection' doctrine was widely adopted in the Choice-of-law Act 2010 to enhance flexibility and justice in individual cases of marriage, engagement to marry, divorce and the matrimonial property regime.[27]

---

17. Choice-of-law Act 2010, Arts 1–8.
18. Choice-of-law Act 2010, Arts 9–14.
19. Choice-of-law Act 2010, Arts 15–19.
20. Choice-of-law Act 2010, Arts 20–37.
21. Choice-of-law Act 2010, Arts 38–44.
22. Choice-of-law Act 2010, Arts 45–57.
23. Choice-of-law Act 2010, Arts 58–61.
24. Choice-of-law Act 2010, Arts 62–63.
25. Rong-Chwan Chen, *The New Way of Thinking for Codification of Private International Law: The Substantive Justice in Conflicts Rules*, 89 Taiwan Law Review (月旦法學雜誌) 50–61 (October 2002).
26. *See* Rong-Chwan Chen, *The Recent Development of Private International Law in Taiwan*, in *Codification in East Asia* 235–245 (Wen-Yeu Wang ed., Springer 2014).
27. Choice-of-law Act 2010, Arts 45, 47, 48 & 50.

§5. Domestic Authorities Involved, Interpretation and Application of PIL

20. The Choice-of-law Act applies to all civil matters involving foreign elements.[28] The 'civil matters' refer to commercial, family and other civil matters which are neither criminal nor administrative in nature. No courts are nowadays specifically responsible for such matters involving foreign elements. Rather, all courts and non-judicial authorities such as public notaries, commercial and property registrars, and authorities in charge of civil registries, are under a duty to apply and interpret the Choice-of-law Act *ex officio*. The applicable law is to be ascertained accordingly. However, all disputes on the application of the Choice-of-law Act are decided by the courts.

28. Choice-of-law Act 2010, Art. 1.

Part I. General Principles (Choice of Law Technique)

Chapter 1. Sources of PIL

§1. PUBLIC INTERNATIONAL LAW

21. Given the fact that both Taiwan and the Mainland China adhere to the 'one China' policy, and the PRC has represented 'China' in the United Nations since 1970, Taiwan is not a UN member and thus is neither accepted as a Contracting State to the Hague Conference on Private International Law, nor allowed to accede to any of its conventions. However, the explanatory comments on the Choice-of-law Act 2010 refer to several relevant Hague Conventions, including the Hague Agency Convention,[29] the Hague Products Liability Convention,[30] the Hague Securities Convention,[31] the Hague Matrimonial Property Convention,[32] the Hague Child Protection Convention,[33] the Hague Maintenance Applicable Law Convention 1973,[34] the Hague Testamentary Dispositions Convention.[35] In addition the explanatory comments refer to the UN Convention on the Rights of the Child[36] and certain multilateral treaties adopted by the Organization of American States such as the Inter-American Checks Convention 1979,[37] the Inter-American Support Obligations Convention,[38] and the Inter-American Bills of Exchange Convention.[39] Such

29. Hague Convention of 14 March 1978 on the law applicable to agency, *Collection of Conventions (1951–2009)* 268 (Hague Conference of Private International Law ed., Intersentia 2009).
30. Hague Convention of 2 October 1973 on the law applicable to products liability, 1056 UNTS 191.
31. Hague Convention of 5 July 2006 on the law applicable to certain rights in respect of securities held with an intermediary, 46 ILM 649.
32. Hague Convention of 14 March 1978 on the law applicable to matrimonial property regimes, 16 ILM 14.
33. Hague Convention of 19 October 1996 on jurisdiction, applicable law, recognition, enforcement and co-operation in respect of parental responsibility and measures for the protection of children, 35 ILM 1391.
34. Hague Convention of 2 October 1973 on the law applicable to maintenance obligations, 1056 UNTS 204.
35. Hague Convention of 5 October 1961 on the Conflicts of Laws relating to the Form of Testamentary Dispositions, 510 UNTS 175.
36. UN Convention on the Rights of the Child of 20 November 1989, 1577 UNTS 3.
37. Inter-American Convention of 8 May 1979 on Conflicts of Laws concerning Checks, 1439 UNTS 1986.
38. Inter-American Convention on Support Obligations of 15 July 1989, 29 ILM 73.

references indicate that the spirit of these conventions was adopted so as to modernize and internationalize Taiwanese conflicts rules. Only a few bilateral treaties between Taiwan and other countries cover specific issues of private international law and remain effective in protecting the mentioned rights.[40]

§2. Supranational Law

22. With an exception of World Trade Organization (WTO), Taiwan is not a party to any supranational organization or international organization aiming at formulating transnational legal norms. The supranational law adopted by such organizations as the European Union is apparent not binding on Taiwan. However, the private international law rules and principles formulated in such supranational regulations, directives and conventions are highly valued in its legislative process and sometimes are referred to as a foreign resource in judicial practice. Some supranational norms that have been regarded as established international customary norms for international professional transactions, e.g. letters of credit, are recognized as *lex mercatoria* and applicable in the judicial process.

§3. National Law

23. According to Article 107 of the ROC Constitution[41], the legislation and administration of civil law, commercial law and the financial and economic matters involving foreign elements fall within the exclusive competence of the central government, as opposed to provinces and cities. Provisions on private international law may be found in a significant number of statutes on various fields of law. The major legislation on choice of law is no doubt the Choice-of-law Act of 1953 and of 2010. The recognition and enforcement of foreign court judgments are provided for respectively in Article 402 of the Code of Civil Procedure (the CCP)[42], and Article

39. Inter-American Convention of 30 January 1975 on Conflict of Laws concerning Bills of Exchange, Promissory Notes and Invoices, OAS, Treaty Series, No 40; 1438 UNTS 211.
40. For instance, the 1948 Treaty of Friendship, Commerce and Navigation between the United States of America and the Republic of China provides the right of access to justice among other things. Art. VI, s 4 of it, 63 Stat. 1300, states in relevant part: 'The nationals, corporations and associations of either High Contracting Party shall enjoy freedom of access to the courts of justice and to administrative tribunals and agencies in the territories of the other High Contracting Party, in all degrees of jurisdiction established by law, both in pursuit and in defense of their rights.'
41. The ROC Constitution (Zhong-Hua Min-Guo Xian-Fa, 中華民國憲法) was adopted on December 25, 1946, by the National Assembly convened in Nanking. It was promulgated by the National Government on 1 Jan. 1947, and put into effect on 25 December of the same year. In addition to the preamble, the Constitution comprises 175 articles in 14 chapters. Intended for the entire territory of the ROC as it was then constituted, it was never extensively nor effectively implemented due to the outbreak of the Chinese Civil War in mainland China at the time of the constitution's promulgation. The Additional Articles of the Constitution was passed from 1991 to 2005 to reflect the government's actual jurisdiction and realization of cross-Strait relations, and to change the structure of the government as the basis of a multiparty democracy in Taiwan.
42. The Code of Civil Procedure (Min-Shi-Su-Song-Fa, 民事訴訟法, hereinafter 'CCP') was adopted in 1930 and last revised in 2021.

4-1 of the Compulsory Enforcement Act.[43] The general rules of recognition and enforcement of foreign arbitral awards are contained in Arts 47 to 51 of the Arbitration Act of 1998[44] to replace the Commercial Arbitration Act of 1961[45].

24. According to Article 10 of the Additional Articles of the ROC Constitution, the relations between Taiwan, Chinese Mainland, Hong Kong and Macau are the subject of legislation. Conflicts between these four territories are dealt with in the Act on the Taiwan Area and the Mainland Area, as well as the Act Governing Relations with Hong Kong and Macau. These provisions establish the legal scheme of interregional conflict rules or 'quasi private international law'.

§4. Case Law

25. Case law is an integral part of Taiwan's private international law. Supreme Court decisions on the Choice-of-law Act are *de facto* binding on the lower courts. They play an important role in clarifying the relevant underlying policy and spirit of provisions in the Choice-of-law Act, and have a significant gap-filling role in the field of international jurisdiction. Besides interpreting the statutory concepts and applying relevant provisions by analogy to the unprovided-for facts, the Supreme Court also introduced through its precedents the theory of the incidental (preliminary) question[46] and the forum *non conveniens* doctrine.[47]

§5. Doctrine

26. Scholarly writings have traditionally had significant influence on Taiwanese legislation and judicial practice. They introduce and explore the latest legal development and academic findings to lead the thoughts on legal reform. They also analyse and criticize the court decisions and judgements to push judicial reform in the field of private international law. The numbered scholars are all counted on to contribute their opinions through the legislative and judicial processes. This author was relied on heavily to draft the provisions and their explanatory comments of the

43. The Compulsory Enforcement Act (Qiang-Zhi Zhi-Xing Fa, 強制執行法) was adopted in 1940 and last revised in 2019.
44. The Arbitration Act (Zhong-Cai Fa, 仲裁法) was adopted in 1998 to replace the Commercial Arbitration Act of 1961 and was last revised in 2015.
45. The Commercial Arbitration Act (Shang-Wu Zhong-Cai Tiao-Li, 商務仲裁條例) was adopted in 1961 and was replaced by the Arbitration Act in 1998.
46. Supreme Court's Civil Judgment, Tai-Shang 1804 of 2007. For a short comment, *see* Rong-Chwan Chen, *The Law Applicable to Torts and Maintenance Obligations*, 71 Taiwan Jurist (月旦法學教室) 24–25 (2008).
47. Supreme Court's Civil Decision, Tai-Kang 188 of 2013. For a short comment, *see* Rong-Chwan Chen *Cautiousness in Applying the Principle of Forum Non Conveniens*, 142 Taiwan Jurist (月旦法學教室) 36–38 (August 2014).

Choice-of-law Act 2010.[48] In judicial practice, the Taiwanese courts at times followed or cited scholarly writings to support their decisions.

§6. Customary Law

27. Customary law is a supplementary source to the legislation governing the civil, commercial and family matters. Taiwan's Civil Code (CC)[49] provides that 'If there is no applicable statute for a civil case, the case shall be decided according to customs. If there is no such custom, the case shall be decided according to the principles of law.'[50] 'Only those customs which are not against public policy or morals shall be applied to a civil case.'[51] Apparently, 'customs' mean customary law in the above provisions. The applicability of customary law is limited due to its nature of supplementary source. Its permissibility is scrutinized by the standards embodied in the relevant legal policy and good morals.

28. Some principles have their origin in interterritorial practices and customary norms. Yet, customary law is not specifically addressed in the Choice-of-law Act. It is stated that 'civil matters involving foreign elements are governed, in the absence of any provisions in this Act, by the provisions of other statutes; in the absence of applicable provisions in other statutes, by the principles of law.'[52] The supplementary source to statutory conflicts rules is the jurisprudence of private international law from which the relevant provisions result. The 'principles of law' mentioned above are thus the basic principles on which the private international law develops and the Choice-of-law Act 2010 prescribes. All the gaps between the statutory provisions, no matter in what form, are going to be filled with the principles that can be found and traced in the pool of jurisprudence of private international law.

29. Although private international law only applies in the civil matters involving with foreign elements, the customary rules in this field were mostly embodied into statutory provisions during the process of codification. The missed customary rules, if any, cannot find their own space in the Choice-of-law Act 2010. However, they are no doubt a part of the private international law jurisprudence, and can be asserted as the 'principles of law' to resolve the questions at issue.

---

48. For the tentative drafts and related discussions, *see* Judicial Yuan (ed.), 1 *Materials on Studying and Revising the Choice-of-law Act by the Judicial Yuan* (Si-Fa-Yuan She-Wai Min-Shi Fa-Lyu Shi-Yong Fa Yan-Jiu Xiu-Zheng Zi-Liao Hui-Bian, 司法院涉外民事法律適用法研究修正資料彙編) (Judicial Yuan 2002); 2 *Materials on Studying and Revising the Choice-of-law Act by the Judicial Yuan* (Judicial Yuan 2011).
49. The Civil Code (Min-Fa, 民法) is composed of the following five Parts: General Principles (總則), Obligations (債), Rights in Rem (物權), Family (親屬), and Succession (繼承). Parts 1–3 were adopted in 1929 and Parts 4 & 5 in 1930. The Civil Code was adopted by the ROC when Taiwan was under the rule of Japan, but it applies only in Taiwan now. It was last revised in 2021.
50. CC, Art. 1.
51. CC, Art. 2.
52. Choice-of-law Act 2010, Art. 1.

Chapter 2. Determination of the Applicable Law

§1. Conflict of Laws Rules

30. The conflict of laws rules are embodied in the Choice-of-law Act. The Taiwanese courts are required to determine and apply *ex officio* the applicable law, domestic or foreign, to the civil cases or matters in accordance with the provisions of it.[53] A conflict of laws rule contains two parts similar to the rules in other fields. The effect of a main conflict of laws rule that can be relied upon to directly ascertain the applicable law is different from a substantive rule. Instead of pure description of facts that can result in a legal effect on duties and rights of the parties, the first part of a conflict of laws rule only states one kind or certain kinds of legal relationship as the operating facts that the rule is provided for. The second part of a conflict of laws rule is a direction from which the governing law can be ascertained. It basically uses a certain connecting factor on which a legal system can stand to govern the civil matter involving with foreign elements.

31. Article 10 Paragraph 1 of the Choice-of-law Act 2010 can serve as an illustration. It states: 'The capacity of a person to act is governed by his/her national law.' In this paragraph, the first part is 'the capacity of a person to act', while the second part is 'governed by his/her national law.' Unlike the substantive rules, the first part does not provide or mention the factual situation and the status or age of the person in issue. The question whether the person is capable and the criteria or age for a person to capably act are left to the applicable legal system. The second part only mentions that the law applicable to such a question is his/her national law. The term 'national law' means the law of the country of which the person is a national. The connecting factor which connects the applicable law and the person is his/her nationality. There is no such legal effect as the person is or is not legally capable. The legal effect in such a sense is just a direction to the legal system that governs the civil matter.[54]

I. Types of Conflict of Laws Rules

32. The Choice-of-law Act 2010 adopts two types of conflict of laws rules: one-sided and all-sided rules.[55] One-sided rules are only formulated exceptionally to meet some specific national need or interests. Article 11 Paragraph 3 states that '[t]he effect of a declaration of death decreed under either of the preceding two paragraphs is governed by the law of the ROC' to acknowledge the principle that the *lex fori* is the origin of effects of the decrees rendered by the Taiwanese courts. Article 15 states that 'if an alien legal person establishes a branch under the law of the ROC, the internal affairs of that branch are governed by the law of the ROC' to

53. Rong-Chwan Chen, *supra* n. 26, at 237.
54. Liu & Chen, *supra* n. 12, at 232.
55. Liu & Chen, *supra* n. 12, at 233.

emphasize that such a branch is established for the sole purpose of doing business in Taiwan and the local law shall therefore govern its internal affairs.

33. Apparently, the legislature considers in one-sided rules only the particular situations in which the Taiwanese law shall be applied. It inevitably leaves some questions unanswered when Taiwanese law does not govern. It is this author's opinion that the unilateral rules aforementioned can be applied in analogy to such questions involving other foreign elements.[56] Therefore, the effects of a declaration of death decreed by a court of State A according to State A's law is governed by State A's law; the internal affairs of a branch established under State B's law are governed by State B's law.

34. All-sided rules designate the applicable law with a connecting factor that can direct to domestic law or any foreign law. It covers all the laws that can be designated with the chosen connecting factor. Article 10 Paragraph 1 of the Choice-of-law Act 2010 aforementioned illustrates that the governing law of the capacity of a person to act is his/her national law, no matter it is domestic or a foreign law. The nationality of the person is chosen as a connecting factor to designate the governing law.

35. Article 38 Paragraph 1 is another example. It states: 'A property right in a thing is governed by the law of the place where the thing is located.' The chosen connecting factor is the place where the thing is located. Its multilateral nature signals the messages that any foreign law has the same possibility as the domestic law to be chosen as the applicable law. This type of conflict of laws rules is no doubt better since it does neither focus too much on the applicability of domestic law nor create the gap of applicability of foreign laws.

II. Connecting Factors

36. The connecting factors adopted in Choice-of-law Act 2010 can be grouped into the following four categories: personal connecting factors, territorial connecting factors, the parties' choice as connecting factor, and mixed connecting factors.[57]

37. Personal connecting factors are those that connect the applicable law with the person. Unlike most countries around the world, nationality is preferred over one's domicile to determine his/her personal law in Taiwan. One of the reasons is that the modern approach to identify a person's nationality is sufficient to guarantee the genuine linkage between the person and his/her national law. The other includes

56. Liu & Chen, *supra* n. 12, at 234.
57. Liu & Chen, *supra* n. 12, at 69–71.

the reality that an independent citizenship of Taiwan means a lot more to the Taiwanese people than any foreign citizenship to a foreigner.[58] The *lex patriae* principle is thus adopted in the all-sided type of conflict of laws rules in order to meet the special interest in applying Taiwanese law to Taiwanese people. The rule of *renvoi* is also adopted to harmonize the tension between such a principle and a foreign conflicts rule that deems nationality inappropriate to connect a person with the law of a country.

38. Domicile is also a personal connecting factor. However, it is supplementary to nationality in determining the personal law. The Choice-of-law Act does not provide or mention the idea of habitual residence that has been adopted by the Hague Conference on Private International Law. The reason is that the definition of domicile in the Civil Code is similar to habitual residence. It states: 'A person who resides in a place with the intention of remaining there permanently, upon presence of supporting fact, is to establish his domicile at that place.' 'Every person has at all times one domicile, and no person has more than one domicile at a time.'[59]

39. Territorial connecting factors comprise the factors that connect the legal relationship with specific territories. The Choice-of-law Act 2010 adopts the 'place where the thing is located' in Article 38 Paragraph 1, the 'place where the tort was committed' in Article 25, and the 'place where the fact occurred' in Article 30. Those connecting factors direct basically the seat of the particular legal relationship which is stated as the first part in the conflict of laws rule.

40. The parties' choice can be the connecting factor to apply the chosen law in some circumstances. It is one of the aspects of the principle of party autonomy. The Choice-of-law Act 2010 adopts the parties' choice as a connecting factor in Articles 20, 21, and 43.

41. A mixed connecting factor is a mix of different categories of the above connecting factors. The Choice-of-law Act 2010 provides that 'the law which is the most closely connected' with the juridical act or tort is its governing law.[60] The connecting factor underlying such a clause is 'the closest connection'. This is a soft connecting factor that is to be ascertained after considering all the personal and territorial connections, the parties' intention, the interests of relevant legal systems and other factors.

III. Time Factors

42. The time factors in conflict of laws result in three major types of problems. Firstly, when there is a change in the content of the conflict rule of the forum, they

58. Rong-Chwan Chen, *supra* n. 16, at 211–212.
59. CC, Art. 20.
60. Choice-of-law Act 2010, Arts 20 and 25.

are significant as to apply provisions of the revised version or old version. Secondly, when the connecting factor (for example, a person's nationality or domicile) has changed, they are significant as to adopt the latest connecting factor or the older one to ascertain the governing law. Thirdly, when there is a change in the content of the *lex causae* or the governing law to which the connecting factor refers, they are relevant in applying provisions of its revised version or old version.[61]

43. The Choice-of-law Act stipulates the first type of problems in Article 62. It reads: 'The provisions of this Revised Act do not apply to civil matters which occurred prior to its entering into force. However, where a part of the legal effect of a civil matter does not occur until after this Revised Act has entered into force, the Revised Act applies to such part.' The courts have interpreted this Article to determine whether the new provisions added or revised in 2010 can be applied to the facts or legal effects at issue. The Supreme Court ruled that the old Act applies to the facts or juridical acts taken place and their effects resulted before the Act was revised; if the facts or juridical acts taken place before the Act was revised, but some of their effects resulted after the Act was revised, the new Act applies to such effects.[62]

44. In a case ruled in 2013, a tort was committed in Australia in 2003, and the trial court erred in applying Article 31 of the Choice-of-law Act 2010 which provides the basis of the parties' agreement to choose the *lex fori* as the governing law. The Supreme Court ruled that the facts taken place before the new provisions came into effect shall ascertain the applicable law in accordance with Article 62 of the Choice-of-law Act 2010, the lower court was therefore erroneous in applying the provisions of its Article 31 which did not exist when the tortious act was committed.[63]

IV. *Dépeçage*

45. Dépeçage is an approach that the courts can deploy to apply different laws to different facts. As a discretionary approach, it was left behind in the Choice-of-law Act to give the discretion and resilience to the courts.

46. In a case decided in 2008,[64] a Vietnamese worker lost his left arm when operating a machine in Taiwan and claimed damages against his employer. The trial court characterized the legal relationship as a tort and ascertained that Taiwanese law was applicable to it. The Supreme Court ruled in this judgment that the problem of damages is separable from the problem of tortious liability, their governing laws are thus not necessarily the same one. [65] In this case, the law applicable to the

61. Liu & Chen, *supra* n. 12, at 594.
62. Supreme Court's Civil Decision, Tai-Shang 1913 of 2011.
63. Supreme Court's Civil Judgment, Tai-Shang 90 of 2013.
64. Supreme Court's Civil Judgment, Tai-Shang 1838 of 2008.
65. Supreme Court's Civil Judgment, Tai-Shang 1838 of 2008.

tortious liability is Taiwanese law. It governs whether and how the tortfeasor is liable. The measurement of damage by losing labour forces is a separate and independent question that is subject to the law of the place where the Vietnamese worker is supposed to work. Besides the period that he has been permitted to work in Taiwan, his damage by losing labour forces shall be governed by his national law or law of domicile in Vietnam.

47. The Supreme Court explained in the above case that a major legal relationship in a civil matter may be composed of several different minor legal relationships. If the civil matter involves complex and diverse connecting factors, it will be inappropriate to ascertain the governing law simply according to a single conflict of laws rule. Under such circumstances, the courts may apply different conflict of laws rules respectively to the minor legal relationships included in the major legal relationship. The reasonableness of a judgment for an individual case can only be achieved with such an approach.[66]

48. The major legal relationship in this case is tortious liability which is subject to Taiwanese law under Article 9 of the Choice-of-law Act 1953. It is ruled that it is unfair and improper to subject the measurement of the worker's damage by losing labour forces to Taiwanese law. The measurement of damage by losing labour forces beyond the period that the worker has been permitted to work in Taiwan is governed by his national law, i.e., Vietnamese law. It is this author's opinion that the measurement of damage is an integral part of tortious liability and is subject to the same governing law, i.e., Taiwanese law. However, the measurement of damage by losing labour forces is a question of fact-finding at the place where it was caused. The damage by losing labour forces in Vietnam depends on the protection provided by the Vietnamese legal system and therefore shall be measured in reference to the standards set by the Vietnamese law.[67]

V. Legal Consequences

49. As mentioned above, the second part of a conflict of laws rule is different from the substantive rules. It deals with the legal consequences without providing the rights and duties of the parties. Rather, it designates connecting factors to refer to the governing law. The legal consequences are only directions to the law that can be applied to resolve the substantive problems.

§2. Relevant Contact and Evasion of the Law

50. The connecting factors are deployed in the conflicts rules to refer to the governing law. They are supposed to be genuine links or relevant contacts between the

66. Supreme Court's Civil Judgment, Tai-Shang 1838 of 2008.
67. Rong-Chwan Chen, *The Law Applicable to Compensation for Foreign Workers*, 80 Taiwan Jurist (月旦法學教室) 22–23 (June 2009).

civil matter and its governing law. In case the neutral connecting factor is intentionally manipulated, the designation of governing law will be unfair to certain interested parties and shall be corrected by the court.

51. The Choice-of-law Act 2010 recognizes that conflicts justice shall be restored if it is distorted by evading the law otherwise applicable. To maintain the applicability of domestic compulsory provisions, it states: 'Where a party to a civil matter involving foreign elements evades a compulsory provision or a prohibition of the law of the ROC, that compulsory provision or prohibition is nevertheless applied.'[68] The underlying principle is that a connecting factor manipulated improperly is far from genuineness and fairness. Thus, it shall no more be treated as a decisive connecting factor in the process of choice of law. The above provision aims at declaring that the malicious and fraudulent arrangement of connecting factors is unlawful and prohibited. A domestic compulsory regulation is not evaded as a result of such manipulation. The parties are thus deprived of the interests they otherwise gained because the evaded domestic mandatory rules shall still be applied.[69]

§3. Choice of Law

52. Principle of party autonomy allows the parties to choose the law that will govern their transaction. This option is attractive to the parties of an international contract who may not know which court will have jurisdiction over a future conflict arising from the agreement and which law will be chosen as the governing law. They are afforded some degree of control and predictability by selecting in advance the governing law.

53. The Choice-of-law Act 2010 stipulates the principle of party autonomy in Article 20. 'The applicable law regarding the formation and effect of a juridical act which results in a relationship of obligation is determined by the intention of the parties.'[70] The intention of the parties to choose the governing law is limited to express intention because the implicit intention is taken into account as an element of close connection under the following provisions: 'Where there is no express intention of the parties or their express intention is void under the applicable law determined by them, the formation and effect of the juridical act are governed by the law which is most closely connected with the juridical act.' [71]

54. In addition to the parties' choice of law for a contract or other juridical act which results in a relationship of obligation, the Choice-of-law Act 2010 extends the principle of party autonomy to the settlements in a Taiwanese court proceeding. 'Where the parties with respect to an obligation which arises otherwise than from a

---

68. Choice-of-law Act 2010, Art. 7.
69. Rong-Chwan Chen, *General Provisions in the Taiwanese Private International Law Enactment 2010*, in Basedow & Pissler (eds.), *supra* n. 7, at 65–84.
70. Choice-of-law Act 2010, Art. 20 para. 1.
71. Choice-of-law Act 2010, Art. 20 para. 2.

juridical act agree to the application of the law of the ROC after a suit has been brought on the obligation in a court of the ROC, the law of the ROC is applied.' [72] Notably, the parties' choice in such a case is limited to the *lex fori*, i.e., the law of the ROC.

§4. OBJECTIVE CONNECTING FACTOR

55. The intention of the parties to choose the governing law is a subjective connecting factor. The absence of intention and implicit intention are not treated as subjective connecting factors to directly determine the governing law. Rather, they are facts of connection that may be considered and weighed for ascertaining the closest connecting or other objective connecting factors.

I. Principle of the Closest Connection

56. The principle closest connection is invoked in the Choice-of-law Act 2010 for two purposes. One is to ascertain the designated connecting factor among multiple nationalities or domiciles. 'Where the applicable law in accordance with this Act is the national law of a party, but such party has multiple nationalities, the national law is the law of the nationality most closely connected with the party.' [73] 'Where the applicable law in accordance with this Act is the law of the place in which a party is domiciled, but the party has multiple domiciles, the law of the domicile most closely connected with the party is applied.' [74] A person's nationality or domicile is adopted in those provisions as a connecting factor to designate the governing law, the principle of closest connection is invoked to determine which nationality or domicile is decisive in ascertaining the governing law.

57. The other purpose of closest connection is to serve as a soft connecting factor that can directly designate a governing law. The Choice-of-law Act 2010 stipulates the closest connection as the connecting factor to designate the governing law for contractual obligations and tortious liability. 'Where there is no express intention of the parties or their express intention is void under the applicable law determined by them, the formation and effect of the juridical act are governed by the law which is most closely connected with the juridical act.' [75] 'An obligation arising from a tort is governed by the law of the place where the tort was committed. However, if another law is the law most closely connected with the tort, it governs.' [76] In those provisions, the governing law is the law most closely connected with the juridical act or tortious act.

72. Choice-of-law Act 2010, Art. 31.
73. Choice-of-law Act 2010, Art. 2.
74. Choice-of-law Act 2010, Art. 4 para. 1.
75. Choice-of-law Act 2010, Art. 20 para. 2.
76. Choice-of-law Act 2010, Art. 25.

58. The connection between a law and the juridical act or tortious act at issue can be weighed by dynamic factors. The closest connection test favours the courts' discretion over the parties' efforts of evidence proving and in doctrine arguing. The flexibility enables the courts to assure fairness and justice in individual cases, while the uncertainty of their decisions is under criticism. In Article 20, the idea of characteristic performance is thus invoked to presume the law of closest connection. 'Where among the obligations resulting from a juridical act there is a characteristic one, the law of the domicile of the party obligated under the characteristic obligation at the time he/she undertook the juridical act is presumed to be the most closely connected law. However, where a juridical act concerns immovable property, the law of the place where the immovable property is located is presumed to be the most closely connected law.' [77]

II. Nationality

59. As *lex patriae* is adopted in the Choice-of-law Act 2010 as a person's personal law which governs his/her capacity, status, marriage and other personal matters. The reason why it adheres to such a principle that has been abolished in some countries due to the political nature of nationality is that nationality is treated as a key element of a person's status in Taiwan's legal system. It is more significant than domicile and residence in private international law as well as in other fields.

60. As a person's nationality is determined respectively by nationality of each relevant state, the positive and negative conflicts of nationality raises problems in ascertaining a person's personal law. The Choice-of-law Act 2010 deals with them by invoking closest connection test and domicile as the supplemental connecting factor. 'Where the applicable law in accordance with this Act is the national law of a party, but such party has multiple nationalities, the national law is the law of the nationality most closely connected with the party.' [78] 'Where the applicable law in accordance with this Act is the national law of a party, but the party is stateless, the law of the place in which the party is domiciled is applied.' [79] It is worth mentioning that if the person has nationalities of the ROC and of other countries, Article 26 of the Choice-of-law Act 1953 provides that his/her national law is the law of the ROC. Such prevalence of *lex fori* over foreign laws was abolished by adopting the closest connection test. All nationalities are thus equal in the conflicts rules.

III. Residence

61. The domicile, temporary residence and transient presence are all deployed in the Choice-of-law Act 2010.

77. Choice-of-law Act 2010, Art. 20 para. 3.
78. Choice-of-law Act 2010, Art. 2.
79. Choice-of-law Act 2010, Art. 3.

A. Domicile (of Origin, of Choice, of Dependence)

62. Domicile is significant in deciding a court's jurisdiction. According to the CCP, a defendant may be sued in the court for the place of the defendant's domicile.[80] It is also an important connecting factor to designate the governing law for a civil matter with foreign elements. In the Choice-of-law Act 2010, the law of the place of domicile plays an important role. It is, among other functions, supplemental to designate a person's personal law when he/she is stateless,[81] to designate the governing law of an obligation arising from a tort which was committed by means of publication, radio, television, internet publication or other medium of communication if the place of the tort is unclear,[82] and to designate the governing law of the effect of an engagement to marry, a marriage or a divorce when the parties' common national law is absent. [83]

63. Under Taiwan's Civil Code, every person has at all times one domicile, and no person has more than one domicile at a time.[84] The domicile of a minor child is that of the father and mother.[85] The domicile of a person who has no or is limited in capacity to make juridical acts is the domicile of his guardian.[86] Such a domicile of origin can be changed by his/her domicile of choice when the child comes to full capability. However, the choice of a domicile is not a juridical act that reflects the person's intention. Instead, a person who resides in a place with the intention of remaining there permanently, upon presence of supporting fact, is to establish his domicile at that place.[87] A person, who has left his domicile with the intention of repealing it, upon presence of supporting fact, is to repeal the domicile.[88] Such a domicile of choice is similar to habitual residence adopted by the Hague Conference of Private International Law in its conventions. The domicile of the husband and the wife shall be agreed by mutual agreement; if it has not been agreed or cannot be agreed, it may depend on the court by application. Before the ruling of the court, it will be presumed the common household domicile as the domicile of the husband and the wife.[89]

64. The legal standard for ascertaining a person's domicile in a civil matter with foreign elements leads to some problems in private international law. Choice-of-law Act 2010 acknowledges and provides the positive and negative of domicile. Where the applicable law is the law of the place in which a party is domiciled, but the party has multiple domiciles, the law of the domicile most closely connected with the party is applied. If no domicile of a party can be established, the law of the

80. CCP, Art. 1 para. 1.
81. Choice-of-law Act 2010, Art. 3.
82. Choice-of-law Act 2010, Art. 28 para. 1 Item 1.
83. Choice-of-law Act 2010, Arts 45 & 47.
84. CC, Art. 20 para. 2.
85. CC, Art. 1060.
86. CC, Art. 21.
87. CC, Art. 20 para. 1.
88. CC, Art. 24.
89. CC, Art. 1002.

place in which the party resides is applied.[90] Those provisions contradict with the principle of Taiwan's Civil Code that every person has at all times one domicile, and no person has more than one domicile at a time.[91] The establishment of a person's domicile is thus apparently not governed by the *lex fori*. Instead, it is the law of each relevant place that governs whether the person has a domicile there.[92]

B. Habitual Residence

65. Habitual residence is not adopted in the Choice-of-law Act 2010 because its Taiwanese version is the domicile in Taiwan's Civil Code. It was introduced by the Act on Family Matters (the AFM)[93] for the first time into Taiwanese legal system. It reads: 'With regard to matters concerning determination of the invalidity of a marriage, annulment of a marriage, divorce, or determination of the existence or non-existence of a marriage, the jurisdiction to hear the proceedings exclusively belongs to the courts listed in the following: 1. the court for the place of the domicile of the husband and wife; 2. the court for the place of the joint habitual residence of the husband and wife; or 3. the court for the place of the habitual residence of the husband or the wife from whom the transactions or occurrences that gives rise to the claim take place.'[94]

C. Temporary Residence

66. Residence is treated as a supplemental connecting factor to domicile in Taiwan's Civil Code. A person's residence is deemed to be his/her domicile in either of the following circumstances: (1) when his/her domicile cannot be certified; (2) when he/she has no domicile in Taiwan except when the *lex domicilli* governs.[95] Where a person has chosen a residence for a specific purpose, the residence is deemed to be his domicile with regard to that purpose.[96]

67. Residence is a supplemental connecting factor for determining both a court's jurisdiction and governing law. When the court of the place of the defendant's domicile cannot exercise jurisdiction, the plaintiff can sue in the court for the place of the defendant's residence. A defendant may also be sued in the court for the place of defendant's residence for a claim arising from transactions or occurrences taking

90. Choice-of-law Act 2010, Art. 4.
91. CC, Art. 20 para. 2.
92. Liu & Chen, *supra* n. 12, at 107–108.
93. The Act on Family Matters (Jia-Shi Shi-Jian Fa, 家事事件法, aka Family Act) was adopted in 2012 and last revised in 2019.
94. AFM, Art. 52 para. 1.
95. CC, Art. 22.
96. CC, Art. 23.

place within the jurisdiction of that court.[97] Residence is treated in the Choice-of-law Act 2010 as a supplemental connecting factor to domicile. Positive and negative conflicts of residences are also addressed in it. If no domicile of a party can be established, the law of the place in which the party resides is applied. Where a party has multiple residences, the law of the residence most closely connected with the party is applied. If no residence of a party can be established, the law of the place in which the party is present is applied.[98]

IV. Registered Office

68. A registered office has the legal effects provided by the law which requires the registration. This concept is not deployed as a connecting factor. Principal office and principal place of business are utilized in Taiwan's CCP. A private juridical person or unincorporated association that has the capacity to be a party to an action may be sued in the court for the location of its principal office or principal place of business. A foreign juridical person or unincorporated association may be sued in the court for the location of its principal office or principal place of business in the ROC.[99] In Choice-of-law Act, domicile and residence are deployed for both individual persons and juridical persons. Registered office is just an element to consider where the principal office is.

V. *Lex Loci Delicti*

69. Lex loci delicti was the basic governing law for a tort under the Choice-of-law Act 1953.[100] However, the Choice-of-law Act 2010 has shifted its role to a *prima facie* applicable law which has the closest connection with the tort. It stipulates: 'An obligation arising from a tort is governed by the law of the place where the tort was committed. However, if another law is the law most closely connected with the tort, it governs.'[101] It is noteworthy that this provision takes the form of rigid rule of *lex loci delicti*, but the *lex loci delicti* can only apply when it is the law of the closest connection. *Lex loci delicti* is not necessarily the governing law of the tort. It is in reality a rule of closest connection test for torts with foreign elements.

VI. *Lex Rei (Cartae) Sitae*

70. The Choice-of-law Act 2010 differentiate property rights from obligatory rights and deploys different approaches for them respectively. A property right over a thing is governed by the *lex rei (cartae) sitae*, which is the law of the place where

97. CCP, Art. 1.
98. Choice-of-law Act 2010, Art. 4.
99. CCP, Art. 3.
100. Choice-of-law Act 1953, Art. 9.
101. Choice-of-law Act 2010, Art. 25.

the thing is located.[102] A property right can be created in a right that is alienable, and the location of such a right that does not physically exist is not possible to be found. Ships and aircrafts are objects of property rights, but their locations are too internationally changeable to ascertain a governing law. So, a property right over a right is governed by the law of the place where the right is formed[103]; a property right over a ship is governed by the law of the nationality of the ship, and a property right over an aircraft is governed by the law of the State in which the aircraft is registered. [104]

§5. Changes in the Connecting Factors; Changes in the *Lex Causae*

71. Changes in the connecting factors and the *lex causae* also raise problems of time factor. The changes in the *lex causae* concern which part of the *lex causae* is applicable. It is this author's opinion that the intertemporal conflict of laws rules in the *lex causae* shall govern whether the changed law shall still be applied to the civil matter in issue.[105] The changes in the connecting factors raise the problem which connecting factor in different time is decisive to ascertain the governing law.

72. The Choice-of-law Act 2010 deals directly with some changes in the connecting factors while leaving others to interpretation by the court. To illustrate, where the location of a thing has changed, the acquisition, loss, or change of a property right over a thing is governed by the law of the location of the thing at the time the decisive fact occurred.[106] When the connecting factor to designate common national law has changed, divorce and the effect of divorce are governed by the national law common to the spouses at the time they reach an agreement of divorce or when a suit is brought for the divorce; in the absence of a common national law, by the law of domicile common to them; in the absence of a common law of domicile, by the law of the place most closely connected with the marriage relationship.[107] When the nationality of the testator has changed, the making and effect of a will are governed by the national law of the testator at the time of the making of the will; the revocation of a will is governed by the national law of the testator at the time of revocation.[108]

§6. Combination of Connecting Factors

73. In addition to deploying a single connecting factor to designate the governing law, the Choice-of-law Act 2010 also adopts some combinations of two or more

102. Choice-of-law Act 2010, Art. 38 para. 1.
103. Choice-of-law Act 2010, Art. 38 para. 2.
104. Choice-of-law Act 2010, Art. 38 para. 4.
105. Liu & Chen, *supra* n. 12, at 616.
106. Choice-of-law Act 2010, Art. 38 para. 2.
107. Choice-of-law Act 2010, Art. 50.
108. Choice-of-law Act 2010, Art. 60.

connecting factors in a conflict of laws rule. Such combinations result in distributive, cumulative, and alternative application of two or more governing laws.

74. Distributive combination of connecting factors is deployed for bilateral contracts concerning domestic relations in the following examples. The formation of an engagement to marry is governed by the respective national law of each party. However, an engagement to marry is also effective if it satisfies the formal requisites of the national law of one of the parties or of the law of the place where the engagement is concluded.[109] The formation of a marriage is governed by the national law of each party. However, a marriage is also effective if it satisfies the formal requisites prescribed either by the national law of one of the parties or by the law of the place of ceremony.[110] The formation and termination of an adoption of a child are governed for the adoptive parent and for the adopted child by their respective national laws.[111] In those provisions, the personal laws of both parties can be applied simultaneously and equally to the single domestic relation.

75. Cumulative combination of connecting factors is deployed to make sure all the requirements of relevant governing laws are all complied. For example, 'where there is a valid ground to declare guardianship or curatorship in respect of an alien under both his/her national law and the law of the ROC, a declaration of guardianship or curatorship may be decreed if he/she has a domicile or residence within the ROC.' [112] The ground to declare guardianship or curatorship shall be cumulatively scrutinized under two governing laws, i.e., the alien's national law and the law of the ROC.

76. Alternative combination of connecting factors enables a court to apply all the laws designated by each connecting factor alternatively. It pursues a certain substantive goal through the alternative application of all the relevant laws.[113] The Choice-of-law Act 2010 designates the applicable law for a person's capacity by comparing the resulting differences, if any, between applying the person's national law and applying the *lex fori*.[114] The following alternative reference increases the possibility of validating the juridical act in question: 'The formal requisites of a juridical act; are governed by the law applicable to the act. However, a juridical act that conforms to the formal requisites provided for in the law of the place where the

109. Choice-of-law Act 2010, Art. 45 para. 1.
110. Choice-of-law Act 2010, Art. 46.
111. Choice-of-law Act 2010, Art. 54 para. 1.
112. Choice-of-law Act 2010, Art. 12 para. 1.
113. The material rules and conflicts rules pursue respectively the material goal and conflicts justice, while some conflicts rules in the Choice-of-law Act 2010 also assist to pursue the material justice by allowing the courts to alternatively apply the law which better fulfils the material goal. *See* Rong-Chwan Chen, *supra* n. 25.
114. Choice-of-law Act 2010, Art. 10 para. 3: 'Where an alien of no or limited capacity to act under his/her national law is of full capacity to act under the law of the ROC, he/she is deemed to be of full capacity to act with respect to his juridical acts undertaken within the ROC.'

act was undertaken is also effective; where a juridical act is undertaken at different places, it is effective if it conforms to the formal requisites of the law of any one of the places.'[115]

77. The same methodology was used to preserve to the maximum extent the validity of an engagement to marry[116], a marriage[117], the legitimacy of a child[118], an acknowledgement of a child born out of wedlock[119], and a last will[120] in those cases where the legal relation in question has foreign elements. Those relevant provisions deploy several connecting factors to designate multiple laws for the court to apply one by one until the validity of the act is supported.

---

115. Choice-of-law Act 2010, Art. 16.
116. Choice-of-law Act 2010, Art. 45.
117. Choice-of-law Act 2010, Art. 46.
118. Choice-of-law Act 2010, Art. 51.
119. Choice-of-law Act 2010, Art. 53.
120. Choice-of-law Act 2010, Art. 61.

Chapter 3. Basic Terms

§1. Characterization (Classification)

78. Like many codifications of private international law, the Choice-of-law Act borrowed many legal concepts and categories of legal relationships from Taiwan's Civil Code and other enactments. Before determining the law applicable to a specific legal relationship, the court is required to know exactly which category of legal relationship the case belongs to. The descriptions of categories in the conflicts rules may be identical with the provisions of the Civil Code and other enactments. However, their interpretations may be different due to the standards employed by the different courts. The situation will be more complicated if the court employs foreign legal standards instead of the domestic law to characterize the nature of the legal relationship at issue.

79. The courts inevitably face the problem of which standard shall be adopted to interpret the conflicts rules in cases involving foreign elements. Legislators addressed such problem neither in the Choice-of-law Act 1953 nor in the Choice-of-law Act 2010. It is apparent that they left the courts with discretion to flexibly solve this technical problem on a case-by-case basis. Among others, *lex fori, lex causae* and comparative law are the three most discussed standards.[121]

80. Taiwan's courts exercise their discretion in characterizing legal relations very cautiously. No reported case shows Taiwan's courts having ever expressly adopted the criteria of a foreign law to characterize the legal relationship at issue. Some court judgments have addressed only minimally the decisive criteria for characterization, but their choice of the conflicts rule for determining the applicable law has stood in line with the trend of comparative law. For example, the Supreme Court ruled in case of 2001[122] that the victim's claim for damages resulted from an air crash shall be governed by the law applicable to such a 'tortious act'.[123]

81. Characterization under the criteria of the *lex fori* might be problematic because different concepts were employed by different legislators for the same purpose or the meaning of the same legal concept differs from statute to statute.[124] Therefore, the courts deal in practice with conflict of rules in the *lex fori* more often than the conflict of *lex fori* and *lex causae*. Some prominent examples on guardianship may help to illustrate such phenomenon.

---

121. For standards for characterization, *see* Liu & Chen, *supra* n. 12, at 545–548.
122. Supreme Court's Civil Judgment, Tai-Shang 1365 of 2001.
123. Rong-Chwan Chen, *The Characterization of the Damages Claim for an Air Crash*, 3 Taiwan Jurist (月旦法學教室) 32–33 (2003).
124. In judicial practice, the court has to characterize and deal with the problem of a sham marriage under the framework of whether it is invalid or void. *See* Rong-Chwan Chen, *The Characterization of and Applicable Law to the Sham Marriages Involving with Foreign Elements*, 75 Taiwan Jurist (月旦法學教室) 24–25 (2009).

82. In the *Mosher* case, the divorced parents disputed over the custody of their minor child and their parental rights and duties.[125] The Supreme Court focused on analysing the basic premises and interpretations of related provisions in addition to analysing the characterization problems, and ruled that the effects of divorce cover the questions of the divorced parents' custody over a common child.[126] Such a conclusion is based on interpretations of several related terms. 'The problems of allocating a parental right of custody over a minor child and its method are outcomes resulting incidentally from a judicial decree rendering the parents' divorce. It shall therefore be governed by the applicable law for the effects of divorce.' As demonstrated by the following quote, the criteria for the court's characterization are the substantive rules in the *lex fori*. 'If the guardian of the minor child has been considered and appointed by a court in a decree ordering divorce, but the circumstances have changed afterwards, the parties are not prohibited from applying to court for a change of guardian. It is the natural interpretation in light of the proviso of Article 1055 of the Civil Code.'

83. In another case related to parental rights and duties, the Supreme Court emphasized in the *Mohajer* case that Article 15 Choice-of-law Act 1953 provides that the effects of a divorce shall be governed by the husband's national law; if an ROC woman is married to an alien but has retained her nationality, or if an alien is married to an ROC woman as a Zhui-Fu (adopted husband), the effects of their divorce shall be governed by ROC law. The Court ruled that the effects of divorce under the Article include the custody of children after the divorce and that any change in the status of the person who has custody of the child after the divorce is, by its nature, within the scope of the court's discretion to decide who is granted custody (parental rights) of the child after the parents' divorce. These questions are therefore properly included in the field concerning the effects of divorce. It is reasonable to conclude that the Supreme Court characterized this legal relationship by following the rules of the *lex fori*.[127]

84. The Supreme Court characterizes the post-divorce parent-child relationship as one of the effects of divorce in the two judgments described above. This characterization is not without its doubts in light of the related provisions in the Civil Code and the Choice-of-law Act 1953. The characterization led the court to determine the applicable law under the conflicts rule on the effects of the divorce and finally to apply the *lex fori* to such relationship. This author advocated that the

125. For a detailed discussion of this case, *see* Rong-Chwan Chen, *The Applicable Law of the Assignments and Reassignments of Custodian for Children after Divorce: A Comment on the Supreme Court's Judgment Tai-Shang 1888 of 1993*, in *Selected Essays on Private International Law* (國際私法各論集), 344 et seq. (Wu-Nan Publisher 1998).
126. Supreme Court's Civil Judgment, Tai-Shang 1888 of 1993.
127. Supreme Court's Civil Judgment, Tai-Shang 1207 of 1996.

courts should look into the nature of the legal relationship at issue and characterize it as a matter of parental power or as a parent-child relationship under the Choice-of-law Act 1953.[128]

85. In contrast to disputes regarding the arguments raised by parents seeking guardianship of a child, other relatives' battle for a left-behind child have generated little attention on its characterization. In the case of the guardianship over an orphan (Wu), whose Taiwanese father died of heart disease when the child was taken to pay his first visit to Taiwan years after his Brazilian mother's death, the Kaohsiung District Court dealt with the problem of characterization as a standard procedure before applying specific provisions of the Choice-of-law Act 1953.[129] The plaintiff, Wu's Brazilian grandmother, asserted that she was qualified as the child's statutory guardian according to Article 1094 Paragraph 1 of Taiwan's Civil Code.[130] The court therefore characterized the dispute as a matter of guardianship under the criteria of the *lex fori*, i.e., Taiwanese law. The parties did not dispute the standard or the result of this characterization.[131]

86. A recent case concerns the Taiwanese heirs to succeed to the shares of a BVI corporation left by the deceased Taiwanese and the status of one of the heirs to administer the BVI estate under the BVI court's order. The Supreme Court ruled the status of the administrator to the BVI corporation shall be characterized as one of the internal affairs of the BVI corporation rather than question of succession under this author's suggestion and criticism on the lower court's judgments.[132]

§2. PRELIMINARY QUESTION

87. A conflict of laws rule contains a legal concept in the first part, such as 'succession on death' or 'tort', which is the principal question for the court to ascertain its governing law. The legal requirements for the concept of principal question may contain another concept and raise 'preliminary' or 'incidental' questions. For example, X claims to succeed the descendant Y's estate as Y's spouse, the principal question is succession, and the validity of X and Y's marriage is the preliminary

128. The problem should be solved under Art. 19 of the Choice-of-law Act 1953. *See* Rong-Chwan Chen, *Parental Power Shall Not Be Characterized as Effects of a Divorce*, 32 Taiwan Jurist (月旦法學教室) 42–43 (2005); Liu & Chen, *supra* n. 12, at 445.
129. Kaohsiung District Court's Civil Judgment, Qing 153 of 2001.
130. The Supreme Court affirmed that the grandmother was to be designated as the child's guardian under Brazilian law in its Decision Tai-Shang 2446 of 2003.
131. For comments on this case, *see* Rong-Chwan Chen, *A Comment on The Disputes of Guardianship over the Taiwan-Brazilian Orphan Wu*,76 Taiwan Law Review (月旦法學雜誌) 147–158 (2001); Rong-Chwan Chen, *Second Comment on the Disputes of Guardianship over the Taiwan-Brazilian Orphan Wu*, 17 Chinese (Taiwan) Yearbook on International Law and International Affairs (中國國際法與國際事務年報) 553–572 (2005).
132. Rong-Chwan Chen, *The Inheritance of Stock Shares and Administration of Estate in British Virgin Island: Analytical Comments on the Taiwan High Court's Judgement Shang 493 of 2014*, 366 Taiwan Law Journal (台灣法學雜誌) 1–28 (28 Apr. 2019).

question. It is necessary to resolve the dispute of validity of marriage before the dispute of succession. In an international context, the court has to find a conflict of laws rule to know which law governs the preliminary question before ascertaining the law applicable to the principal question.

88. The principal question and preliminary question are subject to different conflict of laws rules. It is beyond doubt that the preliminary question is not within the scope of the governing law of the principal question. If the principal question is governed by a foreign law, a dilemma raises as to which national choice-of-law system shall apply to the preliminary question, conflict of laws rules of the forum or of the *lex causae* of the principal question?[133]

89. There is no provision addressing the problem of incidental questions or preliminary questions in the Choice-of-law Act 2010. It is left to the court's discretion in practice. However, the Supreme Court has not expressly acknowledged the choice of law dilemma of preliminary question yet. In a case of 2007,[134] while considering the compensatory damages owed to the parents of a victim who lost her life in traffic accident, the Supreme Court ruled that the question of whether the parents of a victim can claim the costs to support their future life shall not be decided directly by the conflicts rule for torts.[135] Trying to remove such questions from the basket of the law applicable to torts, the Supreme Court said:

> 'The ideal of the *lex loci delicti* is to grant prompt and reasonable compensation to the victim and to safeguard the victim with the protection and compensation that he/she is usually granted in the place of his/her domicile. In this case, the question whether the victim is legally bound to support the parents is not an integrated and inseparable part of the principal legal relationship (tort), and therefore is not necessarily subject to the same applicable law designated by the conflicts rule for torts. Since the question of whether the victim is liable to support her parents is not an integrated and inseparable part of the tort in question, and the law relating to the liability for support differs from country to country, we conclude that for the question of whether the defendant is liable to compensate the victim, the applicable law, by designation of Article 9 Paragraph 1 of the Choice-of-law Act 1953, shall be the law of the place of the tortious act; for the issue of compensation or whether the victim is legally liable to support the plaintiffs, the applicable law, by designation of Article 21 of the Choice-of-law Act 1953, shall be the national law of the victim, i.e., the debtor to support.' [136]

90. In the above judgment, theoretically speaking, the tort is the principal question and the maintenance obligation is the preliminary question. This relationship

133. Rong-Chwan Chen, *The Preliminary or Incidental Question in Private International Law*, 12 Taiwan Law Review (月旦法學雜誌) 62–63 (April 1996).
134. Supreme Court's Civil Judgment, Tai-Shang 1804 of 2007.
135. For a short comment, *see* Rong-Chwan Chen, *supra* n. 46.
136. Supreme Court's Civil Judgment, Tai-Shang 1804 of 2007.

did not outstand in the choice-of-law process because instead of a foreign law, the *lex fori* governs the tort which is the principal question. The Supreme Court ruled correctly that the maintenance obligation between the victim and her parents is out of the scope of the governing law of the tortious liability. [137]

91. The same approach was erroneously adopted in a case of 2008.[138] It involves the question of whether a Taiwanese employer must compensate an injured foreign worker with the basic salary provided in Taiwanese Labour Standards Act.[139] The Supreme Court addressed in this case that the measurement of the loss of working capacity, since it is to be decided after the liability for damages is confirmed, is not an integral or inseparable part of the tort in question and can be subject to another applicable law. Although the applicable law of the tort in question as designated by the Choice-of-law Act 1953[140] was Taiwanese law, the Supreme Court ruled that the compensation for the loss of working capacity during the period when the injured victim was not legally permitted to work in Taiwan shall be governed by his own national law, i.e., Vietnamese law. [141] As mentioned above, it is the right case to adopt the *dépeçage* approach. This author concurred with the conclusion of the above judgment while he is of the opinion that the measurement of loss or damage concerns basically an investigation of the victim's living situation in Vietnam, so it is correct to take the victim's legal protection under Vietnamese law into account.[142]

§3. Substance and Procedure

92. The difference between substance and procedure is significant in civil procedure. Disputes of substance are resolved with court judgments, while disputes of procedure are resolved with court decisions. In PIL, questions of procedure are governed inherently by *lex fori*, while questions of substance are governed by the law which is designated by the relevant conflict of laws rule. Before determining the law applicable to a question, the court has to characterize whether it is substantive or procedural.

93. The statute of limitations is a very illustrative example. It is characterized under Taiwanese legal system as a substantive question because Taiwan's Civil Code stipulates a substantive effect to recognize the debtor's right to refuse performance.[143] It is, however, characterized in some countries as a procedural question

137. Rong-Chwan Chen, *supra* n. 46, at 25.
138. Supreme Court's Civil Judgment, Tai-Shang 1838 of 2008.
139. The Labour Standards Act (Lao-Dong Ji-Zhun Fa, 勞動基準法) was adopted in 1984 and last revised in 2020.
140. Choice-of-law Act 1953, Art. 9 para. 1.
141. Supreme Court's Civil Judgment, Tai-Shang 1838 of 2008.
142. For a short comment, *see* Rong-Chwan Chen, *The Law Applicable to Compensation for Foreign Workers*, 80 Taiwan Jurist (月旦法學教室) 22–23 (2009).
143. CC, Art. 144.

to disqualify the creditor's right of access to the courts.[144] Furthermore, the Choice-of-law Act 2010 addresses its governing law in a single Article.[145]

§4. *Renvoi*

I. The Basic Rule

94. The process and result of a court's applying conflicts rules are theoretically result-neutral, while it is the final substantive conclusion that faces potential criticism from the parties and the public. The legislature thus tried to make the conflict of laws rules as reasonable as possible and reserved some general principles for the courts to ease the tension between conflicts justice and material justice (substantive justice).[146] When the court applies a foreign law to a civil matter with foreign elements, and the conflict of laws rules designate the civil matter to law of other country, it raises a dilemma whether to apply such rules or not.

95. If the conflict of laws rules of the relevant countries are the same, they will all direct the civil matter to the same governing law. However, countries around the world have not yet reached a universal agreement on the approach or mode of designating the applicable law in international cases. Private international law basically remains to be embodied in the form of domestic legislation. Conflict of laws legislation differs from country to country in both form and substance. The court therefore faces such differences and what amounts to a conflict of conflicts legislation. The most apparent conflict between the Choice-of-law Act 2010 and private international law of foreign countries is the provisions on personal law: *lex patriae* versus *lex domicilii*, or the national law versus the law of habitual residence.

96. As the conflict of conflicts laws is the reality, it is a consistent policy of the Choice-of-law Act 2010 to adopt some provisions to deal with bridging gap between the conflicts legislations of Taiwan and foreign countries, furthering international harmony of judgments and deterring 'forum shopping' by the parties. *Renvoi* was thus employed.

97. Given the fact that an individual's personal law is designated as the law of his/her habitual residence in many countries, Article 6 of the Choice-of-law Act 2010 focuses only on the international harmony of personal law and simplifies total *renvoi* to certain types of *renvoi*.[147] It states: 'Where this Act provides that the national law of a party is applicable, but the national law of the party indicates that

144. Rong-Chwan Chen, *The Law Applicable to the Statute of Limitation*, 74 Taiwan Law Journal (台灣本土法學雜誌) 111–122 (September 2005).
145. Choice-of-law Act 2010, Art. 36: 'The time limitation of action for a claim is governed by the law applicable to the legal relationship from which the claim arose.'
146. For the conflicts justice and material justice, *see* Rong-Chwan Chen, *supra* n. 25.
147. The Choice-of-law Act 1953 adopted 'total *renvoi*'. In Art. 29 it provides: 'Whenever the national law of a person shall be applied under the present Act, another law shall be applied if under his/her national law the legal relation in question shall be governed by that other law; the other law shall

another law should govern the legal relation in question, such other law is applied. However, if the national law of the party or the other law indicates, in turn, the law of the ROC as applicable, the internal law of the ROC is applied.'

98. Article 6 of the Choice-of-law Act 2010 fills the gap of single *renvoi* or direct reference, which directs the courts to apply the relevant conflicts rule in the person's national law and to refer to the *lex fori* when it is so provided in it.[148] The doctrine of 'double *renvoi*' or total *renvoi* was revised to allow only a certain types of *renvoi*.

II. The Application of *Renvoi*

99. The law of a person's habitual residence has been widely adopted as the law applicable to many personal legal relationships in foreign conflicts legislation. The national law basically prevails over the law of domicile or habitual residence in the framework of the Choice-of-law Act 2010's drafters. The provision 'whenever the national law of a person shall be applied under the present Act' is therefore interpreted according to its spirit as 'the cases whenever the personal law of a person is applicable' and the national law of an alien is expected to be sent back by referring to the whole of his/her national law, including its conflict of laws rules.[149]

100. Taiwanese courts shall apply the law designated by the Choice-of-law Act once they have decided to exercise jurisdiction over a case containing a foreign complexion. If the applicable law is a foreign law, it might be difficult to decide whether its conflicts rules are included in the applicable 'law'. *Renvoi* allows the court to apply the foreign conflicts rules and to refer the case back to the law of the other country. For the purpose of international harmony in conflicts cases, the provision of *renvoi* shall be applied in all situations. But the provisions limit themselves to application only in cases where the person's national law shall be applicable under the Choice-of-law Act. Article 29 of the Choice-of-law Act 1953 signalled the message of limiting its applicability to the legal relationships governed by a person's personal law. The Choice-of-law Act 2010 went further and adopted nationality as a connecting factor to replace habitual residence in conflict of laws rules for legal relationships other than personal capacity or status. Under such circumstances, the provisions of *renvoi* in Article 6 of the Choice-of-law Act 2010 can be applied in cases 'wherever' a party's national law shall be applicable under the Choice-of-law Act.[150]

---

be further applied if under the rules in that other law it shall be governed by such other law. However, the law of the ROC shall be applied if under that other law it shall be governed by the law of the ROC.'

148. Rong-Chwan Chen, *The Legal Foundation of Direct Renvoi*, 13 Taiwan Law Review (月旦法學雜誌) 67–68 (1996).
149. Liu & Chen, *supra* n. 12, at 536.
150. Rong-Chwan Chen, *supra* n. 58, at 27.

III. Court Judgments on *Renvoi*

101. The provisions of *renvoi* in the Choice-of-law Act 1953 have been applied in some reported court decisions. In an illustrative judgment of Taipei District Court,[151] the parents of a child contested its legitimacy. The court confirmed its jurisdiction over the case by applying the rules for determining domestic jurisdiction by analogy before touching on any questions regarding the merits. The father was a citizen of Japan and the mother a citizen of the ROC. The court determined that the law of the ROC should govern by applying the rule of *renvoi* and examining Japanese legislation on private international law. The court ruled pursuant to Article 16 Paragraph 1 Choice-of-law Act 1953 that the child's legitimacy should be governed by the national law of its mother's husband at the time of birth, namely, Japanese law. After ascertaining that the case should be governed by the law of the ROC under Article 21 of the Japanese enactment of private international law (Horei), the court concluded that the rule of *renvoi* should apply in this case. The law of the ROC should thus be finally applied. It is understandable that the legislative preparers of the Choice-of-law Act 1953 preferred to include all types of *renvoi* to emphasize its function of referring from law to law. The *lex fori* is welcome by the court at the expense of refraining from an absolutism of the domestic conflicts policy.

102. In a case decided on May 6th 2021[152], X, a citizen of Macau, and Y, a citizen of Taiwan together sought for an order to overrule an administrative decision refusing their application for same-sex marriage registration. Articles 1462 and 1501 of the Macau Civil Code prohibit same-sex marriage, while Taiwan's Act for Implementing Interpretation 748[153] provides the legal ground and requisites of a same-sex legal relationship. In its judgment, the Taipei High Administrative Court did not apply the substantive rules of Macau to uphold the administrative decision. Instead, it ruled that the law of Taiwan applies not only to Y but also to X by way of *renvoi*. It stated that although Macau is no more a foreign territory after it was handed over to China in 1999, the Choice-of-law Act applies *mutatis mutandis* to the civil matters involving Macau under Article 38 of the Act Governing Relations with Hong Kong and Macau. In pursuance to Article 46 Sentence 1 of the Choice-of-law Act 2010, the formation of X and Y's same-sex marriage is governed by the national law of each party. It means that X's permissibility to enter into a same-sex marriage is governed by his own national law. The conflicts rules in the Macau Civil Code applies ascertain furtherly the governing law of it according to the *renvoi* rule stipulated in Article 6 of the Choice-of-law Act 2010. The Taipei High Administrative Court noted that Article 24 of the Macau Civil Code provides that the family relations shall be regulated by the personal law of the respective persons, and Article 30 of it states that the personal law is that of the habitual residence of an individual. Since X has been living and working in Taiwan from March of 2017 through 2021,

151. Taipei District Court's Civil Judgment, Qing 98 of 1999.
152. Taipei High Administrative Court's Judgment, Su 14 of 2020.
153. *See infra* n. 537.

the Court found X's habitual residence is in Taiwan. The law of Taiwan thus applies to the requisites of X's same-sex marriage as the law designated by the conflicts rule of Macau.

103. When the foreign conflicts rule is applied by way of *renvoi*, the foreign interpretations of connecting factors such as domicile or habitual residence shall also be applied. A further conflict in their characterizations is thus avoided. It is this author's opinion that by way of *renvoi,* the result of ascertaining the governing laws by a Taiwan court might be 'identical' with that of the court of the national state of the person in question.[154] Given the facts that the characterizations might be different, the international harmony of judgments of courts of relevant States can only be reached by adopting the characterization *per se* for the referred conflicts rule. It is obvious that in the case mentioned above, the Taipei High Administrative Court interpreted the habitual residence in conflicts of Macau without referring to the standards adopted in Macau.

§5. General Conflicts Rule / Special Conflicts Rule

104. The first part of a conflict of laws rule is a concept for a legal relation. In the statutist era, all legal norms were categorized into personal law, real law and mixed law, no conflict of laws rule was established for specific legal relation. It was not until the era when a legal relation is subject to the law where its 'seat' locates that each legal relation is subject to a conflict of laws rule.[155] The legal relation is quite general and broad in the beginning. Along with the development of private international law, some conflict of laws principles were established gradually for special legal relations. It is quite normal that a special legal relation and the general legal relation that the former is composed of are both stipulated in the same private international law legislation.

105. The density of the conflicts norms is a legislative policy that has to be considered by the legislature. This policy affects how much a single civil matter is subject to both a general conflicts rule and a special conflicts rule. In Choice-of-law Act 2010, some special conflicts rules are embodied after a general conflicts rule is formulated in the prior place. For example, Article 25 stipulates the conflict of laws rule for torts in general terms; Articles 26 to 28 stipulate, respectively, the following special torts: product liability, anti-competitive conducts, tort which was committed by means of publication, radio, television, internet publication or other medium of communication. The conflict of such general conflicts rules and special conflicts rules is resolved according to the Latin maxim '*lex specialis derogat legi generali*', which means 'special law derogates general laws', the special conflicts rule prevails and applies to the civil matter at issue.

---

154. Rong-Chwan Chen, *The Characterization and Second Characterization in Private International Law*, 40 Taiwan Law Journal (台灣本土法學雜誌) 129–136 (November 2002).
155. Ernst Rabel, 1 *The Conflict of Laws: A Comparative Study* 50 (2d ed., The University of Michigan Press 1958).

106. In practice, the governing law of individual rights also derogates the governing law of a general estate that includes different kinds of property rights. The governing law of succession of estate on death is a general governing law, while the governing law of a property right over a thing or a right to the shares of a corporation is a special individual governing law. The special individual governing laws prevail and are applicable to the specific rights that are comprised in a more general right of which governing law is otherwise applicable.[156]

§6. ASSIMILATION

107. Given the diversity of private international laws and the plurality of municipal laws around the world, a domestic court faces difficulty in coordinating the domestic law and the relevant foreign laws. As the court is required to ascertain the governing law and to apply specific provisions in it, the institutions unfound in the domestic PIL have to be assimilated to the institutions stipulated as the operating facts or first part in the conflicts rules; and a foreign vested right unknown in the governing law has to be adapted to the closest equivalent right in it.[157]

108. The problem of assimilation or adaptation in PIL has long drawn the attention of this author.[158] The Choice-of-law Act 2010 neither utilizes the terminology nor addresses it in general. However, a foreign vested right *in rem* is adapted to a closest equivalent right *in rem* if the object was moved from abroad into Taiwan. It is stated that the law of the ROC governs the effect of a property right over a movable thing formed in accordance with the law prevailing in the foreign location from which it is brought into the ROC.[159] In other words, a foreign right *in rem* over a movable property can be directly recognized as the same right *in rem* in Taiwan if there is an equivalent one under the Taiwanese law of property. It is why the effects of a foreign right *in rem* are governed by the Taiwanese law.

109. Following the same direction of thinking, if the foreign right *in rem* has no counterpart in Taiwanese law of property, it is up to the court to adapt it to the closest equivalent right *in rem* or to recognize it as an obligatory claim between the parties. Likewise, the effects of a foreign trust or legacy over the properties composed in it and situated within Taiwan need to be adapted for the purpose of taking effect in Taiwan. A foreign trust which is of *in rem* effects in that foreign country is to be adapted to a fiduciary obligation if that trust is missing some requisites to be recognized as a trust of *in rem* effects in Taiwan. A foreign legacy which transfers the title directly to the legatee at the time of the legator's death is to be adapted to have effects of creating an obligatory claim to transfer the properties in question.[160]

---

156. Liu & Chen, *supra* n. 12, at 499.
157. Liu & Chen, *supra* n. 12, at 589.
158. Rong-Chwan Chen, *The Problem of Adaptation or Adjustment in Private International Law*, 145 China Law Journal (法學叢刊) 111 (January 1992).
159. Choice-of-law Act 2010, Art. 40.
160. Art. 31 of the EU Succession Regulation 2012 addresses 'Adaptation of rights in rem' and emphasizes 'the aims and interests pursued by the specific right in rem and the effects attached to it':

§7. *Ordre Public* (Public Policy)

110. 'Conflicts justice' rather than 'material justice' (substantive justice) has been the main objective of the Choice-of-law Act 1953.[161] Material or substantive justice plays a more important role in the Choice-of-law Act 2010 even though conflicts justice is still adhered to. In contrast to facilitating domestic moral values or public policy by way of applying the law favouring the same goal, the provision on public order operates to exclude foreign law that is incompatible with the public order or *boni mores* of Taiwan. It is emphasized that the designated foreign law shall still be applied even if differences exist between it and the *lex fori*; it can be excluded only if it will lead to a 'result' that cannot be accepted in the domestic legal system.[162]

111. It has been established by Taiwan's Supreme Court that, unless the result of applying the foreign law in question is incompatible with the Taiwanese public order or *boni mores*, mere differences in the provisions of foreign law as compared to its Taiwanese counterpart is not sufficient to exclude its application.[163] As an example, even though gambling is legal in the US state of Nevada and such law is literally incompatible with the Taiwanese public order or *boni mores* under which gambling is prohibited, the court concluded that the result of applying state law of Nevada was not incompatible with the Taiwanese public order or *boni mores*, and its application should not be excluded.[164]

112. 'Public order or *boni mores*' is an indefinite legal concept that needs to be interpreted on a case-by-case basis. Although the provision stipulates the standard of exclusion as being based on a literal comparison of the provisions of Taiwanese law and foreign law, the defensive spirit of the rule is always emphasized in its application.[165]

'Where a person invokes a right in rem to which he is entitled under the law applicable to the succession and the law of the Member State in which the right is invoked does not know the right in rem in question, that right shall, if necessary and to the extent possible, be adapted to the closest equivalent right in rem under the law of that State, taking into account the aims and the interests pursued by the specific right in rem and the effects attached to it.' Regulation (EU) No 650/2012 of the European Parliament and of the Council of 4 July 2012 on jurisdiction, applicable law, recognition and enforcement of decisions and acceptance and enforcement of authentic instruments in matters of succession and on the creation of a European Certificate of Succession. OJ L 201 (27.7.2012), pp. 107–134.

161. For a general discussion on conflicts justice and substantive justice, *see* Rong-Chwan Chen, *supra* n. 25.
162. Choice-of-law Act 2010, Art. 40.
163. Liu & Chen, *supra* n. 12, at 226.
164. Supreme Court's Civil Judgment, Tai-Shang 130 of 1994. Two reported cases of lower courts, Taiwan High Court's Civil Judgment, Shang 396 of 2000 and Taipei District Court's Civil Judgment, Su 4566 of 2007, followed the opinions stated in this precedent. *See also* Rong-Chwan Chen, *The Problem of Gambling Debt in Private International Law*, 2 Taiwan Law Review (月旦法學雜誌) 52–53 (1995).
165. Rong-Chwan Chen, *The Application of the Ordre Public Clause*, 1 Taiwan Law Review (月旦法學雜誌) 70–71 (1995).

113. The contents of 'public order or *boni mores*' evolve along with the development of law. The legal policy and development on same-sex marriage is illustrative in this regard. When the parties to a marriage are required to be a man and a woman under the provisions of Taiwan's Civil Code, the foreign law legalizing same-sex marriages is deemed against Taiwan's 'public order or *boni mores*'. It is noteworthy that the freedom of forming a same-sex union has been established as part of Taiwan's 'public order or *boni mores*' due to the promulgation of the Act for Implementing Interpretation 748.[166] The foreign law that prohibits or does not recognize same-sex marriages is shifted to be contradictory to Taiwan's 'public order or *boni mores*'. In a case decided on March 4th 2021,[167] the Taipei High Administrative Court ruled that the law of Malaysia which prohibits same-sex unions are contrary to Taiwan's 'public order or *boni mores*' and can be excluded when it is otherwise applicable to the substantive requisites of a same-sex union of which a citizen of Taiwan is a party. [168]

§8. Overriding Mandatory Rules

114. Overriding mandatory rules are not addressed in the Choice-of-law Act 2010. Their application is left to the court's discretion on a case-by-case basis. Although there has not yet been any reported case on this provision, it is believed that the overriding character of domestic mandatory rules will be established as a reflection of the spirit of such rules.

115. In a case decided in 2012,[169] the parties disputed on a patent licensing agreement in which the parties had chosen the law of a foreign country (the Netherlands) as the governing law. The Supreme Court ruled that all the issues around such licensing agreement shall be governed by the chosen law. [170] It is this author's opinion that since the agreement is so closely connected with Taiwan and since the market influenced by the monopolized licensing is in Taiwan, Taiwan's domestic competition regulation (Fair Trade Act) [171] shall apply directly to regulate the anti-competitive conduct of foreign companies.[172] It is also this author's opinion that the regulation on food safety of a foreign country can be applied directly if is closely connected with the resulted claim, regardless of its nature of public law.[173]

166. *See infra* n. 537.
167. Taipei High Administrative Court's Judgment, Su 1805 of 2019.
168. *See* Rong-Chwan Chen, *The Ordre Public in a Same-Sex Marriage: A Comment on Taipei High Administrative Court's Recent Judgment*, 219 Taiwan Jurist (月旦法學教室) 27–31 (May 2021).
169. Supreme Court's Civil Judgment, Tai-Shang 883 of 2012.
170. Supreme Court's Civil Judgment, Tai-Shang 883 of 2012.
171. The Fair Trade Act (Gong-Ping Jiao-Yi Fa, 公平交易法) was adopted in 1991 and last revised in 2017.
172. Rong-Chwan Chen, *The Immediate Application of Fair Trade Act to the International Licensing Contracts*, 131 Taiwan Jurist (月旦法學教室) 36–38 (2013).
173. Rong-Chwan Chen, *Application of Foreign Public Law in Civil Matters with Foreign Elements*, 147 Taiwan Jurist (月旦法學教室) 30–32 (January 2015).

§9. Evasion of the Law

116. Given the fact that conflicts justice might be distorted if evasion of compulsory provisions were tolerated, Article 7 was added in the Choice-of-law Act 2010 to maintain the applicability of domestic compulsory provisions. It states: 'Where a party to a civil matter involving foreign elements evades a compulsory provision or a prohibition of the law of the ROC, that compulsory provision or prohibition is nevertheless applied.'

117. To evade a law it requires the malice to evade and the fraudulent change of the connecting factor that will otherwise be accepted and designating to a governing law.[174] The above provision proclaims that manipulated connecting factors are far from genuine and fair to designate governing laws and shall be disregarded in the process of choice of law. The provision just states that a domestic compulsory regulation is not evaded as a result of such efforts. The parties are thus deprived of the interests they otherwise gained because the evaded domestic mandatory rules shall still be applied. The evasion of a compulsory provision or a regulatory law of a foreign country is not explicitly stipulated. The above provision can apply by analogy to fill the gap.

§10. Reference to the Law of States with Multiple Legal Systems

118. As the *lex patriae* is adopted as a person's personal law, his/her nationality is the decisive connecting factor. The court will therefore face the problem of how to ascertain the governing law when the national law includes multiple legal systems. In other words, even though a person's *lex patriae* has been ascertained, the problem of choice of law may still arise if the person is a subject of a country which is composed of several distinct legal territories or legal systems. The test of nationality, in this case, may not offer a final answer in itself.

119. PIL legislations deal with such problem either by designating directly a municipal law in the national law or by referring to the internal conflict of laws rules and designating the governing municipal law indirectly. Choice-of-law Act 2010 replaced the direct designation rule of its 1953 version with an indirect designation rule. Article 5 states: 'Where reference is made by this Act to the national law of a party, but the national law of the party differs by reference to sub-national region or another factor, the applicable law is the law as indicated by the rules on choice of law of that national law; if the rules on choice of law of that national law are unclear, the law with which the party is most closely connected, whether by region or by the other factor, is applied.'

120. The above provisions offer a solution which delegates the matter to the internal choice-of-law rules in such national law. This policy will inevitably cause the courts to conduct an extensive search on the applicable law because the internal

174. Liu & Chen, *supra* n. 12, at 567.

conflict of laws rules adopted in federal states, divided states or other multi-legal-system countries – no matter whether interterritorial, interpersonal or intertemporal in nature – are consequently relevant for designating the applicable legal system within such countries. The indirect designation serves to fulfil conflicts justice and increase the reasonableness in ascertaining the governing law by referring to the 'applicable' internal conflicts law of foreign countries.[175] The time factor problem caused by change of the governing law is essentially an intertemporal conflict of a new internal law and an old internal law. It can also be resolved by referring to the conflicts rule to ascertain the governing internal law.

175. Liu & Chen, *supra* n. 12, at 514.

Part II. Conflict of Laws Rules

Chapter 1. Persons

§1. Natural Persons

I. Legal Capacity

121. There are two kinds of legal capacity for a natural person in Taiwan's Civil Code. One is the capacity to enjoy rights and to be liable to duties. The other is the capacity to effectively make juridical acts. The former legal capacity of a person commences from the moment of live birth and terminates at death.[176] An unborn child is considered as if it were already born with regard to its interests, except it was subsequently born dead. [177] A foetus has the capacity to be a party in an action concerning the entitlement of its interests. [178] The latter legal capacity is granted basically when a person attains majority upon reaching the eighteenth (or twentieth before 2013) year of age. [179] The minor, who has not reached their seventh year of age, has no capacity to make juridical acts. The minor, who is over seven years of age, has a limited capacity to make juridical acts. The married minor has the capacity to make juridical acts. [180]

122. The conflict of laws rules to the above two kinds of legal capacity are stipulated respectively in Choice-of-law Act 2010. The legal capacity of a person to enjoy rights is governed by his/her national law. [181] A person's capacity to act is also governed by his/her national law, while the capacity of a person to act is not lost or limited because of a change of nationality by him/her. In order to protect the third parties and the public order in the forum state, where an alien of no or limited capacity to act under his/her national law is of full capacity to act under the law of the ROC, he/she is deemed to be of full capacity to act with respect to his juridical acts undertaken within the ROC. However, a person's juridical act under family law or law of succession is governed absolute by his/her national law; a juridical act

176. CC, Art. 6.
177. CC, Art. 7.
178. CCP, Art. 40 para. 2.
179. CC, Art. 12. This Article was revised in 2021 to lower the age of majority to eighteen. The revised provisions are set to come into effect from January 1st 2023.
180. CC, Art. 13.
181. Choice-of-law Act 2010, Art. 9.

regarding immovable property located in a foreign State is under the courts' exclusive jurisdiction in such State. The law of the ROC is thus unnecessary to be taken into account in determining a person's capacity to make such acts. [182]

123. In Taiwan's Civil Code, an absent person who has disappeared for more than seven years may be declared dead by the court upon the application of any interested person or the public prosecutor; if the absent person was over eighty years of age and has disappeared for more than three years, he may be declared dead; if the absent person was in a catastrophe, he may be declared dead when it has been over a year after the end of the catastrophe.[183] A person who had been declared dead is presumed to be dead at the date fixed in the judgment.[184] Such provisions apply to the ROC citizens that can be confirmed absent within its territory. Whether and how a court may decree over a foreigner or alien remains problematic.

124. The Choice-of-law Act 2010 thus provides: '1. Where an alien having a domicile or residence within the ROC has disappeared, a declaration of death of that alien may be decreed with respect to his property located within the ROC or with respect to those legal relations affecting him that are required to be determined by reference to the law of the ROC. 2. A declaration of death of an alien may be decreed in accordance with the law of the ROC and without regard to the limitations mentioned in the preceding paragraph, upon the application of the spouse or a lineal relative by blood of the disappeared alien if the spouse or lineal relative is a national of the ROC and has a domicile or residence within the ROC. 3. The effect of a declaration of death decreed under either of the preceding two paragraphs is governed by the law of the ROC.'[185]

125. Similar situation and problems happen to the courts' decree to declare an adult's guardianship or curatorship (assistantship). According to the Civil Code, with respect to any person who is not able to make declaration of intention, receive declaration of intention, or who lacks the ability to discern the outcome of the declaration of intention due to mental disability, the court may order the commencement of guardianship at the request of the person in question, his/her spouse, any relative within the fourth degree of kinship, a prosecutor, a competent authority, an organization of social welfare, an assistant, an agent of adult guardianship by agreement or any other interested person. If the cause of guardianship ceases to exist, yet assistantship is necessary, the court, may order the commencement of assistantship to replace the commencement of guardianship.[186] A person who has become subject to the order of the commencement of guardianship has no capacity to perform any

182. Choice-of-law Act 2010, Art. 10
183. CC, Art. 8.
184. CC, Art. 9.
185. Choice-of-law Act 2010, Art. 11.
186. CC, Art. 14.

juridical act.[187] A person under assistance must obtain the consent of his/her assistant if he/she intends to perform acts specified by the Civil Code; provided, however, that, this shall not apply to any act relating to pure legal benefit or the necessity based on the person's age, status, and daily life.[188]

126. With regard to a ROC court's decree to declare an alien's commencement of guardianship or curatorship, the Choice-of-law Act 2010 provides: '1. Where there is a valid ground to declare guardianship or curatorship in respect of an alien under both his/her national law and the law of the ROC, a declaration of guardianship or curatorship may be decreed if he/she has a domicile or residence within the ROC. 2. The effect of a declaration of guardianship or curatorship decreed under the preceding paragraph is governed by the law of the ROC.'[189]

127. It is noteworthy that if a person's national law is applicable to his/her legal capacity, guardianship or curatorship, the rules of *renvoi* applies accordingly.[190] The conflicts rule for such issue in that person's national law shall be applied to consider its further reference to other law. The rigidness of the nationality as a connecting factor can thus be softened.

II. Name

128. Under the household registration system, a person is identified by his/her name. The Name Act[191] provides that in all legal matters that require the use of a name, a person's legal name must be used.[192] The legal name of a citizen of the ROC shall be that entered in the household registration system; a citizen may have just one legal name. The name of a Taiwan indigenous person or member of another ethnic minority may be registered in accordance with his/her culture and customs. If the Han Chinese name of an indigenous person has already been registered, he/she may apply to restore his/her ethnic name. Following a person's legal restoration of an ethnic name, he/she may reapply to restore his/her original Han Chinese name. Each type of restoration is allowed one time only. If an ROC national marries a foreign national or stateless person, the spouse and all children, if any, must take a Chinese name that conforms to ROC practices. This shall also apply to a foreign national or stateless person applying for naturalization.[193] The ethnic name or Han Chinese name of a Taiwan indigenous person or other ethnic minority may be listed in Romanized form together with the name in Chinese characters. When taking a Chinese name during the naturalization process, a foreign national or a

187. CC, Art. 15.
188. CC, Art. 15-2.
189. Choice-of-law Act, Art. 12.
190. Choice-of-law Act 2010, Art. 6.
191. The Name Act (Xing-Ming Tiao-Li, 姓名條例) was adopted in 1953 and last revised in 2015.
192. Name Act, Art. 5.
193. Name Act, Art. 1.

stateless person may have his/her original foreign name registered in Romanized form alongside the name in Chinese characters.[194]

129. In private legal aspect, the Civil Code provides the protection of a person's right to his/her name and the remedies for a tort infringing it. When one's personality is infringed, one may apply to the court for removing. When one's personality is in danger of being infringed, one may apply for prevention. In such circumstances, an action for damages for emotional distress may be brought only it is otherwise provided by the law.[195] The rights protected under these provisions are the personal right to be identified by the name and the right to defend from misusing the name.

130. The Civil Code also stipulates some basic principles on the decision of a child's surname and the change of surname after change of a person's legal status. Parents should agree in writing before filing the child's birth registration regarding if the child assumes the father's or mother's surname. Without such an agreement or when the agreement cannot be made, the surname should be determined by drawing lots at the Household Registration Office. After filing the child's birth registration and prior to the child reaching maturity, the parents may in writing change the child's surname to either the father's or mother's. Where the child reached his/her maturity, he/she may change his/her surname to either the father's or mother's surname.[196] A child born out of wedlock shall assume the mother's surname. [197] The husband and the wife should keep his or her own surname. Unless one party shall prefix to his or her surname that of the spouse in writing at the household administration authority. The party who prefixed to his or her surname that of the spouse shall return to his or her own surname. But only one time for change during the continuance of the marriage relationship. [198]

131. The problem of a person's name is not specifically addressed in Choice-of-law Act 2010. The tortious liability for infringing the victim's right of name is governed by the applicable law to the tort which is the law most closely connected with it. [199] The problems of how to carry a surname are interpreted to be respectively within the scope of parents-children relation, personal effects of marriage, adoption, and acknowledgments, which is basically subject to the personal law, i.e., national law of the person.

132. According to the Name Act, a person who meets one of the following requirements may apply to alter his/her surname: 1. the applicant's paternity has been acknowledged by the natural father or the acknowledgement thereof has been revoked; 2. the applicant has been adopted or his/her adoption has been annulled or terminated; 3. the applicant is a Taiwan indigenous person or other ethnic minority

194. Name Act, Art. 4.
195. CC, Art. 18.
196. CC, Art. 1059.
197. CC, Art. 1059-1.
198. CC, Art. 1000.
199. Choice-of-law Act, Art. 25.

member and the adopted Han Chinese surname leads to misapprehension of the family name; 4. the transliteration is too long; or 5. the applicant's surname has been changed in accordance with other laws or regulations. After marrying, a person may apply to take the spouse's surname or reinstate his/her original surname. As for the latter, a person may apply to reinstate his/her original surname only once per marriage.[200]

III. Nationality / Habitual Residence / Domicile

133. A person's nationality is the link between him/her and the relevant State. The regulation and policy of a State's nationality law decides whether and how it will grant a person its nationality. A person's nationality is thus governed by the nationality law of the relevant States respectively rather than his/her own personal law.

134. A person's domicile is the connecting factor between him/her and the place where it locates. Due to the policy that the courts at the defendant's domicile may exercise their jurisdiction over his/her law suits and the Choice-of-law Act 2010 acknowledges the positive and negative conflict of domiciles, the governing law of a person's domicile is the law of the place where it locates rather than his/her personal law or national law.[201] Habitual residence is only deployed in AFM to decide a court's jurisdiction. It has no legislative definition and is up to the court's interpretation on a case-by-case basis.

135. According to Taiwan's Civil Code, a person who resides in a place with the intention of remaining there permanently, upon presence of supporting fact, is to establish his/her domicile at that place. Every person has at all times one domicile, and no person has more than one domicile at a time. [202] The domicile of a person who has no or is limited in capacity to make juridical acts is the domicile of his/her guardian. [203] The domicile of the husband and the wife shall be agreed by mutual agreement; if it has not been agreed or cannot be agreed, it may depend on the court by application. Before the ruling of the court, it will be presumed the common household domicile as the domicile of the husband and the wife. [204] The domicile of a minor child is that of the father and mother. [205] A person, who has left his/her domicile with the intention of repealing it, upon presence of supporting fact, is to repeal the domicile. [206] A person's residence is deemed to be his/her domicile in either of the following circumstances: (1) when his/her domicile cannot be certified; (2) when he/she has no domicile in Taiwan except when *lex domicilli* governs.

200. Name Act, Art. 8.
201. Liu & Chen, *supra* n. 12, at 107–108.
202. CC, Art. 20.
203. CC, Art. 21.
204. CC, Art. 1002.
205. CC, Art. 1062.
206. CC, Art. 24.

[207] Where a person has chosen a residence for a specific purpose, the residence is deemed to be his/her domicile with regard to that purpose. [208]

IV. Stateless Persons and Refugees

136. Stateless persons and refugees are all foreigners or aliens in Taiwan's private international law. In terms of choice of law in a civil matter with foreign elements, they are subject to the same rules for other foreigners. The Choice-of-law Act 2010 provides particularly that the law of domicile will be applicable when the court is required to apply the national law of a stateless person. [209] The AFM also specifies the ROC courts have international jurisdiction over the marriage matter where either the husband or the wife is a stateless person but has habitual residence within the territory of the ROC. [210]

137. Although refugees are not specifically identified in private international law, a refugee may be deemed as a stateless person if he/she has and will have no political connection as nationality at all in the future. In public legal aspects, however, refugees are regulated in Taiwanese law as a call to protect them. The National Immigration Agency of the Ministry of the Interior is empowered by its Organization Act[211] to formulate laws and regulations regarding refugees, and to handle matters relating to their identification, asylum, sheltering, safeguarding, settling, and management. The employers are encouraged to hire refugees that are permitted to stay in the ROC.[212] Under the Employment Service Act[213], if the refugees are so duly employed, the employers are exempted from paying the employment security fees and many other duties and legal requirements.[214]

V. Transsexuals

138. The right to change gender is protected as a part of the right of personality in finding who and what a person is either from male to female or from female to male. The transsexuals are required to seek a medical review and approval for the transgender surgery. Their privacy and basic rights are protected under the effective

207. CC, Art. 22.
208. CC, Art. 23.
209. Choice-of-law Act 2010, Art. 3.
210. AFM, Art. 53 para. 1 Item 3.
211. The Organization Act of the National Immigration Agency, Ministry of the Interior (Nei-Zheng-Bu Yi-Min-Shu Zu-Zhi Fa, 内政部移民署組織法) was adopted in 2005 and last revised in 2013.
212. *Ibid.*, Art. 2 para. 1 Item 9.
213. The Employment Service Act (Jiu-Ye Fu-Wu Fa, 就業服務法) was adopted in 1992 and last revised in 2018.
214. *Ibid.*, Art. 51 para. 1.

laws. After the change of gender, according to the Household Registration Act[215], the transsexuals are entitle to apply for alteration of gender in the household registration.[216]

139. As gender is not considered as a connecting factor in private international law, change of gender is not going to have effect in the sense of choice of law. The law governing his/her personal affairs remains the same. However, the transsexuals from foreign countries are regulated in some public legal aspects. For example, the Regulation Governing the Detention of the Aliens[217] provides the security inspection of a foreign transsexual detainee. 'Upon entering a detention centre, each detainee shall have a body security inspection, and have his/her fingerprint pressed and photograph taken by detention centre officers. If the detainee is a woman, the inspection shall be conducted by female officers. Male detainees shall be separated from female detainees in detention centres. If a detainee is found to be a transgender, he/she will be detained separately in a solitary room in detention centre (according to the gender showing on his/her identification certificate).'[218] The same standards apply to transsexual detainees from the Mainland China, Hong Kong and Macau under Article 3 of the Regulations Governing the Detention of the People of the Mainland China Area and the Residents of Hong Kong and Macau.[219]

§2. Legal Persons

I. Incorporated Organizations

140. An incorporated organization is established in accordance with the laws in a particular legal system. Its existence, personality and legal functions are well recognized within the territory it was incorporated, while it will face the problem whether it will be recognized in other countries.

141. The basic rules dealing with foreign legal persons are stipulated in the Enforcement Act of the Part of General Principles of the Civil Code.[220] In states that unless otherwise provided by the law, the establishment of the foreign legal person shall not be recognized.[221] If the foreign legal person, the establishment of which has not been recognized, makes a juridical act with another in the name of a foreign legal person, the actor shall be jointly liable for this juridical act with the foreign

215. The Household Registration Act (Hu-Ji-Fa, 戶籍法) was adopted in 1931 and last revised in 2015.
216. *Ibid.*, Art. 21.
217. The Regulation Governing the Detention of the Aliens (Wai-Guo-Ren Shou-Rong Guan-Li Gui-Ze, 外國人收容管理規則) was promulgated in 2000 and last revised in 2015.
218. *Ibid.*, Art. 3.
219. The Regulations Governing the Detention of the People of the Mainland China Area and the Residents of Hong Kong and Macao (Da-Lu Di-Qu Ji Xiang-Gang Ao-Men Ju-Min Shou-Rong Guan-Li Ban-Fa, 大陸地區人民及香港澳門居民收容管理辦法) was adopted in 2000 and last revised in 2017.
220. The Enforcement Act of the Part of General Principles of the Civil Code (Min-Fa Zong-Ze Shi-Xing Fa, 民法總則施行法) was adopted in 1929 and last revised in 2021.
221. Enforcement Act of the Part of General Principles of the Civil Code, Art. 11.

legal person.[222] A recognized foreign legal person, within the limits of the laws and regulations, has the same legal capacity as the legal person of Taiwan of the same kind has. The duty of a recognized foreign legal person to obey the law of Taiwan is the same as the duty of a legal person of Taiwan.[223]

142. In Choice-of-law Act 1953, Article 2 provided that the law of the place of domicile of a foreign legal person that has been recognized by the ROC is deemed to be its national law. The Choice-of-law Act 2010 specifies: 'The national law of a legal person is the law under which it was incorporated.'[224] Under this provision, a legal person's national law is not ascertained on the basis of its nationality which is debatable with the criteria to decide it, and a foreign legal person is not required to petition for the ROC's recognition before its courts ascertain its national law. In simple terms, a Taiwanese legal person is subject to all the relevant laws of Taiwan; likewise, a foreign legal person is governed by its personal law which is its national law under the principle of *lex patriae*.[225]

143. It is noteworthy that the Company Act[226] followed the policy of Article 13 of the Choice-of-law Act 2010 to abolish the system of recognizing foreign companies and replace with a requirement to establish and register its branch office in Taiwan in 2018. It stipulates that a foreign company which establishes its branch office in the territory of ROC shall translate its name into Chinese and indicate the class to which it belongs as well as its nationality.[227] A foreign company without making branch office registration may not conduct its business operation in the name of a foreign company in the territory of the ROC. A person who violates the above provision shall be punished with imprisonment for a period of not more than one year, detention, or in lieu thereof or in addition thereto a fine of not more than NT$ 150,000 and shall assume on his own the civil liabilities arising therefrom, or shall be jointly and severally liable therefor, in case there are two or more violators. In addition, the company shall be enjoined by the competent authority from using its foreign corporate name.[228]

144. However, a foreign company shall not be registered as a branch office under any of the following circumstances: 1. if its objective or business is in contrary to the law, public order or *boni mores* of the ROC; or 2. if any information or statement contained in the items or document of registration application filed by it is found false.[229] A foreign company which establishes its branch office in the territory of the ROC is required to set appropriate funds exclusively for its operation of business therein and shall designate a representative to serve as its responsible person in the territory of the ROC. Where the responsible person of a foreign company

222. Enforcement Act of the Part of General Principles of the Civil Code, Art. 15.
223. Enforcement Act of the Part of General Principles of the Civil Code, Art. 12.
224. Choice-of-law Act 2010, Art. 13.
225. The rule on *renvoi* in Act. 6 of the Choice-of-law Act 2010 shall thus apply.
226. The Company Act (Gong-Si Fa, 公司法) was adopted in 1929 and last revised in 2018.
227. Company Act, Art. 370.
228. Company Act, Art. 371.
229. Company Act, Art. 373.

in the territory of the ROC refunds the funds to the foreign company or such funds are withdrawn by the foreign company at will after the registration of the branch office, the responsible person of a foreign company in the territory of the ROC shall be liable, jointly and severally with the foreign company, for the damages to be sustained by the third party or parties therefrom.[230]

II. Unincorporated Organizations

145. An unincorporated organization is an organization that does not enjoy legal personality and the status as a legal person. It has not been granted the legal status of a legal entity by any law. The question whether it is an incorporated organization is governed by each relevant law respectively. An unincorporated organization has no legal capacity *per se* and finds no way to be recognized as a legal person.

III. Scope of the *Lex Societas*

146. The *lex societas* of a legal person, pursuant to the Choice-of-law Act 2010, is its national law, i.e., the law under which it was incorporated.[231] It is beyond doubt that Taiwan's law applies to the personal affairs of a domestic legal person. Article 14 thus states: 'The following internal affairs of an alien legal person are governed by its national law: 1. the incorporation, legal nature, legal capacity and capacity to act of the legal person; 2. the acquisition or withdrawal of membership in the corporation; 3. the rights and obligations of membership in the corporation; 4. the organs and organization of the legal person; 5. the representative of the legal person and the limitation on his/her power of representation; 6. the internal distribution of liability toward a third person between the legal person and its organs; 7. the amendment of the bylaws; 8. the dissolution and liquidation of the legal person; and 9. other internal affairs of the legal person.'

147. The above specified internal affairs of a foreign legal person are governed by the law under which it is incorporated. In practice, such affairs may mingle together. It is this author's opinion that the questions whether a vice CEO can represent the foreign corporation[232], whether the liquidator can represent the foreign corporation during its liquidation[233], and whether the administrator designated by foreign court for the foreign company can act as its director[234], can all be characterized as 'the representative of the legal person and the limitation on his/her power of representation' in Item 5 above.

230. Company Act, Art. 372.
231. Choice-of-law Act 2010, Art. 13.
232. Rong-Chwan Chen, *The Representatives of the US Corporations*, 1 Taiwan Jurist (月旦法學教室) 34–35 (November 2002).
233. Rong-Chwan Chen, *The Domestic Effects of an Insolvency Decree of Foreign Court*, 154 Taiwan Jurist (月旦法學教室) 30–32 (August 2015).
234. Rong-Chwan Chen, *supra* n. 132.

148. A branch of a foreign legal person is not qualified as a separate and independent entity, while it is required by the law of the place where it locates to comply some basic local rules. The internal affairs of such branch, if any, are subject to the law by which it was established. Therefore, if an alien legal person establishes a branch under ROC law, the internal affairs of that branch are governed by ROC law.[235]

IV. Liability

149. The tortious or contractual liability of a legal person toward a third party relates both to its internal affairs such as legal capacity and capacity to act, and to external relation with the third party. The internal affairs are still governed by the *lex societas*, while the liability is governed by the law applicable the legal relation at issue. In other words, whether and how a legal person is liable to a third party is within the scope of the governing law of the legal relation from which the liability results. It may be ascertained in pursuance with the conflicts rule for such legal relations in the Choice-of-law Act 2010.

V. Relocation

150. Relocation of a legal person relates to its freedom of movement and the recognition of it in the new location. It is the policy of the *lex societas* how much freedom of movement the legal person enjoys and whether it can move out of its territory and relocate in another country. Again, the national law of the country on which is targeted to relocate governs all questions on its side. As relocation is not stipulated in the Choice-of-law Act 2010, a Taiwanese legal person relies on the Taiwanese law to relocate, a foreign legal person cannot transform itself into a Taiwanese legal person without being incorporated under the Taiwanese law.

VI. Cross-Border Transformation

151. Transformation of a legal person relates to the fundamental principle of freedom of establishment. The Business Mergers and Acquisitions Act[236] 2002 was enacted to facilitate merger /consolidation and acquisition by a business for purposes of reorganization and optimal operation efficiency. It states that any merger/consolidation and acquisition by a company shall be done pursuant to this Act.[237] Cross-border transformation is not stipulated in the Choice-of-law Act 2010, there is no such rules as the Directive (EU) 2019/2121 of the European Parliament and of the Council of 27 November 2019 amending Directive (EU) 2017/1132 as regards

235. Choice-of-law Act 2010, Art. 15.
236. The Business Mergers and Acquisitions Act (Qi-Ye Bing-Gou Fa, 企業併購法) was adopted in 2002 and last revised in 2015.
237. *Ibid.*, Art. 2.

cross-border conversions, mergers and divisions,[238] so the traditional conflicts rules will be relied on to decide the related questions.

152. It is evident that the Business Mergers and Acquisitions Act applies to the transformation if it involves a Taiwanese business in its specific part and dimension.[239] A foreign legal person who is involved in it basically has to comply the requirements specified in its *lex societas*. This results in the distributive application of multiple *lex societas*.

238. Directive (EU) 2019/2121 of the European Parliament and of the Council of 27 November 2019 amending Directive (EU) 2017/1132 as regards cross-border conversions, mergers and divisions, OJ L 321, 12.12.2019, p. 1–44.
239. Wang-RuuTseng, *Private International Law in Taiwan – Company Law*, in Basedow & Pissler (eds.), *supra* n. 7, at 361).

Chapter 2. Obligations

153. Obligations are obligatory claims and duties that one party can claim against the other. They are distinguishable from the rights *in rem* over things which can be enforced against the third parties.

§1. Contractual Obligations

154. Contractual obligations can be interpreted as obligations resulted from obligatory contracts or juridical acts in a broader sense. Taiwan's Civil Code adopts the narrow sense of contracts and recognizes the obligations arisen from juridical acts other than contracts, i.e., unilateral and multilateral acts. The Choice-of-law Act 2010 put them together and formulates a relationship of obligation resulted from 'a juridical act' in Article 20. For the purpose of the following discussion, contractual obligations and the legislative wording will be used interchangeably.

I. Party Autonomy

155. The Choice-of-law Act 2010 enshrines the principle of party autonomy. Article 20 Paragraph 1 states that the formation and effect of a juridical act resulting in a relationship of obligation are determined by the parties' intention. The existence of the parties' intention must be proved by the parties in the court. There is always a problem to prove the existence of an implicit intention.

156. In Taiwan's Civil Code, mere silence is distinguished from an implicit intention that can be proved by supporting facts.[240] Before the Choice-of-law Act was revised in 2010, Article 6 Paragraph 2 of its version of 1953 provided that in case the parties' intention cannot be duly proved, it is governed by the parties' national law, if they have a common nationality; by the law of the place of their act, if their nationalities are different; by the law of the place where the intention of offer was sent, if the places of their acts are different; by the law of the place of the offeror's domicile, if the offeror did not know from where the offer was sent at the time when the acceptance was conducted. The rigid rule above is potential to result in an applicable law which is far from reasonable and appropriate. This author was therefore of the opinion that the implicit intentional shall be recognized as a subjective connecting factor and found to better designate the governing law.[241] Under such situation, the parties' implicit intention is a subjective connecting factor to ascertain the governing law of the contractual obligation.

240. Supreme Court's Civil Judgment, Yu-Shang 762 of 1940.
241. Rong-Chwan Chen, *The Principle of Party Autonomy*, 6 Taiwan Law Review (月旦法學雜誌) 56–57 (1995).

157. Article 20 Paragraph 1 of the Choice-of-law Act 2010 addresses the fundamental principle of party autonomy. Yet, the policy in the scope of subjective connecting factors is adjusted as the former rigid rule of objective connecting factors was revised by the flexible approach adopted in Paragraph 2: 'Where there is no express intention of the parties or their express intention is void under the applicable law determined by them, the formation and effect of the juridical act are governed by the law which is most closely connected with the juridical act.' Under the above provisions, the parties' choice of applicable law is limited to those in explicit terms. The problematic implicit intention to choose the governing law is considered as an important element in ascertaining the closest connection with a particular place. This reduces the tension in ascertaining the implicit intention and softens the rigidness of objective connecting factors.

158. The above provision specifies the governing law of the parties' intention or choice-of-law clause by stating 'their express intention is void under the applicable law determined by them'. In other words, the intention is governed by the law designated by that intention. In absence of the parties' express intention or where their express intention is void under the applicable law determined by them, they are governed by the law most closely connected with the juridical act. The law most closely connected with the juridical act is ascertained through weighing and comparing all connections that the juridical act has with each law. All objective personal and territorial factors such as nationality, domicile, residence, place of property, business, financial assets, education and family activity, are all taken into consideration in this process. As mentioned earlier, the subjective factor of unexpressed or implicit intention is significantly considered as well.

159. To ascertain 'the most closely connected law', the court is required to explore the relevant connecting factors unlimitedly. The major issue is the certainty and predictability of the outcome. To increase the concreteness in ascertaining it, 'characteristic performance' was added in Article 20 Paragraph 3 as a supplemental criteria.[242] Where there is a characteristic obligation among those resulting from a juridical act, the law of the domicile of the party obligated under the characteristic obligation at the time they performed the juridical act is presumed to be the most closely connected law. Where a juridical act relates to an immovable property, the law of the place where the immovable property is located is presumed to be the most closely connected law. This *prima facie* rule helps in deciding the closest connection while the court is not deemed as erred in ruling if it jump over the test of characteristic performance to the ascertainment of the most closely connected law.[243]

242. The test of characteristic performance may play a decorative role only since the courts may look directly to the test of closest connection and bypass it. David J.W. Wang, *The Revision of Taiwan's Choice-of-Law Rules in Contracts*, in Basedow & Pissler (eds.), *supra* n. 7, at 187.

243. Liu & Chen, *supra* n. 12, at 319.

160. The test of characteristic performance was borrowed from the European Rome Convention 1980 [244] and EU Rome I Regulation 2008,[245] their provisions concerning the law governing the contract under such test or centre of gravity are accordingly followed spiritually. It is therefore agreed that the following contracts are presumed to be governed by the prescribed law[246]: a contract for the sale of goods is presumed to be governed by the law of the country where the seller has his/her domicile; a contract for the provision of services is presumed to be governed by the law of the country where the service provider has his/her domicile; a contract relating to a right *in rem* in immovable property or to a tenancy of immovable property is presumed to be governed by the law of the country where the property is situated; a tenancy of immovable property concluded for temporary private use for a period of no more than six consecutive months is presumed to be governed by the law of the country where the landlord has his domicile, provided that the tenant is a natural person and has his/her domicile in the same country; a franchise contract is presumed to be governed by the law of the country where the franchisee has his/her domicile; a distribution contract is presumed to be governed by the law of the country where the distributor has his/her domicile; a contract for the sale of goods by auction is presumed to be governed by the law of the country where the auction takes place, if such a place can be determined.

II. Form

161. It is an ancient Chinese proverb that a person has to follow the custom within the territory into which he/she just entered (Ru-Jing Sui-Su, 入境隨俗). This is echoed by the Latin maxim '*locus regit actum*', which means the place governs the act. Under such a soft rule, the law of the place where a contract is entered into governs the manner in which it shall be formally solemnized.

162. The Choice-of-law Act 2010 adopts the above rule alternatively as to favour the formal validity of a contract or juridical act. Article 16 states that formal prerequisites of a juridical act are governed by the law applicable to the act. However, a juridical act that conforms to the formal prerequisites provided for in the law of the place where the act was undertaken is also effective. Where a juridical act is undertaken at different places, it is effective if it conforms to the formal prerequisites of the law of any one of the places.

163. Apparently, the basic rule is that the formal requisites of a juridical act are governed by the law applicable to the substantive requisites of the act. This makes all the formal and substantive requisites subject to the same governing law while the formal validity is alternatively supported by the supplementary maxim '*locus*

244. Convention 80/934/EEC on the law applicable to contractual obligations opened for signature in Rome on 19 June 1980
245. Regulation (EC) No 593/2008 of the European Parliament and of the Council of 17 June 2008 on the law applicable to contractual obligations (Rome I Regulation).
246. Liu & Chen, *supra* n. 12, at 317.

regit actum'. Where a contract is negotiated and concluded during a long time at different places, the *lex loci contractus* or the law of the place where the act was undertaken is hard to be ascertained. It is specified that each law of the places can support the formal validity the *lex loci contractus*. This provision clarifies the spirit of the conflicts rule on formality of a juridical act and eliminates the possible doubt in its interpretations.

III. Validity and Formation

164. Contracts are the main sources of consensual obligations. Taiwan's Civil Code states that when the parties have reciprocally declared their concordant intent, either expressly or impliedly, a contract shall be constituted; if the parties agree on all the essential elements of the contract but have expressed no intent as to the non-essential elements, the contract shall be presumed to be constituted; in the absence of an agreement on the above-mentioned non-essential elements, the court shall decide them according to the nature of the affair. [247]

165. Under the above provisions, the fundamental key of a contract is meeting of intents of the parties no matter declared expressly or impliedly. Consideration is not a requirement to the validity of a contract. So, a contract of gift is valid if the parties agree accordingly. However, Article 408 stipulates that so long as the right of the gift has not been transferred to the donee, the donor may revoke the gift. If the thing given has been partially transferred, the donor may revoke the gift for the portion has not been transferred. Such provision shall not apply to gifts notarized or to gifts made for the discharge of a moral obligation.[248]

166. Article 20 Paragraph 1 of the Choice-of-law Act 2010 specifies that the issues relating to formation or validity of a contract, which is in nature a juridical act, are governed by the same governing law as if it were valid. The parties' intent to choose the applicable law is separated from the intent to conclude the contract. It's possible that the contract at issue is invalid under that governing law while the agreement to choose the governing law is valid, or vice versa, the agreement to choose the governing law is void while the contract at issue is valid under other law that is ascertained as applicable in the absence of the parties' choice. Legality is basically governed by the law applicable to the contract, but the mandatory law of the place with which the contract has close connection may intervene to apply as an overriding mandatory law.

IV. Performance

167. The principal effects of a contract are that the parties are under duty to honour it and the debtor is obliged to perform in conformity with the forbearance.

247. CC, Art. 153.
248. CC, Art. 408.

Article 20 Paragraph 1 of the Choice-of-law Act 2010 stipulates the making and performance together and subject them to the applicable law of the contract as a whole. The 'effects' mentioned here is the direct obligatory effects resulting from the contract. The indirect effects based on other factual event or act are not within its scope.

168. An act to perform an obligatory contract is sometimes a juridical or factual act separated from the contract itself, and is pertinent to another conflicts rule. For example, a debtor of a contract governed by the law of State X is obliged to transfer to the creditor certain rights that are governed by the law of State Y. The debtor's performance has to comply all requisites and regulation prescribed in the law of State Y, although it results from the contract and the obligatory duty is governed by the applicable law of the contract. In other words, the alienability of such rights, the requisites and effects of the transfer of such rights are governed by the applicable law of them rather than the applicable law of the contract.

V. Breach of Contractual Obligations (Including Damages)

169. According to Article 20 Paragraph 1 of the Choice-of-law Act 2010, the law governing the contract determines all its effects, including the rights and duties around performance. As nonperformance constitutes breach of contractual obligations, the legal requisites of default, excuses for nonperformance, and the effects of unexcused failure to perform are all subject to the same law.

170. Taiwan's Civil Code stipulates several effects of breach of contractual obligations. The debtor shall be responsible for his acts, whether intentional or negligent. The extent of responsibility for one's negligence varies with the particular nature of the affair; but such responsibility shall be lessened, if the affair is not intended to procure interests to the debtor. [249] The debtor will be released from his obligation to perform if the performance becomes impossible by reason of a circumstance to which he/she is not imputed. [250] If the performance becomes impossible by reason of a circumstance to which the debtor is imputed, the creditor may claim compensation for any injury arising therefrom. [251] If a debtor incompletely performs his/her obligation by reason of a circumstance to which the debtor is imputed, the creditor may execute his/her right according to the provisions of the default or the impossibility of the performance. [252] If there is change of circumstances which is not predictable then after the constitution of the contract, and if the performance of the original obligation arising therefrom will become obviously unfair, the party may apply to the court for increasing or reducing his/her payment, or altering the original obligation. [253] In an international case, these provisions can only apply when the case is governed by the Taiwanese law.

249. CC, Art. 220.
250. CC, Art. 225.
251. CC, Art. 226.
252. CC, Art. 227.
253. CC, Art. 227-2.

171. The compensation or damages for nonperformance of a contract is characterized as a substantive issue rather than a procedural question. In Taiwan's Civil Code, they are subject to the basic rule of compensatory damages. Unless otherwise provided by the statutes or by the contract, the compensation shall be limited to the injury actually suffered and the interests which have been lost. Interests which could have been normally expected are deemed to be the interests which have been lost, according to the ordinary course of things, the decided projects, equipment, or other particular circumstances.[254] In case a foreign law which allows punitive damages is applicable, the court will be asked to consider whether the result of its application is contradictory to the public order or *boni mores* of Taiwan.

VI. Rescission

172. Once a contract is concluded, it is effective and binding on the parties. Nonperformance and impossibility do not make it void automatically. It is necessary to acknowledge right of a party to cancel or rescind the contract. Taiwan's Civil Code states that when a party to a contract is in default, the other party may fix a reasonable period and notify him/her to perform within that period. If the party in default does not perform within that period, the other party may rescind the contract.[255] If according to the nature of the contract or the expression of intent of the parties, the purpose of the contract cannot be accomplished if not performed within the fixed period, and if one of the parties does not perform the contract within that period, the other party may rescind the contract without giving the notice.[256] If the performance becomes impossible by reason of a circumstance to which the debtor is imputed, the creditor may rescind the contract.[257]

173. The right of rescission is characterized as a substantive right rather than an equitable remedy or procedural measure. It is not specified particularly in the Choice-of-law Act 2010. Under the policy to end the contract fairly and legally, the right of rescission is acknowledged as a right inherent in the contract. The conflict of laws issues arise on whether a party is entitled to rescind a contract and what restitution is due in this case by either party. Those issues are governed by the law of the contract which is ascertained according to Article 20.

VII. Representation

174. Representations lie in the core of a juridical act or contract. In this sense, a representation is an expression of intent which is relied on by the receiving party and induces them to enter into the contract. It requires two representations to form a contract, an offer and an acceptance. The representation of an offer is binding if

254. CC, Art. 216.
255. CC, Art. 254.
256. CC, Art. 255.
257. CC, Art. 256.

it is effective. According to Taiwan's Civil Code, a person who offers to make a contract shall be bound by his offer except at the time of offer he/she has excluded this obligation or except it may be presumed from the circumstances or from the nature of the affair that he/she did not intend to be bound. Exposing goods for sale with their selling price shall be deemed to be an offer. However, the sending of pricelists is not deemed to be an offer. [258] An offer ceases to be binding if it is refused. [259]

175. A representation or an expression of intent is the key element in making a juridical act. It comprises a real intent to create a legal effect, an act and consciousness of the expression. Taiwan's Civil Code thus states that an expression of intent inter presents becomes effective at the moment when the person to whom it is made understands it well. [260] An expression of intent inter absents becomes effective at the moment when the notification of the expression reaches such other party, except when the withdrawal of the notification previously or simultaneously reaches such other party. [261]

176. With regard to the quality of an expression of intent, Taiwan's Civil Code states similarly to a juridical act that the effectiveness of an intent lies on the genuineness and completeness of that intent. However, an intent shall not be void for the expresser did not intend to be bound by it, except the fact was known to the other party. [262] A fictitious expression of intent made by the expresser in collusion with other party is void, but the voidance cannot be a valid defence against any *bona fide* third party. If the fictitious expression of intent was intended to conceal another juridical act, the provisions of the act with respect to such another juridical act shall apply. [263] If the expression was acting under a mistake as to the contents of his/her expression of intent, or had known the situation of affairs, he/she would not make the expression; he/she may revoke the expression; provided that the mistake or the ignorance of the affairs was not due to his/her own fault. If a mistake in respect to the qualification of the other party or the nature of a thing is regarded as essential in trade, it shall be deemed a mistake as to the contents of the expression of intent. [264] An expression of intent which is procured by fraud or by duress may be revoked by the expresser. If the fraud was done by a third party, the expression may be revoked only under the circumstances that the other party knew, or might know the affairs. The revocation of an expression of intent on the ground of fraud cannot be a valid defence against the *bona fide* third party. [265]

177. A party may claim misrepresentation where a false representation has been made. As the laws on the requisites, effectiveness, quality and the effects of a misrepresentation differ from country to country, conflict of laws problems arise as to

258. CC, Art. 154.
259. CC, Art. 155.
260. CC, Art. 94.
261. CC, Art. 95.
262. CC, Art. 86.
263. CC, Art. 87.
264. CC, Art. 88.
265. CC, Art. 92.

whether the sending party is entitled to revoke or has the contract to be set aside and whether the receiving party is entitled to damages to put them back into the position they would have been had the contract never been entered into.

178. The Choice-of-law Act 2010 does not provide specifically the law to govern the issues of a representation. Since it is a substantive component of a juridical act or contract, it is within the scope to apply the law which governs the 'formation' of the contract. Article 20 applies to the issues of a representation accordingly.

VIII. Interpretation

179. When a contract is effective, disputes may still arise in what its contents are. It depends on the courts to interpret or construe the undisputed part and decide what concrete effects the contract results in. The interpretation or construction of a contract has to find the 'genuine' meaning of the contract when it is unclear. The conflict of the true intention and the literal black letters is on one hand, the difference between one party's interpretation and the other party's interpretation of the same term or paragraph is on another hand. It relates to the court's exercise of power and discretion to resolve the factual dispute and some principles that are embodied in substantive legislations for certain valuable purposes.

180. Taiwan's Civil Code stipulates in Article 98 that in the interpretation of an expression of intent, the real intention of the parties must be sought rather than the literal meaning of the words. This is a basic guideline to solve the conflict of common intention of the parties and the words they expressed literally. A further problem arise in conflict of the 'real' subjective intention that one party really intended and the objective intention that reasonable parties of the same kind as the parties would intend in the same circumstances.

181. Special concerns are addressed for consumer contracts in Taiwan's Consumer Protection Act.[266] It state that the terms and conditions adopted in the standard contracts shall be conformed to the principles of equality and reciprocity. Where there is any ambiguity in the wording of the standard terms and conditions, interpretations shall be made in favour of consumer. (Article 11) The interpretation or construction of ambiguous wording by the court is thus no more looking to the original intent of the preparer or the reasonable objective meaning.

182. It's natural for the court to characterize it as a procedure of exercising its adjudicating power and subject it to the *lex fori*. Because during the process of the court's interpretation of a contract term, it is required to discover the true or proper meaning under full observation of all circumstances. The factors taken into account by the court to make its own determination are, *inter alia*, the nature and purpose of the contract, the conduct of the parties, the meaning commonly given to contract

266. The Consumer Protection Act (Xiao-Fei-Zhe Bao-Hu Fa, 消費者保護法) was adopted in 1994 and last revised in 2015.

terms and expressions in the trade concerned, the relation between the parties and their usage and practice in the past experiences. However, as interpretation relates to the presentation and contents of the contract, all questions about who obtains what rights through the contract and the extent of the contractual duties shall be governed by the law that is applicable to the whole contract. It is inappropriate for the court to apply the *lex fori* and infer different meanings to the same contract.

IX. Third Parties and Multiparty Agreements

183. The obligations resulted from a contract are basically obligatory in nature and are binding only between the parties under the doctrine of privity or relativity. Some legal systems exceptionally stipulates that a third party can enforce a contract or a party can enforce the contract against the third parties. Taiwan's Civil Code states that one of the parties to a contract who has undertaken that an obligation shall be performed by a third party shall be responsible for the injury if the third party does not perform the obligation. [267] When it is provided in a contract that an obligation shall be performed to a third party, the offeror may demand the debtor to perform the obligation to the third party, and such third party also has the right to demand performance direct from the debtor. So long as the third party has not expressed his intent to take such advantage of the contract, the parties may modify the contract or revoke it. If the third party expresses to either of the parties his/her intent not to take advantage of the contract, he/she is deemed to never have any right under the contract. [268]

184. Conflict of laws problems may arise as to the contractual rights and duties of a third party, yet they are not specifically addressed in the Choice-of-law Act 2010. As they are part of the 'effects' of the contract or juridical act, the governing law of the whole contract shall be applicable to them.

185. Multiparty agreements result in plural creditors or plural debtors in a contractual obligation. Theoretically speaking, the rights and duties of each party can only be ascertained by looking into the agreement on which the obligatory relation was created. If the agreement is concluded multilaterally by a resolution of multiple parties, it will bind equally all the parties. If several persons are grouped together to form a party to a contact, the problems arise as to how internally they share the single right or duty and externally how they exercise their right or perform the duty.

186. Taiwan's Civil Code focuses on plural creditors or plural debtors as a party and addresses the basic principle. When several persons undertake the same obligation, and if the prestation is divisible, each of them shall be responsible for or be entitled to the prestation equally, unless otherwise provided by the statutes or by the

267. CC, Art. 268.
268. CC, Art. 269.

contract. The same rule shall be applied when a prestation is converted from an indivisible one to a divisible one.[269] When there are several persons undertaking the same obligation and expressing that each of them is bound to the creditor for the whole of the prestation, this obligation is a joint obligation. If there is no such expression, a joint obligation is constituted only in the cases provided by the statutes. [270] The creditor of a joint obligation is entitled to demand one or several or all of the debtors simultaneously or successively to tender total or partial performance. Before the complete performance of the obligation, all of the debtors are jointly bound to tender the performance. [271] When several persons entitled by the statutes or by the juridical act to a claim of the same obligation that each of them may demand the whole of the prestation from the debtor, this claim is a joint claim. [272] The debtor to a joint claim may at his option perform wholly in favour of any of the joint creditors. [273]

187. Conflict of laws problems may arise in the rights and duties of anyone of the plural creditors or plural debtors. There may be a certain legal relation on which the plural creditors or plural debtors relied to form as a group party to the contract. But the contract is separated from their grounding relation. Their contractual rights or duties resulted from the contract are part of its effects that shall be governed by the law applicable to the contract as a whole. The internal relation between the group members are subject to the governing law of the underlying relation that make them as a group to be a party to the contract.

X. Assignment and Subrogation

188. The assignment of an obligatory claim relates to three interested parties: the assignor, the debtor, and the assignee. Although there is potential possibility of conflicts between two or more assignees and their creditors, it has been recognized in almost every legal system. The parties of assignment enjoy the flaw and mobilization of values of the assigned obligation, while protection of the debtor from altering his/her interests without consent or being noticed is needed to balance. Taiwan's Civil Code thus stipulates that the transfer of a claim will not be effective as against the debtor until the debtor has been notified of it by the transferor or by the transferee, unless otherwise provided by the law. The effect of tendering by the transferee to the debtor the deed of transfer executed by the transferor is equivalent to the effect of notice. [274]

189. The assignment of a claim is usually based on another underlying contract such as a sale contract of the claim. It is noteworthy that the governing law of the underlying contract is separated from the assignment. As the methods of dealing

269. CC, Art. 271.
270. CC, Art. 272.
271. CC, Art. 273.
272. CC, Art. 283.
273. CC, Art. 284.
274. CC, Art. 297.

with the specific problems of assignment of a claim are not identical among the municipal laws, the conflict of laws problems arise in many perspectives. The Choice-of-law Act 2010 states in Article 32 Paragraph 1 that where a claim has been transferred, the effect of the transfer on the debtor is determined by the law governing the formation and effect of the transferred claim. This provision regards only the assignment of claim itself, and focuses on the effect on the debtor. The assignability of the claim, the requisites and effects of the assigned claim are governed by the governing law of such claim. The underlying relation is subject to its own applicable law. The security attached to the transferred claim is governed by its own governing law. Paragraph 2 of it therefore specifies that where a third person has provided security for a claim, the effect on the third person of a transfer of the claim is determined by the law governing the formation and effect of the security.

190. The assumption of a debt changes the debtor rather than the creditor. It is on the other side of the coin of assignment. In contrast, the interests of the creditor is in particular need to be protected. In Article 33 of the Choice-of-law Act 2010, the related issues are addressed similarly. Paragraph 1 states the where a contract of assumption is concluded between an assuming person and the debtor, the effect of the assumption on the creditor is governed by the law applicable to the formation and effect of the assumed obligation. Paragraph 2 provides that where a third person has provided security for the performance of an obligation to a creditor, the effect on the third person of an assumption of the obligation is governed by the law applicable to the formation and effect of the security.

191. Subrogation, the substitution by law of one who pays a debt in place of the creditor, happens when a claim is satisfied by a third party or a debtor pays more than his/her personal share. Taiwan's Civil Code states that if a third party who has interest on the performance of the obligation has performed the obligation, the third party is subrogated to the rights of the creditor to the amount of the performance, but such third party shall not exercise them to the detriment of the creditor.[275] If one of the joint debtors has caused the other joint debtors to be released from the obligation by virtue of his performance, prestation in lieu of performance, lodgement, offset or merger, he/she is entitled to demand from the other debtors the reimbursement of their respective shares in the prestation, plus interest from the date of release. The debtor entitled to claim the reimbursement is subrogated to the rights of the creditor to the amount of the reimbursement which the said debtor is entitled to demand, but such debtor shall not exercise them to the detriment of the creditor.[276]

192. The conflict of laws problems result from the fact that the requisites of subrogation are not identical among the municipal systems. Article 34 of the Choice-of-law Act 2010 specifies that where a third person satisfies an obligation on behalf of a debtor by reason of a particular legal relationship existing between them, the right of reimbursement of the third person against the debtor is governed by the law

275. CC, Art. 312.
276. CC, Art. 281.

applicable to the legal relationship. Therefore, where an obligation borne by multiple persons has been performed in whole by some of them, the right to reimbursement of those who performed against the others is governed by the law applicable to the legal relationship between the multiple debtors rather than the obligation itself. Subrogation is included in 'the right of reimbursement' in the above provisions and governed by the same law.

§2. Particular Contracts

I. Sales Contracts

193. According to Taiwan's Civil Code, a sales contract is a contract whereby the parties agree that one of them shall transfer to the other his/her rights over property and the latter shall pay a price for it. The contract of sale is completed when the parties have mutually agreed on the object and the price. [277] Although the price is not fixed concretely by the agreement, if it may be decided from the circumstances, it is deemed to be fixed. If it is agreed that the price shall be fixed according to the market price, it is deemed to be fixed according to such market price at the place and time of performance unless otherwise provided by contract. [278]

194. A sales contract is one of the typical obligatory contracts. The object of sale may be movable or immovable properties or intangible rights. As no special provision is provided for it in the Choice-of-law Act 2010, the law that governs it shall be ascertained in pursuance with Article 20. The transfer of titles or rights is a distinguishable juridical act, the issues relating directly to the transfer are basically not included in the law that governs the sales contract. They are subject to the governing law of the relevant rights *in rem* or intangible rights.

195. It is beyond doubt that sale of an immovable connects closely with the *lex rei situs*. Yet, an obligation to transfer rights *in rem* over an immovable is obligatory in nature, rather than the rights in rem that shall be governed by the *lex rei situs*. To the sales contract that does not include the transfer the rights *in rem* over the immovable, the *lex rei situs* is presumably to be the law expected by the parties and the most naturally qualified law, but is not definitely required to be its governing law. It is thus stipulated in Article 20 Paragraph 3 of the Choice-of-law Act 2010 that where an obligatory juridical act concerns immovable property, in absence of the parties' expressly intent, the law of the place where the immovable property is located is presumed to be the most closely connected law.

277. CC, Art. 345.
278. CC, Art. 346.

II. Service Contracts

196. Service contracts cover at least three types of contracts in Taiwan's Civil Code. Firstly, contracts of hire of services: contracts whereby the parties agree that one of them shall service for a fixed or undefined period to the other party, and the latter shall pay remuneration. [279] Secondly, contracts of hire of work: contracts whereby the parties agrees one of them complete a definite work for the other party, who pays him remuneration after the completion of the work. [280] Thirdly, contracts of mandate: contracts whereby the parties agree that one of them commissions the other party to deal with his affairs, and the latter agrees to do so. [281] Since different rules apply respectively to each service contract, the service contract at issue is sometimes required to be characterized as a contract of hire of services, hire of work or mandate in judicial practice.[282]

197. No special provision is provided specifically for the service contracts in the Choice-of-law Act 2010, the general conflicts rule in Article 20 applies accordingly. In absence of the parties' expressly intent to choose the applicable law, the law most closely connected with the contract governs. The characteristic performance of a service contract is the provision of services by the provider. So, the law of the country where the service provider has his/her domicile is presumed to have the closest connection with it.

III. Consumer Contracts

198. 'Consumer contract' is not a legislatively adopted term in Taiwan. Taiwan's Consumer Protection Act defines 'consumer relationship' as the legal relationship arising between consumers and traders for the sale of goods or provision of services; 'consumer' as any person who in relation to a commercial practice, is acting for purposes of consumption to make transactions in exchange for goods or services; and 'trader' as any person who in relation to a commercial practice, is acting for purposes relating to his business in designing, producing, manufacturing, importing or distributing goods, or providing services.[283] It can be easily understood that a consumer contract means a contract concluded between a consumer and

279. CC, Art. 482.
280. CC, Art. 490.
281. CC, Art. 528.
282. In Judicial Yuan's Interpretation 740 of 2016, it was held that the standards to characterize a service contract for the solicitation of insurance business between an insurance solicitor and the insurance company to which the solicitor belongs, are whether the service debtor (the insurance solicitor) may freely decide the manner of the provision of service (including working hours), and will bear business risks on own account (e.g., the remuneration shall be calculated on the basis of insurance premium received from the solicited insurance). It cannot be determined directly in accordance with the Regulations Governing the Supervision of Insurance Solicitors.
283. Consumer Protection Act, Art. 2.

a trader. As the consumer is protected in different approaches and levels around the world, the conflict of laws in consumer contractual relationship remains an issue of private international law.

199. The Consumer Protection Act specifies some special substantive rules on consumer contracts. 'Standard contracts' means the standard terms and conditions prepared by traders which are fully or partially adopted in the contract between the parties. 'Standard terms and conditions' means standard contract clauses unilaterally prepared by traders for entering into contracts with consumers not limited in writing, in any form or by any means, including, but not limited to, via showing captions on the screens, flyers, public postings, and the Internet. It state that the terms and conditions adopted in the standard contracts shall be conformed to the principles of equality and reciprocity. Where there is any ambiguity in the wording of the standard terms and conditions, interpretations shall be made in favour of consumer.[284]

200. Traders shall provide a reasonable period, not longer than 30 days, for consumers to review all contract clauses, before entering into a standard contract. The terms and conditions adopted by traders in standard contracts made consumer waive such right shall be invalid. [285] Any standard terms and conditions in violation of the good faith requirements are unconscionable to consumers, shall be rendered null and void. The use of standard contracts are presumed unconscionable where the terms and conditions provided fall within any of the following: 1. where the terms and conditions of the contracts are in violation of the principle of equality and reciprocity; 2. where the terms and conditions of the contracts which are excluded by the optional rules are obviously contradicted to legislative intent; and 3. where the purposes of the contracts cannot be achieved due to the major rights or obligations of the contracts are restricted by such terms and conditions. [286] For terms and conditions not specified in standard contracts and not foreseeable by the consumers under normal circumstances shall not constitute as part of the contract. [287] Any standard terms and conditions shall be null and void when it is contradicted to individually negotiated terms. [288]

201. No special provision is provided specifically for consumer contracts in the Choice-of-law Act 2010, the governing law is basically ascertained in pursuance with the general conflicts rules in Article 20. The above policy to protect consumers is part of the public order or *boni mores* of the ROC, the choice-of-law clause may be rendered void if it is closely connected with Taiwan and unfair to the consumer. If the foreign law ascertained to be applicable will result in unfairness to the consumer, it may be excluded because it is deemed contradictory to the public order or

284. Consumer Protection Act, Art. 11.
285. Consumer Protection Act, Art. 11-1.
286. Consumer Protection Act, Art. 12.
287. Consumer Protection Act, Art. 14.
288. Consumer Protection Act, Art. 15.

boni mores of the ROC. The protection and interests of the consumer shall be taken into account particularly in the test of the closest connection.

IV. Employment Contracts

202. An employment contract is the contract between an employee and an employer. It is based on private law regarding a contract of hire of services, while it is also regulated by the Labour Standards Act of which purposes are to provide minimum standards for working conditions, to protect workers' rights and interests, to strengthen employee-employer relationships and to promote social and economic development.

203. There are many compulsory rules about labour contracts to protect the employees in the Labour Standards Act. For examples, an employer shall not make an after-resignation business strife limitation agreement with an employee unless the following requirements have been met: 1. the employer has proper business interests that require being protected; 2. the position or job of the employee entitles him or her to have access to or be able to use the employer's trade secrets; 3. the period, area, scope of occupational activities and prospective employers with respect to the business strife limitation shall not exceed a reasonable range; and 4. the employer shall reasonably compensate the employee concerned who does not engage in business strife activities for the losses incurred by him or her. Any agreement in violation of any of the above provisions shall be null and void.[289] No employer shall, even by advance notice to a worker, terminate a labour contract unless one of the following situation arises: 1. where the employers' businesses are suspended, or has been transferred; 2. where the employers' businesses suffers an operating losses, or business contractions; 3. where force majeure necessitates the suspension of business for more than one month; 4. where the change of the nature of business necessitates the reduction of workforce and the terminated employees cannot be reassigned to other suitable positions; or 5. a particular worker is clearly not able to perform satisfactorily the duties required of the position held. [290] Upon termination of a labour contract, neither an employer nor the employer's agent shall reject a request from the worker for proof of service record. [291]

204. As an obligatory contract, the governing law of an employment contract is ascertained according to Article 20 of the Choice-of-law Act 2010. The parties' choice of law is limited to expressly agreement and is subject to the chosen governing law's requirements. In absence of their choice, the law with closest connection governs. It is suggested that the law of the place where the employees perform

289. Labour Standards Act, Art. 9-1.
290. Labour Standards Act, Art. 11.
291. Labour Standards Act, Art. 19.

their work or provide their services weigh significantly in this test.[292] The nature of Taiwan's Labour Standards Act is public and compulsory law, in case the employment contract is closely connected with Taiwan, the relevant provisions can apply as overriding compulsory rules.[293]

V. Contracts of Carriage

205. Contracts of carriage are of obligatory nature and are addressed in Taiwan's Civil Code. In PIL, they are subject to the conflicts rule set up in Article 20 of the Choice-of-law Act 2010. The autonomy of the parties' express intents or agreements, the closest connection and the test of characteristic performance embodied in it are fitful for ascertaining the governing law of both the contract of carriage of persons and the contract of carriage of goods. Unlike the situation in EU and other countries, the courts of Taiwan apply the Choice-of-law Act 2010 and its designated governing law rather than the conventions and international documents to which Taiwan is not a member.

A. Carriage of Persons

206. Taiwan's Civil Code addresses general principles of contract of carriage of persons. They apply to carriage of persons by road, rail, inland waters, sea and air. The Maritime Act[294] specifies some rules on carriage of persons by sea. The Civil Code states that the carrier of passengers shall be liable for any injury suffered by the passenger in consequence of the transportation, and for the delay in the transportation, except the injury or the delay is due to the negligence of such passenger or the injury is due to *force majeure*; if the delay of the transportation is due to *force majeure*, unless otherwise provided by the trade custom, the liability of the carrier of passengers shall be limited to the increased necessary expenses paid by the passenger due to the delay of the transportation.[295] Luggage entrusted to the carrier in time shall be delivered on the arrival of the passenger. [296] The carrier is liable for the loss or damage of the luggage caused by his own negligence or that of his/her employees, even if such luggage has not been entrusted to him/her by the passenger. [297] A statement in a ticket, receipt or other document delivered by the carrier

292. Rong-Chwan Chen, *The Application of Labour Basic Act in Labour Cases with Foreign Elements: Analytical Comments on the Supreme Court's Decision Tai-Shang 1624 of 2017 and Its Prior Judgments*, 358 Taiwan Law Journal (台灣法學雜誌) 23–44 (28 Dec. 2018); Rong-Chwan Chen, *Employment Contracts Involving Foreign Elements – Perspectives from Private International Law*, 166 Taiwan Law Review (月旦法學雜誌) 77 (March 2009), 167 Taiwan Law Review 82 (April 2009).
293. Rong-Chwan Chen, *The Law Applicable to Laying Off by a Foreign Corporation*, 197 Taiwan Jurist (月旦法學教室) 15–17 (March 2019).
294. The Maritime Act (Hai-Shang-Fa, 海商法) was adopted in 1929 and last revised in 2009.
295. CC, Art. 654.
296. CC, Art. 655.
297. CC, Art. 658.

to the passenger, excluding or limiting the liability of the carrier, is ineffective, unless it can be proved that the passenger expressly agreed to such exclusion or limitation of liability. [298]

207. The Maritime Act stipulates that the carrier or shipmaster shall, comply with the tenor of the passenger ticket, transport the passenger to the port of destination; if the carrier or shipmaster is in breach of the provision in it, the passenger may rescind the contract and may also claim for damages, if any. [299] The passenger may rescind the contract where the ship fails to commence the voyage on the scheduled date. [300] Where the ship is unable to continue the voyage due to force majeure, the carrier or shipmaster shall still endeavour to carry the passenger to the port of destination. [301] Where the ship is unable to enter the port of destination for disembarking the passenger due to an act of God, war or disturbances, epidemic or any extraordinary events at that port, the carrier or shipmaster shall be liable, at the option of passenger, to send the passenger to the nearest port or back to the original port of embarkation. [302]

208. By applying Article 20 of the Choice-of-law Act 2010, the governing law of a contract of carriage of persons can be chosen by express agreement. Yet this choice of law is curtailed by the consideration of protecting the passengers as consumers as discussed earlier. The party to perform the characteristic obligation of a contract of carriage is the carrier. Its domicile or principal business place may be presumed to be the place of closest connection.[303] It can also coincide with the place of departure or the place of destination.

B. Carriage of Goods

209. Taiwan's Civil Code addresses on the contract of carriage of goods. It states that if required by the carrier, the sender shall make and issue to him/her a bill of transportation. [304] If required by the sender, the carrier shall make and issue to him/her a bill of lading after receiving the goods of delivery. [305] When a bill of lading has been supplied to the sender the facts concerning the carriage as between the carrier and the holder of the bill are determined by the tenor of the bill of lading. [306] Even though a bill of lading has been made out to a named consignee, it may be transferred by endorsement to another person, except endorsement is forbidden in

298. CC, Art. 659.
299. Maritime Act, Art. 83.
300. Maritime Act, Art. 86.
301. Maritime Act, Art. 88.
302. Maritime Act, Art. 89.
303. Marco Lopez de Gonzalo, *Carriage of Passengers*, in 1 *Encyclopedia of Private International Law* 269 (Jürgen Basedow et al. eds, Edward Elgar 2017).
304. CC, Art. 624.
305. CC, Art. 625.
306. CC, Art. 627.

the bill. [307] The delivery of the bill of lading to a person entitled to accepting the goods has the same effect, as regards the transfer of the ownership of the goods, as delivery of the goods themselves. [308] The consignee shall, on his/her requesting the delivery of goods, surrender the bill of lading. [309] The carrier is liable for any loss, damage or delay in the delivery of the goods entrusted to him/her, except he/she can prove that the loss, damage or delay is due to force majeure, or to the nature of the goods, or to the negligence of the sender or of the consignee. [310] A statement in the bill of lading or other such document delivered by the carrier to the sender excluding or limiting the liability of the carrier is ineffective, unless it is proved that the sender has expressly agreed to such exclusion or limitation of liability. [311]

210. The Maritime Act stipulates also the rules for carriage by sea. It states that where the ship provided by the carrier has defects and therefore incapable of fulfilling the contract of carriage, the shipper may rescind the contract.[312] The carrier or shipmaster, upon demand of the shipper, shall issue a bill of lading after loading of the cargo. [313] The shipper shall not be responsible for the loss sustained by the carrier or the ship owner unless it was caused by the fault of the shipper, his/her agents or servants. [314]If, in cases where there are two or more holders of the bills of lading, the carrier or shipmaster has not yet delivered the cargo, the holder of the part which was forwarded or delivered earliest may exercise his/her right in preference to the others. [315] Where a bill of lading is issued under a contract for the entirety or a proportionate part of a ship for carriage, the legal relationship between the carrier and the holder of the bill of lading other than the shipper is determined in accordance with the terms and conditions of the bill of lading. [316] Where a contract of carriage which is for the purpose of carrying individual cargo or a bill of lading contains a clause, covenant or an agreement diminishing or relieving the carrier or the ship owner from liability for damage to, loss of or delay to the cargo resulting from negligence or a failure to fulfil the obligations provided in this Act, such clause, covenant or agreement shall be null and void. [317] The issuer of a bill of lading shall be responsible for all acts which should be done as stated in the bill of lading.[318]

211. The Choice-of-law Act 2010 does not laid out general provisions for contract of carriage of goods or special rules for carriage by road, rail, inland waters,

307. CC, Art. 628.
308. CC, Art. 629.
309. CC, Art. 630.
310. CC, Art. 634.
311. CC, Art. 649.
312. Maritime Act, Art. 42.
313. Maritime Act, Art. 53.
314. Maritime Act, Art. 57.
315. Maritime Act, Art. 59.
316. Maritime Act, Art. 60 para. 2.
317. Maritime Act, Art. 61.
318. Maritime Act, Art. 74 para. 1.

sea or air.[319] Regardless of the chosen means of carriage, contracts of carriage of goods are obligatory juridical acts resulting obligations between the parties. They are thus subject to Article 20 of the Choice-of-law Act 2010. The protection of individual shipper as a consumer is taken into account in ascertaining the validity of the clauses in a standard contract. Absent of express agreement by the parties, the governing law is ascertained by the closest connection test, while the carrier's domicile or principal business place may be presumed to be the place of closest connection.

212. It is noteworthy that the Maritimes Act specifies not only Article 78 on court jurisdiction which will be dissed later, but also the basic conflicts principle in Article 77. It states that where the port of loading or port of discharge stipulated in the bill of lading is a port of ROC, the applicable law of any legal relationship arising under that bill of lading shall be determined according to the Choice-of-law Act 2010; however, in case any provision in this Act provides a better and more favourable position to the shipper or consignee who is of ROC nationality, this Act shall be applied.

213. Furthermore, the Choice-of-law Act 2010 addresses specifically the conflicts problems of ocean bills of lading and warehouse receipts in Article 43. '(1) The legal relationship arising from an ocean bill of lading is governed by the law specified as applicable on the bill; in the absence of specification, it is governed by the law of the place most closely connected with the bill. (2) Where goods covered by an ocean bill of lading are claimed by multiple persons on the basis either of the bill or of a property right, the priority of the claims to the goods is governed by the law applicable to claims of property right in the goods. (3) The provisions of the preceding two paragraphs regarding ocean bills of lading apply *mutatis mutandis* to determine the law applicable to the legal relationship arising from a warehouse receipt or a bill of lading other than an ocean bill of lading.'

214. Article 43 Paragraph 1 advocates the opinion that the principle of party autonomy applies to ocean bills of lading and other similar documents, which was denied by the Supreme Court on the ground that they were issued by the carrier unilaterally and the parties did not actually agree on the terms.[320] It successfully guides the judiciary to turn to a new page as the Grand Chamber of the Supreme Court ruled that no matter it was issued after or before the Choice-of-law Act 2010 came into effect, the choice-of-law clause on the backside of an ocean bill of lading is valid and binding on the carrier, the sender, and the holders of the ocean bill of lading.[321]

---

319. For discussions on comparative private international law, *see* Monica Brighnardello, *Carriage of Goods by Road, Rail and Inland Waters*, in *Carriage of Passengers*, in 1 *Encyclopedia of Private International Law* 255 (Jürgen Basedow et al. eds, Edward Elgar 2017) 255–261; Paola Ivaldi, *Carriage of Goods by Sea*, *ibid.*, at 261–269.
320. Resolution of the 4th Meeting of the Supreme Court Judges in 1978. For further discussion, *see* Rong-Chwan Chen, *The Clauses Involving Foreign Elements in Bills of Lading*, 164 Taiwan Jurist (月旦法學教室) 27–29 (May 2016).
321. Grand Chamber of the Supreme Court's Civil Decision, Tai-Shang-Da 980 of 2019.

215. The bills of lading and similar documents are the products of obligatory juridical acts and tools for proprietary transactions. Most goods *in transit* are represented by sea waybills, ocean bills of lading, or other transport documents. Those documents function as the evidence of the contract of transportation, the evidence of the owner's title, and an indirect tool to exercise possession over the goods. In some practice, the transfer of those documents is deemed to have the same effects as transfer of title of the goods.

VI. Insurance Contracts

216. According to Taiwan's Insurance Act,[322] an insurance contract is entered into between the proposer who agrees to pay a premium to the insurer, and the insurer who agrees to pay pecuniary indemnification for damage caused by unforeseeable events or *force majeure* to the beneficiary.[323] Insurance contracts are classified into unvalued and valued insurance contracts. An unvalued insurance contract is an insurance contract which expressly states that the value of the subject matter insured must be estimated after occurrence of the insured risk. A valued insurance contract is an insurance contract that expressly states a definite value for the subject matter insured. [324] If the risk associated with the subject matter insured has already occurred or ceased to exist at the time an insurance contract is entered into, the contract shall be void, provided that this rule does not apply when neither of the contracting parties is aware of the occurrence or cessation of existence. If, at the time an insurance contract is entered into, only the proposer knows that the risk has already occurred, the insurer is not bound by the contract. If, at the time an insurance contract is entered into, only the insurer knows that the risk has ceased to exist, the proposer is not bound by the contract. [325]

217. The insurers are much more powerful than the proposers, yet, the principle of party autonomy is still adopted with some limitations on the insurance contracts. The Insurance Act states that the compulsory provisions of this Act may not be modified by contract. However, this restriction does not apply to modifications favourable to the insured. Interpretation of insurance contracts shall seek the true intent of the parties, and may not adhere blindly to the language employed. Where there is doubt, interpretations should in principle be favourable to the insured. [326] Furthermore, it specifies that if an insurance contract contains any term or condition as follows, and such term or condition would have been obviously unfair under the circumstances at the time of signing, such part of the contract shall be void: 1. a term or condition that exempts the insurer from or diminishes its obligations under this Act; 2. a term or condition that causes the proposer, beneficiary, or insured to waive or limit any right they enjoy under this Act; 3. a term or condition that

322. The Insurance Act (Bao-Xian Fa, 保險法) was adopted in 1929 and last revised in 2021.
323. Insurance Act, Art. 1.
324. Insurance Act, Art. 50.
325. Insurance Act, Art. 51.
326. Insurance Act, Art. 54.

increases the obligations of the proposer or the insured; or 4. any other term or condition that is materially disadvantageous to the proposer, beneficiary, or insured. [327]

218. An insurance contract is characterized as an obligatory contract. Its governing law is thus ascertained under Article 20 of the Choice-of-law Act 2010. An expressly and fair choice of law is effective and the policy to protect the weaker parties, including the insured and the proposers, plays a role in Taiwan's *ordre public* to exclude the otherwise applicable foreign law. The situation is similar to an employment contract.

219. It is noteworthy that an insurance contract grants sometimes a third party the right to claim interest as a beneficiary. As the third party is basically a claimant to whom the insured is liable under another legal relation such as a tort, this raises the problem of governing law of the question whether the insurer is directly liable to the third party. It relates to both the insurance contract and the tort in which the third party and the insured involved.

220. To better protect the third party or the victim of that tort, Article 29 of the Choice-of-law Act 2010 adopts the approach of alternative application of two governing laws. It states that the existence of a direct claim of an injured person against the insurer of the person liable for the tort is governed by the law applicable to the insurance contract; however, the injured person also may assert a direct claim if the law applicable to the obligation permits its assertion.

221. The insurer's right of subrogation is addressed in the Insurance Act. It states that if an insured has a right to claim indemnification from a third party due to occurrence of loss for which the insurer bears insurance liability, the insurer may, after paying indemnification, be subrogated to the insured's right of claim against the third party. However, the amount of the subrogated claim may not exceed the amount of the indemnification. If such third party is a family member or employee of the insured, the insurer has no right of claim by subrogation. However, this rule is not applicable when the loss has resulted from the wilful misconduct of such third party. [328]

222. The governing law of the insurer's right of subrogation relates to both the insurance contract and the insured's right of claim against the third party. As discussed earlier, Article 34 of the Choice-of-law Act 2010 specifies that where a third person satisfies an obligation on behalf of a debtor by reason of a particular legal relationship existing between them, the right of reimbursement of the third person against the debtor is governed by the law applicable to the legal relationship. This provision applies also to the right of subrogation. Therefore, the insurer's right of subrogation is governed by the law applicable to the insurance contract rather than the obligation between the insured and the claimant.

327. Insurance Act, Art. 54-1.
328. Insurance Act, Art. 53.

VII. IP Licensing Contracts

223. IP contracts cover all obligatory contracts concerning intellectual properties. They are not specifically specified in the Choice-of-law Act 2010. Article 42 Paragraph 2 of it states that any right in an intellectual property created by an employee in the performance of his/her duties is governed by the law applicable to the contract of employment. Yet, the purpose of such provision is to ascertain the governing law of the ownership attribution for the intellectual properties in question rather than the governing law of the employment contract. No obligatory aspects are touched upon by this provision.

224. The governing law of an IP contract is ascertained in the same way as other obligatory juridical acts. The parties to an IP obligatory contract can expressly choose the law applicable to it. In absence of expressly agreement or if the agreement is void, the law of the intellectual property right will certainly weigh quite a lot in the test of closest connection. The obligatory IP contracts may relate to transfer, using, leasing or licensing of an IP, but it is noteworthy that a contract for transfer can be distinguished from the transfer itself quite as well as in the case of movable properties. The governing law of a right in an intellectual property is the law of the place where the protection of that right is sought ('*lex loci protectionis*'), according to Article 42 Paragraph 1 of the Choice-of-law Act 2010.

225. A licensing contract is a contract between the licensor and licensee, in which the licensor agrees that the licensee may make use of an IP over which he/she holds exclusive right, such as a patent, trademark, copyright, layout in an integrated circuit, or trade secret. The licensor remains holder of the licensed right and may provide exclusive or non-exclusive permission. The licensee acquires a limited permission to make use of the protected subject matter. It may also be restricted territorially or for an agreed specific period.

226. A licensing contract is of bilateral and obligatory nature. It basically entails mutual rights and duties, including the license grant, the license fee to be paid by the licensee, the method of the licensee's exercising the licensed right, the warranties and liabilities with regard to third party rights or other defects in title, choice-of-law and choice-of-court clauses, etc. It is subject to Article 20 of the Choice-of-law Act 2010. The autonomy of the parties' express agreement on choice of law is recognized. In absence of their express agreement, the governing law is ascertained by the test of closest connection. The domicile of the licensor may be presumed to be the place of closest connection.

227. As mentioned above, the license grant of the licensed right is distinct from the licensing contract itself. The formation, validity, interpretation, effects and other contractual issues of the licensing contract are governed by the law ascertained under Article 20 of the Choice-of-law Act 2010. The license grant is a partial transfer of the licensed right in nature. The issues around it such as whether it is transferable and licensable are proprietary rather than contractual.[329] The law applicable to them is the *lex loci protectionis* designated under Article 42 Paragraph 1 of the Choice-of-law Act 2010.

VIII. Hybrid Contracts

228. The ascertainment of the governing law of hybrid obligatory contracts are subject to the general provisions in Article 20 of the Choice-of-law Act 2010. Special emphasis is on the nature of the respective contract in weighing the connection it has with the relevant laws.

A. *Leasing*

229. A leasing is a contract between a lessor and a lessee, in which the lessor hires out an asset to the lessee for a certain period of time and the lessee agrees to pay in return an agreed rental. The ownership of the asset is transferred to the lessee at the end of the lease. The lessor retains the ownership of the asset concerned during the period and will repossess the asset should the client require a replacement. A leasing arrangement can be useful to a lessee in so far as it enables it to employ assets without having to tie up large amounts of capital for long periods of time.

230. A leasing relates heavily to the use and potential transfer of title to the leased object, the *lex locus rei situs* weighs a lot in ascertaining the law of closest connection.

B. *Factoring*

231. A factoring is a contract entered into by a supplier to transfer accounts receivable to a factor who then chase up the debt. Factoring relieves the supplier of a debt for less than the total amount providing them with working capital to continue trading and accelerates the cash flow.

232. A factoring relates to the accounts receivable and the arrangement between the parties. The law applicable to the obligations or accounts receivable that the supplier transferred to the factor might govern the factoring if it is the law of closest connection.

---

329. Alex Metzer, *Licence Contracts*, in 2 *Encyclopedia of Private International Law* 1150 (Jürgen Basedow et al. eds, Edward Elgar 2017).

C. Franchise

233. A franchise is a type of license that a franchisor licenses its know-how, proprietary knowledge, processes, intellectual property, use of its business model, brand, and rights to sell its branded products and services to a franchisee. In exchange for gaining the franchise, the franchisee usually pays certain fees and agrees to comply with certain obligations, typically set out in a Franchise Agreement.

234. Franchising is not an equal partnership, especially due to the legal advantages the franchisor has over the franchisee. The franchisors are thus required by Taiwan's Fair Trade Commission to comply basic principles such as transparency to safeguard the fair competition in the market. As no specific rule is stated in the Choice-of-law Act 2010, the governing law of a franchise is decided according to Article 20 of it. The law of the franchising market weighs significantly in deciding the law of closest connection.

D. Publishing Contract

235. According to Taiwan's Civil Code, a publishing contract is a contract whereby one of the parties agrees to deliver to the other for publishing a literary, a scientific, an artistic, or others of the writings, and the latter agrees to print or in other ways to reproduce and publish the said writings. [330] The right of publishing cedes to the publisher when the person ceding the right of publishing according to the publishing contract delivers the writing to the publisher. The publisher's right of publishing is extinguished at the end of the publishing contract. [331]The rights of the author who are entitled to the intellectual property are exercised by the publisher, in so far as it is necessary for executing the legally authorized rights. [332] A publishing contract is extinguished if, before the completion of the writing, the author died or becomes incapable, or it is impossible to have it completed without his own negligence. [333]

236. Publishing contracts are not specifically addressed in the Choice-of-law Act 2010. The governing law of a publishing contract is ascertained in pursuance with its Article 20. The *lex domicilli* of the author, the *lex domicilli* of the publisher and the governing law of the copyright for the published writing are all relevant in weighing the closest connection.

330. CC, Art. 515.
331. CC, Art. 515-1.
332. CC, Art. 516.
333. CC, Art. 527.

IX. Negotiable Instruments

A. Bills of Exchange and Checks

237. Taiwan's Negotiable Instruments Act[334] defines a 'negotiable instrument' as a bill of exchange, promissory note, or check.[335] A bill of exchange is a negotiable instrument signed and issued by the drawer authorizing the drawee to pay unconditionally at a fixed future date a sum certain in money to the payee or holder. [336] A promissory note is a negotiable instrument signed and issued by the maker engaging himself to pay unconditionally at a fixed future date a sum certain in money to the payee or holder. [337] A check is a negotiable instrument signed and issued by the drawer authorizing a financial institution to pay unconditionally on demand a sum certain in money to the order payee or holder. [338] A person who signs his name to a negotiable instrument is liable on the instrument according to its tenor. [339]

238. The rights and duties arising from a negotiable instrument are obligations. The Negotiable Instruments Act is a special legislation to Taiwan's Civil Code. Thereupon, the law applicable to them may be otherwise ascertained in accordance with Article 20 of the Choice-of-law Act 2010.[340] While Article 21 of it states that where a juridical act results in the creation of rights on a negotiable instrument, the formation and effect of the act are governed by the law determined by the intention of the parties.[341] However, where there is no express intention of the parties or their express intention is void under the applicable law determined by them, the law of the place where the juridical act was undertaken governs; where the place of the juridical act is unclear, the law of the place of payment governs. [342]

239. Due to the purpose of circulation and fair play of the parties, the exercise and preservation of rights in a negotiable instrument are needed to be addressed. The Negotiable Instruments Act thus states that any act required to be done by a party to a negotiable instrument for the exercise and preservation of rights in the instrument shall be performed at the place designated on the instrument; in the absence of a designated place, the acts shall be performed at the party's place of business, or, in the absence of a place of business, at the party's domicile or residence. If the place of business, domicile, or residence of the party against whom a protest is contemplated to be made is unknown, a request may be made to the notary

334. The Negotiable Instruments Act (Piao-Ju Fa, 票據法last revised 1987) was adopted in 1929 and last revised in 1987.
335. Negotiable Instruments Act, Art. 1.
336. Negotiable Instruments Act, Art. 2.
337. Negotiable Instruments Act, Art. 3.
338. Negotiable Instruments Act, Art. 4.
339. Negotiable Instruments Act, Art. 5.
340. For discussion on the relevant judicial practice, *see* Rong-Chwan Chen, *The Applicable Law to the Promissory Notes Involving Foreign Elements: Comments on Some Precedents of the Supreme Court*, 55 Taiwan Law Journal (台灣本土法學雜誌) 149–161 (February 2004).
341. Choice-of-law Act 2010, Art. 21 para. 1.
342. Choice-of-law Act 2010, Art. 21 para. 2.

public office of a court, or a chamber of commerce, or other public office for investigations into the party's whereabouts. If, after investigations, the whereabouts of the party still cannot be ascertained, the protest may be made at the notary public office of the court, the chamber of commerce, or other public office.[343] Conflict of laws problems raise in the formal requisites of such an act. Hence, Article 21 Paragraph 3 of the Choice-of-law Act 2010 stipulates that formal requisites of a juridical act undertaken for the purpose of exercising or preserving a right on a negotiable instrument are governed by the law of the place of the act.

B. Notes and Letters of Credit

240. For bills and notes, Taiwan's Civil Code provides generally basic rules on its two forms. It states that a security payable by an assigned person is an instrument whereby a person directs another person to deliver to a third party money or valuable securities or other fungible things[344]; when the assignee has notified the payee that he/she accepts to perform the order of payment, he/she is bound to perform it in accordance with the tenor of the order[345]; and if a security payable by an assigned person is made by the assignor for the performance of a debt due to the payee, the debt is extinguished when prestation is made by the assignee. [346] The payee may transfer the security payable by an assigned person to a third party, except the assignor has inserted in the securities itself that transfer is forbidden. [347]

241. It also states that a security payable to bearer is securities by which the bearer may claim from the maker a prestation according to the tenor thereof. [348] The maker of a security payable to bearer is bound to make the prestation to the person who presents it. However, he/she shall not make such prestation if he/she knows that the bearer is not entitled to dispose of the securities, or if he/she has been notified of the loss, stolen or destruction of the same. [349] The maker of a security payable to bearer is bound by it toward *bona fide* bearers, even if it has been lost, or stolen by him/her, or has otherwise passed into circulation without his/her consent. [350] The maker of a security payable to bearer may only take the defences which result from the voidance of the securities itself, or for its tenor, or from his/her legal relationship with bearer as valid defences against the bearer. However if the bearer acquires the securities in bad faith, the maker may also take the defences against the former bearer as valid defences against the bearer. [351]

343. Negotiable Instruments Act, Art. 20.
344. CC, Art. 710.
345. CC, Art. 711.
346. CC, Art. 712.
347. CC, Art. 716.
348. CC, Art. 719.
349. CC, Art. 720
350. CC, Art. 721.
351. CC, Art. 722.

242. Conflict of laws problems raise in requisites of a security mentioned above and the rights and duties of the interested parties. Article 22 of the Choice-of-law Act 2010 stipulates that where a juridical act results in an obligation on a security made payable to order or to bearer, and is not governed by Article 21, the formation and effect of the act are governed by the law of the place where the act was performed; where the place of the act is unclear, by the law of the place of payment. Apparently the principle *locus regit actum* is adopted. It is noteworthy that the principle of party autonomy is not expressly adopted, but the private autonomy is the inherent principle for these securities. The validity of a choice of law clause is governed by the law of the place where the act was performed; where the place of the act is unclear, by the law of the place of payment.[352]

243. According to the Banking Act,[353] a letter of credit is an instrument which a bank issues upon the request of a customer to notify and authorize a beneficiary named by the customer to issue a draft or other certificate in accordance with a prescribed form and in an amount not to exceed a certain limit, such draft to be accepted or paid by the bank or its designated correspondent upon the beneficiary performing certain agreed-upon terms and conditions.[354] It is a commitment by a bank on behalf of the importer (buyer) that payment will be made to the beneficiary (seller, exporter) provided that the terms and conditions stated in it have been met, as evidenced by the presentation of specified documents.

244. The letter of credit protects the importer and guarantees financially the exporter since the documents are required to trigger payment and to provide evidence that goods have been shipped as agreed. It is thus widely adopted in international trade. The bank's examination of such documents is critical in the transaction. The strict compliance is required, so the documents of trivial discrepancies are rejected. International Chamber of Commerce (ICC) promulgated the Uniform Customs and Practice for Documentary Credits (commonly called 'UCP') to set up the uniform international standards for dealing with letters of credit.[355]

245. To cope with the international standards, Taiwan leaves the questions of letters of credit open and does not formulate the domestic substantive rules for them. The courts determine the related disputes in pursuance with the UCP[356]. The Supreme Court interpreted the spirit of the UCP to rule that the exporters start to arrange the delivery of goods after receiving the letter of credit in the practice of international trade, so the letter of credit shall be delivered prior to the delivery of

352. Liu & Chen, *supra* n. 12, at 321.
353. The Banking Act (Yin-Hang Fa, 銀行法) was adopted in 1930 and last revised in 2019.
354. Banking Act, Art. 16.
355. The latest (July 2007) revision of UCP, commonly known as UCP 600, is the sixth revision of the rules since they were first promulgated in 1933. Earlier versions of the UCP were published in 1933, 1951, 1962, 1974, 1983, and 1993.
356. Supreme Court's Civil Judgment, Tai-Shang 1367 of 1980.

goods.[357] It also ruled that the issuance of letter of credit is a condition to the validity of the contract of sale while it is an act distinct from the contract, [358] and supported the principle of strict compliance on documents relating to the letter of credit.[359]

246. The UCP is treated in judicial practice as an embodiment of uniform international practice and customs with regard to the letters of credit. Such substantive norms are universally and directly applicable. Since there is no competition or conflict of legal norms in this regard, the Choice-of-law Act 2010 therefore does not address on the letters of credit.

X. Agency Contracts

247. A voluntary agency or authorization operates in the relation between the agent, the principal, and the third party. Taiwan's Civil Code states that an expression of intent which an agent makes in the name of the principal within the scope of his delegated power takes effect directly to the principal. If an expression of intent which is required to be made to the principal is made to his agent, it also takes effect directly to the principal. [360] If the authority of agency is conferred by a juridical act, it shall be made by an expression of intent to the agent or to the third party with whom the delegated act is transacted. [361]

248. The conferring act is unilaterally conducted by the principal and is distinguishable from the underlying agency contract between principal and agent upon which the authority of agency is conferred. The underlying agency contract is included in, for instance, a contract of hire of services whereby the parties agree that one of them shall service as an agent for a fixed or undefined period to the other party, and the latter shall pay remuneration[362], and a contract of mandate whereby the parties agree that one of them commissions the other party to deal with his affairs as an agent, and the latter agrees to do so. [363]

249. In conflict of laws, the distinction of the three dimensions of a voluntary agency is also established. Article 17 of the Choice-of-law Act 2010 states that where an agent's authority is conferred by a juridical act, the formation of the agency and the relationship between the principal and the agent are governed by the law expressly chosen by them; in the absence of an express choice, by the law of the place with which the agency relationship is most closely connected. Despite the

357. Supreme Court's Civil Judgment, Tai-Shang 206 of 1974.
358. Supreme Court's Civil Judgment, Tai-Shang 3206 of 1978.
359. Supreme Court's Civil Judgment, Tai-Shang 2210 of 1978.
360. CC, Art. 103.
361. CC, Art. 167.
362. CC, Art. 482.
363. CC, Art. 528.

governing law of the conferring act is independent from governing law of the underlying agency contract, the approach to ascertain the former is quite similar to the latter.

250. Taiwan's Civil Code addresses the effects of an agent's act to the principal largely. An emphasis is on the case that the power of agency lacks foundation in the internal relation or agency contract. The limitation or withdrawal of the delegated power shall not be a valid defence against any *bona fide* third party, except the ignorance of the third party is due to his fault. [364] However, a person, who by his own acts represents he has conferred the authority of agency to another person, or who knows that another person declares himself to be his agent and failed to express a contrary intent, shall be liable to the third party as a person who has conferred that authority, except the third party knew, or might know of the absence of authority. [365] A juridical act made in the name of an agent by a person of no authority of agency shall not be effective to the principal except it is acknowledged by the principal. [366]

251. The conflict of laws problems of the above legal relations are stipulated in Article 18 of the Choice-of-law Act 2010. It states the where an agent undertakes a juridical act in the name of the principal with a third person, as between the principal and the third person, the existence, extent, and effect of an exercise of the agent's authority is governed by the law as expressly chosen by the principal and the third person; in the absence of an express choice, by the law of the place with which the act undertaken by the agent is most closely connected.

252. The juridical act conducted by an agent takes effects directly on the principal and the third party. But the agent is also liable to the third party for wrongful doings. Taiwan's Civil Code thus provides that if one who has no delegated power to make a juridical act as an agent of another person, he is liable for the injury to the *bona fide* other party. [367] As injury results from the pseudo agent's act with the third party in the capacity of the principal's agent, although it is distinct from the validity of the juridical act at issue, it shall also be governed by the same law. Thereupon, Article 19 of the Choice-of-law Act 2010 states that where an agent undertakes a juridical act in the name of the principal with a third person, as between the third person and the agent, the legal effect of the agent's acting with, in excess of, or without authority is governed by the applicable law as provided in Article 18 of it.

364. CC, Art. 107.
365. CC, Art. 169.
366. CC, Art. 170.
367. CC, Art. 110.

§3. NON-CONTRACTUAL OBLIGATIONS

253. In Taiwan's Civil Code, obligations may arise from juridical acts,[368] *negotiorum gestio*,[369] unjust enrichments,[370] and torts.[371] It is the general consensus that the act to confer power of agency[372] does not result in any obligation. In the Choice-of-law Act 2010, a similar structure was adopted, so that the non-contractual obligations denote the obligations beyond Article 20 and includes the other three causes. Due to the uncertainty of characterization, a catch-all provision is inserted in Article 30 to address any obligation arising from a 'legal fact' other than the four causes mentioned above. If any such obligation exists, it is governed by the law of the place where the legal fact took place.

I. Party Autonomy

254. The principle of party autonomy is adopted for contractual obligations to decide their governing laws. The non-contractual obligations are not outcomes of party autonomy. However, the parties' disputes regarding such obligations are eligible for settlement by mutual agreement in or outside the court. As a partial settlement to resolve the dispute, the choice of law is an accepted reality in judicial practice. Article 31 of the Choice-of-law Act 2010 thus states that where the parties with respect to an obligation which arises otherwise than from a juridical act agree to the application of the law of the ROC after a suit has been brought on the obligation in a court of the ROC, the law of the ROC is applied.

255. Apparently, the aforementioned rule of party autonomy applies in the court proceedings.[373] It is distinguishable from the party autonomy in contractual obligations that applies to the contracts or juridical acts. The parties may not agree on the governing law of obligations caused by a *negotiorum gestio*, unjust enrichment or tort before or at the time such a legal fact occurred.

II. Objective Connection

256. The traditional rule to ascertain the governing law of a non-contractual obligation is to find out its seat or to weigh and compare the relevant objective connections. The Choice-of-law Act 2010 basically follows this methodology and refines the rules to adopt the closest connection test in ascertaining the objective connecting factor. In contrast to the general principle that a non-contractual obligation is governed by the law of the place where the legal fact from which it arise, it

368. CC, Art. 153.
369. CC, Art. 172.
370. CC, Art. 179.
371. CC, Art. 184.
372. CC, Art. 167.
373. It aims at reducing litigation costs. En-Wei Lin, *New Private International Law in Taiwan: Negotiorum Gestio, Unjust Enrichment and Tort*, in Basedow & Pissler (eds.), *supra* n. 7, at 245.

addresses respectively the connecting factor to ascertain the governing law of an obligation resulted from a *negotiorum gestio*, unjust enrichment, tort or other legal facts. The objective connecting factors deployed includes the place where the management was undertaken[374], the place where the enrichment was received[375], the place where the tort was committed, the closest connection[376], and the place where the fact occurred. [377]

III. Law of Torts

257. Taiwan's Civil Code lays down some basic principles for torts. 'A person who, intentionally or negligently, has wrongfully damaged the rights of another is bound to compensate him for any injury arising therefrom. The same rule shall be applied when the injury is done intentionally in a manner against the *boni mores*. [378] This provision addresses the basic concept, requisites and effects of a tort. It is, however, applicable to an international tort case on the premise that the Taiwanese law governs.

258. There are many types of torts or delicts, ranging from murdering, negligent driving, nuisance, defamation, fraudulent misrepresentation, unfair competition and mismanagement of properties, to infringement of intellectual property rights and torts involving ships, aircraft or internet. The conflict of laws problems of torts are dynamic because they relate simultaneously to many different connecting factors: the residence, habitual residence, domicile, or nationality of the actors and the victims, the place where the tort was committed, the place where the injury occurred, the place of the closest connection, and the place of the forum. It is apparently inappropriate to apply a single rigid conflicts rule, regardless of the type of tort involved. The combination of rigid and soft connecting factors and diverse conflicts rules for different types of tort are thus adopted in modern legislations.

A. Lex Loci Delicti

259. Taiwan's Choice-of-law Act adopted the *lex loci delicti* principle which denotes that a tort is governed by the law of the place where the alleged tort occurs in both its versions of 1953 and 2010. This principle was compulsory and part of the system of double actionability with the *lex fori* in 1953[379], but it was totally revised by introducing the closest connection test in 2010.

374. Choice-of-law Act 2010, Art. 23.
375. Choice-of-law Act 2010, Art. 24.
376. Choice-of-law Act 2010, Art. 25.
377. Choice-of-law Act 2010, Art. 31.
378. CC, Art. 184 para. 1.
379. Choice-of-law Act 1953, Art. 9.

260. The Choice-of-law Act 2010 states: 'An obligation arising from a tort is governed by the law of the place where the tort was committed. However, if another law is the law most closely connected with the tort, it governs.'[380] The first sentence remains as if it were still rigid and compulsory, while the second sentence speaks the truth that the closest connection test is the ultimate and real criteria. Under such a structure, the *lex loci delicti* is *prima facie* applicable, but it governs only when it is the law of closest connection with the tort.

B. Scope of Application

261. As mentioned above, the *lex loci delicti* is no more a general conflict of laws rule for torts. Furthermore, as the closest connection test is as soft as it can be the approach to ascertain the applicable law for every case, some special half-rigid conflicts rules are stipulated for several types of torts. For example, Taiwan's Civil Code states that the manufacturer is liable for the injury to another arising from the common use or consumption of his merchandise, unless there is no defectiveness in the production, manufacture, process, or design of the merchandise, or the injury is not caused by the defectiveness, or the manufacturer has exercised reasonable care to prevent the injury.[381] Such products liability of the manufacturer relates to the reasonable distribution of risk to the manufacturer and the protection of consumers. The ascertainment of its governing law excludes the general closest connection test to reflect the governmental interests of the relevant laws.

262. The Choice-of-law Act 2010 states that the products liability is basically governed by the manufacturer's national law,[382] but the injured person can choose among the three options below as the applicable law provided the manufacturer has agreed in advance or where the manufacturer could reasonably have foreseen that the product would be sold in such place: (i) the law of the place of injury, (ii) the law of the place where the injured person purchased the product, or (iii) the injured person's national law.[383] This provision is a combination of several conflicts rules including the *lex loci delicti*.

263. The obligation arising from a ubiquitous tort committed by means of publication, radio, television, internet publication or other medium of communication is another example.[384] According to the Choice-of-law Act 2010, it is governed by the most closely connected law as follows: either (i) the law of the place where the tort was committed or the law of the tortfeasor's domicile, (ii) the law of the place where the injury occurred, provided the tortfeasor could reasonably have foreseen that place, or (iii) the injured person's national law, provided the injury was done to

380. Choice-of-law Act 2010, Art. 25.
381. CC, Art. 191-1 para. 1.
382. The rule on *renvoi* in Act. 6 of the Choice-of-law Act 2010 shall thus apply.
383. Choice-of-law Act 2010, Art. 26.
384. From a practical view point, this new provision is evaluated as a big progress. En-Wei Lin, *supra* n. 373, at 253.

his individual personality rights. If such tortfeasor is in the business of publication, radio, television, internet publication, or other medium of communication, then the law of the place of their business governs. [385]

C. Damages (Compensation)

264. The governing law of a tort is applicable to all respects regarding the obligation arising from it. It basically applies to the capacity to commit a tort, the unlawfulness of the act, the requirements of causation and fault, and the legal effects of it. In Taiwan's legal system, damages or compensation is part of the material legal effects of a tort, rather than the remedial sanction granted by a court. It is, along with other substantive questions, subject to the governing law of the tort, and not necessarily governed by the *lex fori*.

265. Before the court awards any measures to compensate the damage or injury caused by the tort, it is necessary to look into what the actual damage or injury is. The question whether the victim suffered a legal loss or damage is basically governed by the law applicable to the said loss or damage. Special problems arise when the loss or damage is governed by a law other than the law of the tort.

266. In a case of 2008, the Supreme Court ruled that the problem of damages is separable from the problem of tortious liability, their governing laws are thus not necessarily the same one. In this case, a Vietnamese worker lost his left arm when operating a machine in Taiwan and claimed damages against his employer.[386] The law applicable to the questions of whether and how the tortfeasor is liable is Taiwanese law, while the measurement of damage by losing labour forces beyond the period that the worker has been permitted to work in Taiwan is governed by his national law, i.e., Vietnamese law.

267. In a case of 2007, the Supreme Court ruled that the question of whether the parents of a victim can claim the costs to support their future life shall not be decided directly by the conflicts rule for torts, when considering the compensatory damages owed to the parents of a victim who lost her life in a traffic accident.[387] As the law relating to the liability for support differs from country to country, the issue of compensation or whether the victim is legally liable to support the plaintiffs is subject to the law of the obligation of maintenance or support, and falls out of the scope of the governing law of the tort.

385. Choice-of-law Act 2010, Art. 28.
386. Supreme Court's Civil Judgment, Tai-Shang 1838 of 2008.
387. Supreme Court's Civil Judgment, Tai-Shang 1804 of 2007.

D. Insurance and Social Security Law

268. The victims of a tort may be covered by contracts of insurance and the social security law. It is noteworthy that insurance is an independent legal relation to torts no matter whether the policyholder is the victim or the tortfeasor. The social security law applies to the victims it covers by nature of its effects as a public law, and is out of the scope of Taiwan's Choice-of-law Act.

269. For private contracts of liability insurance held by the victim, the victim can claim directly under the terms of their contracts. The construction of the terms is governed by the governing law of the insurance contract in question. If the victim is claiming under the liability insurance contract held by the tortfeasor, the question of whether the victim may claim directly against the insurer may be governed by the applicable law of tort or liability insurance contract, depending on its characterization.

270. In order to better protect the victim and to avoid the potential contradictory results of applying the different laws, the Choice-of-law Act 2010 therefore adopts the methodology of alternative application of them both. It states that the existence of a direct claim of an injured person against the tortfeasor's insurer is governed by the law applicable to the insurance contract; however, the injured person may also assert a direct claim if the law applicable to the obligation permits its assertion.[388]

IV. Unfair Competition

271. Unfair competition and restraints of competition are regulated in Taiwan's Fair Trade Act.[389] They both are prohibited by the administrative provisions of it. Unfair competition is essentially a concept of tortious act which comprises several types of acts. They are all prohibited by the Fair Trade Act. To name a few, no enterprise shall make or use false or misleading representations or symbols on the matter that is relevant to goods and is sufficient to affect trading decisions on goods or in advertisements, or in any other way make it known to the public[390]; no enterprise shall have any of the following acts with respect to the goods or services it supplies: 1. using in the same or similar manner in the same or similar category of merchandize, the personal name, business or corporate name, or trademark of another, or container, packaging, or appearance of another's goods, or any other symbol that represents such person's goods, commonly known to the public, so as to cause confusion with such person's goods; or selling, transporting, exporting, or importing goods bearing such representation; or 2. using in the same or similar manner in the same or similar category of services, the personal name, business or corporate name,

388. Choice-of-law Act 2010, Art. 29.

389. The Fair Trade Act (Gong-Ping Jiao-Yi Fa, 公平交易法) was adopted in 1991 and last revised in 2017.

390. Fair Trade Act, Art. 21.

or service mark of another, or any other symbol that represents such person's business or services, commonly known to the public, so as to cause confusion with the facilities or activities of the business or service of such person[391]; no enterprise shall compete for trading opportunities by means of improper offerings of gifts or prizes[392]; no enterprise shall, for the purpose of competition, make or disseminate any false statement that is capable of damaging the business reputation of another[393]; no enterprise shall otherwise have any deceptive or obviously unfair conduct that is able to affect trading order. [394]

272. Taiwan's Fair Trade Act stipulates that if any enterprise violates any of the provisions of this Act and thereby infringes upon the rights and interests of another, the injured may request the removal of such infringement; if there is a likelihood of infringement, prevention may also be claimed.[395] Any enterprise that violates any of the provisions of this Act and thereby infringes upon the rights and interests of another shall be liable for the damages arising therefrom. [396] In response to the request of the injured person, a court may, taking into consideration of the nature of the infringement, award compensation more than the actual damages if the violation is intentional; provided that no award shall exceed three times of the amount of damages that is proven. Where the infringing person gains from its act of infringement, the injured may request to assess the damages exclusively based on the monetary gain to such infringing person. [397] Such civil legal effects apply to unfair competition and restraints of competition as well.

273. Given the facts that the regulations on unfair competition and restraints of competition differ from country to country, the conflict of laws problems arise in the perspectives of private law. The Choice-of-law Act 2010 hence states that where an obligation has resulted from a disruption of the order of a market by an act of unfair competition or of restraint of competition, the obligation is governed by the law of the place where the market is located; however, where the unfair competition or restriction of competition is produced by a juridical act, and where the law governing the juridical act is more beneficial to the injured person, said law is applied.[398]

274. Under the above provision, the civil liability for anti-competitive conduct is governed by the law of the place where the affected market is located. Despite the nature of public law, foreign anti-trust law or competition law can be applied for the purpose of determining the type and amount of remedies for such anti-competitive conduct. It is noteworthy that the local authority can only apply the local public law to impose administrative sanction or criminal penalty while it may

391. Fair Trade Act, Art. 22.
392. Fair Trade Act, Art. 23.
393. Fair Trade Act, Art. 24.
394. Fair Trade Act, Art. 25.
395. Fair Trade Act, Art. 29.
396. Fair Trade Act, Art. 30.
397. Fair Trade Act, Art. 31.
398. Choice-of-law Act 2010, Art. 27.

apply to an act which is committed abroad and has resulted in some local effects.[399] The so-called extraterritoriality theory is transformed into the rule stating the local law applies to the acts committed within the jurisdiction or an act committed abroad and resulted in effects within the jurisdiction.

V. *Negotiorum Gestio*

275. *Negotiorum gestio* is management of affairs of another person without a mandate or obligation. According to Taiwan's Civil Code, a person, who manages an affair of another person without a mandate or obligation, shall manage the affair in conformity with the principal's expressed or presumptive wishes and in the manner beneficial to the principal. [400] If the undertaking of the management of the affair is against the principal's expressed or presumptive wishes, the manager is bound to compensate the principal for any injury arising from his/her management, even if no negligence is in his act. [401] If the management of the affair is beneficial to the principal and is not against his/her expressed or presumptive wishes, and where the manager has, for the principal, made necessary or beneficial expenses, or assumed debt, or suffered injury, he/she is entitled to claim against the principal for the reimbursement of such expenses plus interest commencing from the date of outlay, or the payment of such debt, or compensation for the injury sustained. [402]

276. As the legal fact of managing affairs of another without mandate is evaluated differently from country to country, the problem of conflict of laws on obligation of *negotiorum gestio* remains to be resolved. The Choice-of-law Act 2010 states that an obligation arising from a management of the affairs of another without mandate ('*negotiorum gestio*') is governed by the law of the place where the management was undertaken.[403] This provision acknowledges that the management is the centre of the legal fact and the law of the place of management is applicable to the requisites and effects of the *negotiorum gestio*.

277. In the Supreme Court's Civil Judgment, Tai-Shang 1031 of 2002, a ship owned by a Korean company sank to the bottom within Taiwan's territorial sea and was abandoned by its owner. The local navigation authority removed and disposed of the wreck of it without the owner's mandate, and then sued the owner to compensate the expenses for the removal and disposal. The Supreme Court ruled that the obligation arising therefrom is governed by the Taiwanese law which is the law of place where the legal fact occurred.[404]

399. For further discussion, *see* Rong-Chwan Chen, *Jurisdiction and Law Applicable to Anti-competition Conducts*, 22-2 Fair Trade Quarterly (公平交易季刊) 93–162 (April 2014).
400. CC, Art. 172.
401. CC, Art. 174.
402. CC, Art. 176.
403. Choice-of-law Act 2010, Art. 23.
404. For detailed information and further discussion, *see* Rong-Chwan Chen, *The Obligation Arisen from Clearing the Foreign Sunken Ship*, 19 Taiwan Jurist (月旦法學教室) 30–31 (May 2004).

VI. Unjust Enrichment

278. Unjust enrichment is a legal fact resulting in an obligation between the parties. According to Taiwan's Civil Code, a person who acquires interests without any legal ground and prejudice to the other shall be bound to return it.[405] In addition to the interests received, a recipient unjustly enriched shall return whatever he acquired by virtue of such interests. If restitution is impossible by reason of the very nature of the interests or by reason of any other circumstance, he shall be bound to reimburse the value. [406] When the recipient unjustly enriched transferred gratuitously whatever he has received to a third party, and therefore the recipient is released from his obligation to return the interests, such third party shall be bound to make restitution to the extent which the recipient is released from his/her obligation. [407]

279. The recipient unjustly enriched is obligated to return the interests as mentioned above, other than being removed by a court's equitable remedy of the interests. However, the laws of countries vary on the requisites of such an obligation, the relation of the transferred interests and their legal grounds, the exceptional circumstances in which the interests may not be claimed to return, and the extent of interests that shall be returned. In addition, the conflict of laws problem arises also in its nature of substantive right or equitable remedy, and the existence of the legal ground on which the interests were transferred.

280. The Choice-of-law Act 2010 states: 'An obligation arising from an unjust enrichment is governed by the law of the place where the enrichment was received. However, if the unjust enrichment arises from an intended performance of an obligation, the obligation of the enriched party is governed by the law applicable to the legal relationship which gave rise to the intended performance.'[408] The first sentence is based on the fact that the enrichment is the centre and the recipient was enriched under the law by which such enrichment took effect. It applies to the non-prestation unjust enrichments. An unjust enrichment arising out of a prestation is closely connected with its underlying legal relationship, and is therefore governed by the law applicable to such legal relationship.[409]

281. In a case of 2019[410], an Indonesian company asserted that it was deceived and thus erroneously wired a certain sum of money to the account of a Taiwanese citizen and sued him in a Taiwanese court for returning the unjust enrichment under the Taiwanese law. The Taiwanese defendant contended that he legally dealt with the said money in conformity with the terms of a contract with a foreign company, and the said unjust enrichment, if any, shall be governed by the law applicable to

405. CC, Art. 179.
406. CC, Art. 181.
407. CC, Art. 183.
408. Choice-of-law Act 2010, Art. 24.
409. For further discussion, *see* Rong-Chwan Chen, *A Study on the Applicable Law to the Unjust Enrichments*, 8-2 Soochow Law Review 143 (April 1995).
410. Supreme Court's Civil Judgment, Tai-Shang 819 of 2019.

the contract. The Supreme Court ruled that there is no underlying contractual relationship between the parties, and the Indonesian company was deceived and transferred the said money to the account, so it is correct to characterize it as a non-prestation unjust enrichment and to ascertain its governing law under the first sentence of Article 24 of the Choice-of-law Act 2010. Taiwanese law is applicable since the said account is a local account opened in a Taiwanese bank.

VII. *Culpa in Contrahendo*

282. *Culpa in contrahendo* concerns good faith and fair dealing in negotiation and conclusion of a contract. The violation of relevant duties raises the pre-contractual liability of the violating party. Taiwan's Civil Code stipulates: 'Even though the contract is not constituted, one of the parties is responsible for the injury caused to the other party who without his own negligence believed in the constitution of the contract when he, in order to prepare or negotiate for the contract, has done either of the following: 1. hidden in bad faith or dishonestly explained the gravely relevant matter of the contract when the other party inquired; 2. intentionally or gross negligently spilt out the other party's secret known or held by himself which the other party has explicitly expressed to be kept in secret; or 3. any other matter obviously against good faith.'[411] This provision is prescribed under the heading of 'contracts', *culpa in contrahendo* is thus characterized as a question of contract other than tort in Taiwanese substantive law.

283. As no prescription of *culpa in contrahendo* is addressed in the Choice-of-law Act 2010, its characterization and applicable law remain problematic.[412] It is this author's opinion that in Taiwan's private international law, *culpa in contrahendo* is separate from the problems of validity and effects of the contract that might ensue after the negotiation, and hence does not fall into the concept of a contract or a juridical act which is stated in Article 20. Its governing law can be ascertained by the closest connection test which is adopted for torts involving foreign elements.[413] It is also possible to characterize it as a *sui generis* obligation and apply the law of the place where the fact occurred. [414]

VIII. Other

284. Some general rules concerning the scope of the law applicable to an obligation are also provided in the Choice-of-law Act 2010. It states: 'The extinction of an obligation is governed by the law applicable to the formation and effect of the obligation.'[415] This provision recognizes the extinction of an obligation is severable

411. CC, Art. 245-1.
412. En-Wei Lin, *supra* n. 373, at 247.
413. Choice-of-law Act 2010, Art. 25.
414. Choice-of-law Act 2010, Art. 30.
415. Choice-of-law Act 2010, Art. 37.

to its formation, validity and effects, and is governed by the same law. In this sense, the set-off of two obligations shall apply simultaneously the laws applicable respectively to the two obligations in question.

285. Statute of limitation or extinction by prescription of a claim is problematic in its characterization in private international law. The conflicts rule varies as it is characterized as an issue of procedure which is subject to the *lex fori* or an issue of substantive law of which governing law is ascertained according to the relevant conflicts rule. Taiwan's Civil Code addresses it as a substantive legal question. It states that after the completion of a prescription, the debtor is entitled to refuse to perform his obligation; if any prestation is made in satisfaction of a claim extinguished by a prescription, the debtor may not demand the return of the prestation on the ground that he was ignorant of the prescription.[416] Unless shorter periods are provided by the enactments, a claim is extinguished by prescription if it is not exercised within fifteen years.'[417] So, the general period of extinctive prescription is 15 years.

286. Following the way of thinking in Taiwanese substantive law, the Choice-of-law Act 2010 states that the extinctive prescription for a claim is governed by the law applicable to the legal relationship from which the claim arose.[418] By this provision, it is proclaimed that the problem of statute of limitation is not a procedural question as to apply the *lex fori*. In contrast, it is in nature a substantive question of the claim and is governed by the law applicable to its effect.[419]

416. CC, Art. 144.
417. CC, Art. 125.
418. Choice-of-law Act 2010, Art. 36.
419. For further discussion, *see* Rong-Chwan Chen, *Choice of Law and Statute of Limitation*, 74 Taiwan Law Journal (台灣本土法學雜誌) 111 (September 2005).

Chapter 3. Property

§1. *Lex Rei Sitae*

287. The Latin principle *lex rei sitae* or *lex loci rei sitae* means the transfer or rights over a property is governed by the law of the place where the property is situated. This principle acknowledges the law under which the rights *in rem* are created and transferred is mandatory to them. Such a globally recognized principle relates more or less to the distinction between a property right and an obligatory claim.

288. *Lex rei sitae* is adopted in the Choice-of-law Act 2010. It states that a property right over a movable or immovable thing is governed by the law of the place where the thing is located.[420] A property right over a right is governed by the law of the place where the right is formed. [421] A property right over a ship is governed by the law of the nationality of the ship, and a property right over an aircraft is governed by the law of the state in which the aircraft is registered. [422]

§2. Moveable Property

289. Things are physical objects that are distinguishable from persons that are subjects to rights. They are further divided into immovable property (real property) and movable property (personal property) in Taiwan's Civil Code. Immovable property is land and things which are constantly affixed thereto. The products of the immovable property, if they are not separated therefrom, constitute a part of the immovable property.[423] A movable property is a thing other than the said immovable property. [424]

290. For the purpose of ascertaining the governing law in cases involving foreign elements, the distinction of an immovable property and a movable property is of very little practical importance. Because the conflicts rule for the rights *in rem* is unitary to follow the *lex rei sitae*, the movables do not follow the person and are not governed by his/her *lex domicilli.*

291. Several aspects have to be added to address the issues of the *lex rei sitae.* The transfer of a right *in rem* over a movable property is distinguishable from the obligatory contract between the parties. The *lex rei sitae* applies to the proprietary

420. Choice-of-law Act 2010, Art. 38 para. 1.
421. Choice-of-law Act 2010, Art. 38 para. 2.
422. Choice-of-law Act 2010, Art. 38 para. 3.
423. CC, Art. 66.
424. CC, Art. 67.

juridical act, and the contractual obligations are subject to the conflicts rule for obligations. The Choice-of-law Act 2010 states that the formal requisites of a juridical act concerning a right *in rem* are governed by the law applicable to the right, i.e., the *lex rei sitae*.[425]

292. The change of *situs* raises special problems of the *lex rei sitae*. A single fact that is divided and partly took place in different *situs* is in need of a suitable criterion to evaluate. The Choice-of-law Act 2010 adopt the principle of distributive application and states that where the location of a thing has changed, the acquisition, loss, or change of a property right in the thing is governed by the law of the location of the thing at the time the decisive event occurred.[426]

293. The mandatory nature of property law, the variance in types and contents of rights *in rem* of different states, and the mobility of movables from one state to another raise the unique problem of adaptation or adjustment. The effects of a right *in rem* are exclusive and valid against all third parties within the territory of the *lex rei sitae*. If the movable property is removed from country A to country B, the *lex rei sitae* of the same right changes from the law of country A to the law of country B. Under the fundamental policy to protect the existing rights of the owner and to harmonize the property laws of different countries, the Choice-of-law Act 2010 states that the ROC law governs the effect of a right *in rem* over a movable thing formed in accordance with the law prevailing in the foreign location from which it is brought into the ROC.[427] It recognizes on one hand the validity of the rights *in rem* created under a foreign law, and stipulates on the other hand that the governing law of the transformation of such foreign rights into domestic rights is the ROC law. If the existing foreign right *in rem* is not known in the ROC law, as the new *lex rei sitae* of the right *in rem*, a substantially similar right *in rem* in the ROC law shall be recognized and enforced.

I. Collateral

294. The difference between the law on rights *in rem* and the law of contracts is significant in both substantive law and private international law. The parties to obligatory contracts enjoy the freedom of contract while the rights *in rem* are subject to the statutory limitation of *numerus clausus*. Taiwan's Civil Code stipulates that no rights *in rem* shall be created unless otherwise provided by the statutes or customs.[428] The formation and effects of a right *in rem* over movable properties and their collateral are all governed by the *lex situs*.

425. Choice-of-law Act 2010, Art. 39.
426. Choice-of-law Act 2010, Art. 38 para. 4.
427. Choice-of-law Act 2010, Art. 40.
428. CC, Art. 757.

295. Movable properties may be collateral of certain security rights *in rem.* 'A pledge of movable property is a preferential right of a creditor to receive satisfaction of a claim from the proceeds from sale of movable property the possession of which has been transferred by a debtor or a third party as security for the claim.'[429] 'The right of retention is the right of a creditor who is in possession of the personal property of another to retain that personal property if there is a nexus between the occurrence of the creditor's claim and that property and the creditor has not received payment upon maturity of the claim.' [430]

296. Besides, Taiwan's Movable Property Secured Transactions Act[431] provides three different secured transactions over movable properties. A 'mortgage over movable property' means a mortgage right over the movable property that secures a claim in favour of the mortgagee without transfer of possession of the property by the debtor or a third party. If the debtor fails to perform the contract, the mortgagee may take possession of the mortgaged property and may sell the property to satisfy the mortgagee's claims from the sale proceeds with priority over other claims.[432] A 'conditional sale' means a transaction in which a buyer first takes possession of the subject property of the sale, under a stipulation that ownership of the subject property will pass to the buyer only upon the partial or full payment of the price of the property, or upon the fulfilment of a specific condition. [433] 'Possession in trust' means a transaction in which a trustor provides funds or credit to a trustee, and a claim is secured with ownership of the subject personal property originally placed in trust, while the trustee takes possession of and disposes the property under a trust receipt. [434]

297. In conformity with the principle of *numerus clausus* mentioned above, the security rights *in rem* can be created accordingly over the movable properties in Taiwan. This echoes the conflicts principle of *lex rei sitae*, and reaffirms that the security rights *in rem* over the movable properties in Taiwan shall be governed by the Taiwanese law. The creation, transfer, disposal and effects are governed by the *lex rei sitae*. The nature of the collateral, i.e., the characterization of it as a movable property or an immovable property, and whether such a security right *in rem* can be created over it, are also governed by the *lex rei sitae*.

II. Goods in Transit

298. The transfer of rights *in rem* over a movable property effects at the point of time stipulated by the law of its *situs*. For example, Taiwan's Civil Code states: 'The

---

429. CC, Art. 884.
430. CC, Art. 928.
431. The Movable Property Secured Transactions Act (Dong-Chan Dan-Bao Jiao-Yi Fa, 動產擔保交易法) was adopted in 1963 and last revised 2007.
432. *Ibid.*, Art. 15.
433. *Ibid.*, Art. 26.
434. *Ibid.*, Art. 32.

transfer of rights *in rem* of movable property will not effect until the movable property has been delivered. However, if the transferee has been in possession of the movable property, the transfer effects when the parties agree to such transfer. In the transfer of a right *in rem* of movable property, where the transferor is still in possession of it, a contract causing the transferee to acquire its indirect possession may be made between the parties in the place of its delivery. In the transfer of a right *in rem* of movable property, where a third party is in possession of it, the transferor may transfer the claim against such third party for the return of it to the transferee in place of its delivery.'[435] In the course of transit, the *situs* of the movable property changes from time to time, the different laws of *situs* may conflict in provisions of the requisites and time of its transfer, not to mention the question of its next transfer. The ascertainment of its governing law is thus more complex and problematic.[436]

299. The *situs* of goods in transit starts from the place of dispatch, to the place of actual situation, and finally, to the place of destination. The place of dispatch weakens its connection with the goods from the beginning of the route. The place of the actual situation is too inconstant and uncertain to be a suitable connecting factor. The law of the stipulated destination is appropriate to ascertain the governing law from the moment of dispatch. The Choice-of-law Act 2010 thus states that the acquisition, creation, loss, or change of a property right in a movable thing during its transit is governed by the law of its destination.[437] The destination is interpreted as the stipulated place of destination before dispatch, however, if it changed before arrival, the law of the last stipulated place or the actual final destination governs.

III. Cultural Property

300. Taiwan's Cultural Heritage Preservation Act[438] was codified to preserve, conserve and promote cultural heritage, and to regulate the transfer of the relevant rights.[439] It defines 'cultural heritage' as the designated or registered tangible or intangible cultural heritages which are of cultural value from the point of view of history, art or science, and further divides it into tangible cultural heritages and intangible cultural heritages. Tangible cultural heritages denotes similarly to 'cultural properties' and includes: (1) monuments, (2) historic buildings, (3) commemorative buildings, (4) groups of buildings, (5) archaeological sites, (6) historic sites, (7) cultural landscapes, (8) antiquities, and (9) natural landscapes and natural monuments. [440]

435. CC, Art. 761.
436. Yao-Ming Hsu, *Property Law in Taiwan*, in Basedow & Pissler (eds.), *supra* n. 7, 119, at 122–123.
437. Choice-of-law Act 2010, Art. 41.
438. The Cultural Heritage Preservation Act (Wen-Hua Zi-Chan Bao-Cun Fa, 文化資產保存法) was adopted in 1982 and last revised in 2016.
439. *Ibid.*, Art. 2.
440. *Ibid.*, Art. 3.

301. In private international law, conflict of laws problems arise in the rights *in rem* over the tangible cultural heritages or cultural properties and in the contracts about them. The Choice-of-law Act 2010 does not stipulate those problems specifically. The governing laws of the rights *in rem* over immovable and movable tangible cultural heritages or cultural properties are ascertained according to the general conflicts rule for rights *in rem*, i.e., the *lex rei sitae*. But the transient stay of movable cultural property at an airport for transfer is not closely connected with the transfer of rights *in rem* over it as to designate the law of the place as the governing law.[441] It is noteworthy that the tangible cultural heritages or cultural properties are subject to the cultural property law of the country that designated or registered them as such, so the law of the country of their origin (*lex originalis*) could play as overriding mandatory rules in the related contracts.[442]

IV. Other

302. A Ship or seagoing vessel is a movable property in Taiwan's Civil Code, but it is treated as a part of virtual territory of the state that grants it license. Likewise, an aircraft is movable and is deemed as an extension of the territory of the state that it is registered. The rights *in rem* over such vehicles for international transportation are thus particularly addressed and subject to other conflicts rules than the general rules for movable properties. The Choice-of-law Act 2010 stipulates that a right *in rem* over a ship is governed by the law of the nationality of the ship, and a right *in rem* over an aircraft is governed by the law of the State in which the aircraft is registered.[443] The nationality of a ship is determined by the laws of the relevant states and is basically the state of which flag is flown or by which the ship is registered and licensed.

§3. Immoveable Property

303. The rights *in rem* over an immovable property are governed by the *lex rei sitae* and the related disputes are subject to the exclusive jurisdiction of the court at the place where it is situated. Taiwan's law applies hence to the rights *in rem* over lands and buildings within its territory. According to Taiwan's Civil Code, unless otherwise restricted by the laws and regulations, ownership of land extends to such height and depth above and below the surface of the land within the range advantageous to the exercise of such ownership. Interference from others shall not be excluded if it does not obstruct the exercise of the ownership. [444] A condominium

441. Rong-Chwan Chen, *The Bona Fide Acquisition of a Movable Property in Transit*, 11 Taiwan Law Review (月旦法學雜誌) 53 (March 1996).
442. For further discussion, *see* Rong-Chwan Chen, *The Recovery of Stolen Cultural Objects in Private International Law*, 14-1 Soochow Law Review 67–128 (August 2002); Rong-Chwan Chen, *International Trade and Export Control of Cultural Properties*, 13 Chinese Yearbook of International Law and International Affairs 20–75 (August 2002).
443. Choice-of-law Act 2010, Art. 38 para. 4.
444. CC, Art. 765.

building is a building that is partitioned by several persons. Each of these persons owns an individual unit of it and has individual ownership of the individual unit, and the common elements of the building and its accessories is held tenancy in common by all the owners. [445]

I. Mortgage

304. Taiwan's Civil Code provides two kinds of mortgages. A general mortgage is a preferential right of a creditor to receive satisfaction of a claim from the proceeds from sale of immovable property that a debtor or a third party has provided, without transferring possession, as security for the claim. [446] A line of credit mortgage is a mortgage created for not more than a specified maximum amount on immovable property belonging to a debtor or a third party and provided thereby to secure a creditor's unspecified claim within a specific scope against the debtor. Claims secured by line of credit mortgages shall be limited to claims deriving from specific legal relationships or to rights deriving from negotiable instruments. [447]

305. The security interests resulting from a mortgage is distinguishable from the secured claim to which it is attached. Mortgage is not specifically addressed in the Choice-of-law Act 2010 and is within the scope of rights *in rem* over a thing, and is governed by the *lex rei sitae*. The secured claim is governed by the law applicable to the legal relation from which it resulted. Taiwan's Civil Code provides that a mortgage may neither be transferred nor furnished as security for any other claim by separating it from the claim that it secures.[448] In conflict of laws, whether the mortgage is accessory to the secured claim falls into the effects of the right *in rem* (mortgage), which is governed by the *lex rei sitae*. As a mortgage is a security to a claim, where a third person has provided a mortgage for a claim, the effect on the third person of a transfer of the secured claim concerns basically the nature or effects of the mortgage, and is therefore governed by the law of the mortgage. Article 32 Paragraph 2 of the Choice-of-law Act 2010 echoes this point of view.

II. Emissions

306. Emissions from an immovable property often cause injury or nuisance to the neighbouring properties. They relate to the criteria and requirements maintaining and managing such immovable property by the owner or user. Taiwan's Civil Code states that the landowner is entitled to prohibit the discharge of gases, steam, odours, smoke, heat, soot, noises, vibrations and other similar nuisances from another person's land, building or other works, except such nuisance is insignificant

445. CC, Art. 799.
446. CC, Art. 860.
447. CC, Art. 881-1.
448. CC, Art. 870.

or is justified by the shape of the land or by local custom.[449] The violator of this provision is liable to compensate accordingly.

307. Emissions encounter problems of characterizing them as tort or neighbouring relations in conflict of laws. No specific provision is addressed in the Choice-of-law Act 2010 in this respect. It is this author's opinion that to apply the conflicts rule based on the closest connection test for tort[450] is preferable, as the fairness and reasonableness can be better achieved through it. The governing law of the ownership of immovable property, i.e., the *lex rei sitae*, may be too rigid to protect the victims. It is as well too problematic to determine the *lex rei sitae* of the source immovable property or the injured immovable property.

III. Easements

308. Easements are interests in immovable property that diminish the power of the owner. Servitude is one of the typical ones. Taiwan's Civil Code states that a servitude of immovable property is the right to use the property of another person for accessing, drawing water, lightening, surveying, telecommunication or other specific convenience of one's own property.[451] A servitude of immovable property cannot be separately transferred from the dominant immovable property or created other right. [452] Where the continuance of all or part of the servitude of immovable property is no longer necessary, the court may, on the application of the owner of the servient immovable property, declare such servitude of immovable property extinguished upon the part of which the continuance is no longer necessary. A servitude of real property is extinguished by virtue of destruction or failure in use of the dominant immovable property. [453]

309. In conflict of laws, the ascertainment of the governing law of a servitude encounters the problem of the *lex rei sitae* of which immovable property, the dominant or the servient, is decisive. As servitude or easement is not specifically addressed in the Choice-of-law Act 2010, and the centre of a servitude is the real interest burdened on the servient immovable property, its *lex rei sitae* governs the creation and effects of the servitude.

§4. Securities

310. A security is a fungible, negotiable financial instrument issued by an entity according to the law of a country. It holds some type of monetary value and represents an ownership position or a creditor relationship. Logically, the security is the

449. CC, Art. 793.
450. Choice-of-law Act 2010, Art. 25.
451. CC, Art. 851.
452. CC, Art. 853.
453. CC, Art. 859.

product of its underlying legal relation and is governed by the law by which it is issued. The problems arise when a security is issued under the law of country A and transacted or publicly traded under the law of country B.

311. Where a security is held by a centralized depositary, the owner possesses it indirectly through the records in the account of the depository. The seller and buyer of such a security do not have to deliver it directly. Besides the distinction of the contractual obligations and the rights in the security, here emerges the legal relationship between the depository and the account holders. As the depository is established under the law of its incorporation and opens the account for the holders by the contracts between them, the rights in the deposited securities are presumed to be in closest connection with the contracts.

312. The Choice-of-law Act 2010 provides that where a security is held by a centralized depositary, the acquisition, loss, disposition, or change of a right in the security is governed by the law expressly specified as applicable in the contract of centralized deposit; in the absence of express specification, the law of the place most closely connected with the security governs.[454] The closest connection test applies also by analogy to the case in which the choice of law in the contract is void.

§5. TRUST

313. A trust is legislatively defined in Taiwan's Trust Act[455] as 'the legal relationship in which the settlor transfers or disposes of a right of property and the trustee agreed to administer or dispose of the trust property according to the stated purposes of the trust for the benefit of a beneficiary or for a specified purpose'.[456] Unlike the fiduciary contract between two parties, a trust is a three-party legal relationship. But, a trust is not an independent legal entity which is separate from the parties. No trust in respect of a property right that requires trust registration shall be valid against third parties unless trust registration of the right has been duly completed.[457] A trust property is held by the trustee for the benefits of the beneficiary and is legally separated from the trustee's properties. No trust property shall appertain to the trustee's estate upon the death of the trustee.[458] No trust property shall appertain to the bankrupt estate when the trustee becomes bankrupt.[459]

314. Trusts can be created by law or by juridical acts. Voluntary trusts include trusts *inter vivos* and testamentary trusts. A testamentary trust is based on a valid

---

454. Choice-of-law Act 2010, Art. 44. Taiwan is not a member to the Hague Convention of 5 July 2006 on the Law Applicable to Certain Rights in Respect of Securities held with an Intermediary. This provision does not incorporate or reflect the rules adopted in the Hague Convention. Liu & Chen, *supra* n. 12, at 408.
455. The Trust Act (Xin-Tuo Fa, 信託法) was adopted in 1996 and last revised in 2009.
456. Trust Act, Art. 1.
457. Trust Act, Art. 4.
458. Trust Act, Art. 10.
459. Trust Act, Art. 11.

testament. The creation and validity of the testamentary trust are governed by the law applicable to the testament.[460] *Inter vivos* trusts are not specifically dealt with in the Choice-of-law Act 2010, the governing law depends on the characterization of it as a question of obligation or right *in rem*. If a trust is established by creating or transferring a right *in rem*, it shall be characterized as a right *in rem* and governed by the *lex rei sitae*.[461] If only an obligation is created, the conflicts rule for obligatory juridical acts applies.[462] This author is of the opinion that the problem of characterization shall be determined by the *lex rei sitae*. The trustee's management of the trust property is part of the effects of the trust, it is governed by the law applicable to the trust, i.e., the *lex rei sitae* in case the trust is characterized as a proprietary arrangement.

§6. Expropriation

315. An expropriation is an action by the state or an authority to take a property from its owner for public use or benefit. Such exercise of public function of a state raises the problems of its reasonableness and promptly adequate compensation. A state can only dispossess someone of property with its territory. The conditions and effects of an expropriation are governed by the public law of the state exclusively. Foreigners whose property were nationalized or taken by the state can only challenge it by means of diplomatic protection. An action in the International Court of Justice can be initiated only by their own national state. The effects of and expropriation in private respect, such as when and how the title of the property was changed, are governed by the law applicable to the rights *in rem* over the expropriated property, which is the *lex rei sitae* under Article 38 of the Choice-of-law Act 2010.

460. Choice-of-law Act 2010, Arts 60 & 61.
461. Choice-of-law Act 2010, Art. 38 para. 1.
462. Choice-of-law Act 2010, Art. 20.

Chapter 4. Intangible Property Rights

316. Intangible property rights are distinguishable from the tangible property rights which comprise movable and immovable property rights. In a broad sense, they include obligatory claims, rights of negotiable instruments, shares and securities. They denote a narrower meaning here as to include only rights of personality and intellectual property rights.

§1. RIGHTS OF PERSONALITY

317. Rights of personality are protected in Taiwan's Civil Code in both general and special ways. The general rule is that when one's personality is infringed, one may apply to the court for removing; when one's personality is in danger of being infringed, one may apply for prevention; in such cases, an action for damages for emotional distress may be brought only it is otherwise provided by the law.[463] If one's right to use his name is infringed, one may apply to the court for removing of infringement and for damages for emotional distress. [464] Furthermore, some special personality rights are specified and stated. If a person has wrongfully damaged to the body, health, reputation, liberty, credit, privacy or chastity of another, or to another's personality in a severe way, the injured person may claim a reasonable compensation in money even if such injury is not a purely pecuniary loss. If it was reputation that has been damaged, the injured person may also claim the taking of proper measures for the rehabilitation of his reputation. Such a claim shall not be transferred or inherited, except a claim for compensation in money has been promised by contract or has been commenced. [465]

I. Applicable Law

318. The right of personality is not generally addressed in the Choice-of-law Act 2010 due to the fact that such right is fundamental and relates closely to the person's status and capacity and shall naturally be governed by the person's personal law, i.e., his/her national law. However, the rights of personality are basically protected from infringement by the law of torts. The conflict of laws problems arise in applying the governing law of the tort or the person's national law. This question is unanswered and left to the closest connection test of tort. In other words, the person's national law is applicable because it is the governing law of the infringed right or the law of closest connection with the tortious act.

319. The Choice-of-law Act 2010 tries to balance the interests and expectations of the relevant parties. It stipulates that an obligation arising from infringement of right of personality by a tort which was committed by means of publication, radio,

463. CC, Art. 18.
464. CC, Art. 19.
465. CC, Art. 195.

television, internet publication or other medium of communication is governed by the law mentioned below which is the most closely connected with the tort: 1. the law of the place where the tort was committed; if the place of the tort is unclear, the law of the tortfeasor's domicile; 2. the law of the place where the injury occurred, if such place could have been foreseen by the tortfeasor; and 3. the national law of the injured person.[466] Where the tortfeasor is in the business of publication, radio, television, internet publication, or other medium of communication, then the law of the place of his/her business governs. [467]

II. Remedies

320. The remedies for infringement of a person's right of personality are part of its effects. They are substantive questions that are governed by the law applicable to the tortious act, rather than a procedural question that is governed by the *lex fori.*

§2. Patents

321. A patent is a form of intellectual property that gives its owner the right to exclude others from making, using, selling, offering for sale, or importing the patented invention for a limited period of years in exchange for publishing an enabling public disclosure of the invention. According to Taiwan's Patent Act[468], a patent may be: 1. an invention patent, 2. an utility model patent; or 3. a design patent.[469]

322. The Choice-of-law Act 2010 does not address individual intellectual property rights such as patent, trademark and copyright separately. Instead, it provides a general conflicts rule for all intellectual property rights and states that a right in an intellectual property is governed by the law of the place where the protection of that right is sought ('*lex loci protectionis*'); any right in an intellectual property created by an employee in the performance of his/her duties is governed by the law applicable to the contract of employment.[470]

I. Creation

323. A patent is created by the competent authority's approving the patent application filed by the applicant. Apparently, it is created by a government's official or public act which is functioned under the law of the country. Therefore, creation of a patent is governed by the law of the country to which the applicant applied for patent, i.e., the *lex loci protectionis.*

466. Choice-of-law Act 2010, Art. 28 para. 1 Item 3.
467. Choice-of-law Act 2010, Art. 28 para. 2.
468. The Patent Act (Zhuan-Li Fa, 專利法) was adopted in 1944 and last revised in 2019.
469. Patent Act, Art. 2.
470. Choice-of-law Act 2010, Art. 42.

II. Protection

324. After a patent is granted by a country, it is effective and protected within the territory of that country. Protection of the patent is thus governed by the state's law under which the plaintiff asserts it shall be effective and protected, i.e., the *lex loci protectionis*.

III. Ownership and Transfer

325. The ownership of a patent belongs basically to its inventor after it is granted according to the law. Taiwan's Patent Act basically applies to the ROC applicants. Foreign applicants are permitted to apply under some conditions. It provides that a patent application filed by a foreign applicant shall not be accepted if the home country of such foreign applicant is not a signatory to an international treaty for protection of patent right to which the ROC is a signatory, or if the home country did not conclude with the ROC a treaty or an agreement for reciprocal protection of patent rights, or if no patent protection agreement was concluded by and between organizations or institutions of the ROC and said foreign country and approved by the respective competent authorities, or if the laws of said foreign country do not accept patent applications filed by ROC nationals.[471] Unless otherwise prescribed or the covenants otherwise set forth in an agreement, an inventor, a utility model creator, a designer, or the assignee or successor thereof enjoys the right to apply for a patent. [472]

326. A special problem arises in the case of work for hire. Taiwan's Patent Act stipulates that where an invention, a utility model or a design is made by an employee in the course of performing his/her duties, the right to apply for a patent and the patent right thereof shall be vested in his/her employer and the employer shall pay the employee reasonable remuneration; where there is an agreement providing otherwise, such agreement shall prevail.[473] Where an invention, utility model or design made by an employee has no connection to the course of performing his/her duties, the right to apply for a patent and the patent right for such invention, utility model or design shall be vested in the employee. However, if such invention, utility model or design is made through the utilization of the employer's resources or experiences, the employer may, after paying the employee a reasonable remuneration, exploit the invention, utility model or design concerned in the enterprise. [474]

327. The provisions for vesting the ownership of a patent may differ from country to country, and they are closely related to the employment contract. Special conflict of laws problems arise in the process of characterization. According to the

471. Patent Act, Art. 4.
472. Patent Act, Art. 5 para. 2.
473. Patent Act, Art. 7.
474. Patent Act, Art. 8.

Choice-of-law Act 2010, the patent right created by an employee in the performance of his/her duties is governed by the law applicable to the contract of employment rather than such patent right.[475]

328. The transfer of a patent is distinguishable from the underlying contract on which the transfer is performed. It is a part of the effects of the patent right and is governed by the *lex loci protectionis*. Taiwan's Patent Act stipulates that the assigning, entrusting, licensing, or establishing of a pledge on a patent right by the patentee shall have no *locus standi* against any third party unless it is recorded with the competent authority;[476] where a patent right is jointly owned, except for exploitation by each of the joint owners, it shall not be assigned, entrusted, licensed, pledged, or abandoned without the consent of all the joint owners. [477] Such provisions apply only to the patents granted by the Taiwan's competent authority.

IV. Infringement

329. Infringement of a patent right relates to the governing laws of the patent and of the tortious act. The infringement of a patent is governed by the same law of its creation and protection, i.e., the *lex loci protectionis*. It is the law of the place where the plaintiff asserted that the patent is granted and protected, rather than the *lex fori*. It is also the law of closest connection with the tortious act of infringement, which governs the tort of infringement.[478]

330. Taiwan's Patent Act prescribes that a patentee of an invention patent may demand a person who infringes or is likely to infringe the patent right to stop or prevent such infringement; in case an infringement of invention patent occurs due to intentional act or negligence, the patentee may claim for damages suffered therefrom; the patentee may request for destruction of the infringing articles or the materials or implements used in the infringing act, or request for other necessary disposal. [479] It further states that the damages claimed may be calculated according to any of the following methods: 1. the method as set forth in the Civil Code[480]; if no method of proof can be produced to prove the damages suffered, a patentee may claim damages based on the difference between the profit earned through patent exploitation after infringement and the profit normally expected through exploitation of the same patent; 2. the profit earned by the infringer as a result of patent infringement; or 3. the amount calculated on the basis of reasonable royalties that may be collected from exploiting the invention patent being licensed. Where the infringement is found to be intentionally committed, the court may, upon request

475. Choice-of-law Act, Art. 42 para. 2.
476. Patent Act, Art. 62.
477. Patent Act, Art. 64.
478. Choice-of-law Act 2010, Art. 25.
479. Patent Act, Art. 96.
480. CC, Art. 216.

and on the basis of the severity of the infringement, award the damages greater than the loss suffered but not exceeding three times of the proven loss. [481]

§3. COPYRIGHT

331. Copyright is a type of intellectual property that gives its owner the exclusive right to make copies of a creative work for a limited time. It is intended to protect the original expression of an idea in the form of a creative work, but not the idea itself. Taiwan's Copyright Act[482] prescribes that copyright means the moral rights and economic rights subsisting in a completed work which is a creation that is within a literary, scientific, artistic, or other intellectual domain; the completed work may be in form of an oral, literary, musical, dramatic, choreographic, artistic, photographic, pictorial, graphical, audio-visual, or architectural work, or in sound recordings or computer programs.[483]

I. Creation

332. The copyright of authors to their literary or artistic products comes into existence under the relevant laws of a state. It is a privilege accorded by law as an absolute right to the ideal content embodied in the work. Taiwan's Copyright Act states that the author of a work shall enjoy copyright upon completion of the work; provided, where this Act provides otherwise, such provisions shall govern. [484]

333. Taiwan's Copyright Act applies basically to the works created by its citizens, and to works of foreigners under some exceptional conditions. It provides that works of foreign nationals that comply with one of the following conditions may enjoy copyright under this Act; provided, where the terms of a treaty or an agreement that has been ratified by resolution of the Legislative Yuan provide otherwise, such terms shall govern: 1. works that are first published in the territory under the jurisdiction of the ROC, or are published in the territory under the jurisdiction of the ROC within thirty days after their first publication in territory outside the jurisdiction of the ROC; provided, this shall only apply where the country of such foreign national extends protection under identical circumstances to the works of persons of the ROC, and such protection has been verified; and 2. where by treaty or agreement, or under the domestic acts, regulations, or standard practice of the home country of the foreign national, works of persons of the ROC enjoy copyright in such country. [485]

---

481. Patent Act, Art. 97.
482. The Copyright Act (Zhu-Zuo-Quan Fa, 著作權法) was adopted in 1928 and last revised in 2019.
483. Copyright Act, Art. 3.
484. Copyright Act, Art. 10.
485. Copyright Act, Art. 4.

334. Although the national copyright laws are standardized under the umbrella of international treaty, this author's opinion is that copyright is still granted by individual states according to their own copyright laws, including the international treaties that are effective to them. The creation of a copyright is governed by the state's law under which the author asserts the work shall be copyrighted, i.e., the *lex loci protectionis*. A work can be copyrighted in several countries due to the fact that it satisfies the requirements of the laws of such countries respectively and simultaneously.

II. Protection

335. As mentioned above, a copyright is created under the *lex loci protectionis*. The same law governs the protection of it. Taiwan's Copyright Act prescribes that protection for copyright that has been obtained in accordance with this Act shall only extend to the expression of the work in question, and shall not extend to the work's underlying ideas, procedures, production processes, systems, methods of operation, concepts, principles, or discoveries. [486] A creation adapted from one or more pre-existing works is a derivative work and shall be protected as an independent work; protection of a derivative work shall not affect the copyright in the pre-existing work. [487] A compilation work is a work formed by the creative selection and arrangement of materials, and shall be protected as an independent work; protection of a compilation work shall not affect the copyright in the work from which the material was selected and arranged. [488] A performance by a performer of a pre-existing work or folklore shall be protected as an independent work; protection of a performance shall not affect the copyright in the pre-existing work. [489]

III. Ownership and Transfer

336. The author of a work is accorded copyright under the *lex loci protectionis*. Special problems arise in the work for hire. Taiwan's Copyright Act stipulates that where a work is completed by an employee within the scope of employment, such employee is the author of the work; provided, where an agreement stipulates that the employer is the author, such agreement shall govern. Where the employee is the author of a work, the economic rights to such work shall be enjoyed by the employer; provided, where an agreement stipulates that the economic rights shall be enjoyed by the employee, such agreement shall govern. [490] Where a work is completed by a person under commission, such commissioned person is the author of the work; provided, where an agreement stipulates that the commissioning party is the author, such agreement shall govern. Where the commissioned person is the

486. Copyright Act, Art. 10-1.
487. Copyright Act, Art. 6.
488. Copyright Act, Art. 7.
489. Copyright Act, Art. 7-1.
490. Copyright Act, Art. 11.

author, enjoyment of the economic rights to such work shall be assigned through contractual stipulation to either the commissioning party or the commissioned person. Where no stipulation regarding the enjoyment of economic rights has been made, the economic rights shall be enjoyed by the commissioned person. [491]

337. The provisions for deciding the author may differ from country to country, and they are closely related to the employment contract or similar contracts. According to the Choice-of-law Act 2010, the author of the work completed by an employee in the performance of his/her duties is governed by the law applicable to the contract of employment rather than such copyright.[492]

338. The transfer of a copyright can be distinguished from the underlying agreement to transfer it. It is governed by the *lex loci protectionis*, since it is part of its effects. Taiwan's Copyright Act prescribes that moral rights belong exclusively to the author and shall not be transferred or succeeded; [493] economic rights may be transferred in whole or in part to another person and may be jointly owned with other persons; the transferee of economic rights obtains economic rights within the scope of the transfer. [494]

IV. Infringement

339. Infringement of a copyright relates to the existing copyright and the tortious act. The infringement of a copyright is governed by the same law of its creation and protection, i.e., the *lex loci protectionis*. It is the law of the place where the plaintiff asserted that the copyright is granted and protected, rather than the *lex fori*. It is also the law of closest connection with the tortious act of infringement, which governs the tort of infringement.[495]

340. Taiwan's Copyright Act states that the holder of a copyright or the plate right may demand removal of infringement when the right is infringed; where the right is in danger of being infringed, a demand may be made to prevent such infringement.[496] It furtherly stipulates that the infringer of the moral rights of an author shall be liable for damages; in the event of non-pecuniary injury, the injured party may claim a commensurate amount of compensation; for such an infringement, the injured party may demand indication of the author's name or appellation, correction of content, or adoption other appropriate measures necessary for the restoration of its reputation. [497]

491. Copyright Act, Art. 12.
492. Choice-of-law Act 2010, Art. 42 para. 2.
493. Copyright Act, Art. 21.
494. Copyright Act, Art. 36.
495. Choice-of-law Act 2010, Art. 25.
496. Copyright Act, Art. 84.
497. Copyright Act, Art. 85.

§4. TRADEMARKS

341. A trademark consists of a recognizable sign, design, or expression which identifies products or services of a particular source from those of others. It is legally recognized as a type of intellectual property. Taiwan's Trademark Act[498] prescribes that a trademark shall refer to any sign with distinctiveness, which may, in particular, consist of words, devices, symbols, colours, three-dimensional shapes, motions, holograms, sounds, or any combination thereof; the term 'distinctiveness' refers to the character of a sign capable of being recognized by relevant consumers as an indication of the source of goods or services and distinguishing goods or services of one undertaking from those of other undertakings.[499]

I. Creation

342. A right of trademark is created by registration in the competent authority of a country according to its law. Taiwan's Trademark Act provides that any person who wishes to obtain the rights of trademark, certification mark, collective membership mark, or collective trademark shall apply for registration therefor in accordance with such Act. [500] The Act applies basically to Taiwanese citizens' application for trademark registration. It is stated that an application for trademark registration, filed by a national of a foreign country, may be inadmissible if such country did not accede to any international treaty for protection of trademarks, to which the ROC accedes, or did not conclude with the ROC any treaty or agreement for reciprocal protection of trademarks, or does not admit applications for trademark registration filed by nationals of the ROC. [501]

343. It is evident that the creation of a right of trademark is governed by the law of the country where the application is filed, i.e., the *lex loci protectionis*. A trademark can be filed for registration in several countries to seek the protection as a right under the law of each country. The right thus granted is territorial in its nature.

II. Protection

344. A trademark is protected as a right when it is registered and created under the *lex loci protectionis*. So, its protection is governed by the *lex loci protectionis*. According to Taiwan's Trademark Act, unless otherwise prescribed in this Act[502], consent of the owner of a registered trademark shall be required in any of the following: 1. using a trademark which is identical with the registered trademark in relation to goods or services which are identical with those for which it is registered; 2.

498. The Trademark Act (Shang-Biao Fa, 商標法) was adopted in 1930 and last revised in 2016.
499. Trademark Act, Art. 18.
500. Trademark Act, Art. 2.
501. Trademark Act, Art. 4.
502. Trademark Act, Art. 36.

using a trademark which is identical with the registered trademark and used in relation to goods or services similar to those for which the registered one is designated, and hence there exists a likelihood of confusion on relevant consumers; or 3. using a trademark which is similar to the registered trademark and used in relation to goods or services identical with or similar to those for which the registered one is designated, and hence there exists a likelihood of confusion on relevant consumers.[503] A trademark may, if registered, be displayed with the words 'registered trademark' or the internationally used symbol for registration.

III. Ownership and Transfer

345. If an application for trademark registration is accepted and approved by the competent authority of a country pursuant to its law, the right of trademark is conferred on the applicant. The ownership comes into existence under such law, which is the *lex loci protectionis*. According to Taiwan's Trademark Act, the owner of a registered trademark shall have the exclusive right of the trademark for a period of ten years from the date of publication for registration; the period of the trademark right may be renewed, and the duration of each renewal period shall be ten years. [504] The owner of a registered trademark has the exclusive right in the trademark in relation to the designated goods or services. [505]

346. The transfer of a trademark right can be distinguished from the underlying agreement to transfer it. It is governed by the *lex loci protectionis*, as it is included in the effects of such a right. Taiwan's Trademark Act stipulates that the transfer of a trademark right shall not be valid against any third party unless it is registered in the competent authority. [506] If, due to a transfer of trademark right, two or more proprietors use an identical trademark on similar goods or services or similar trademarks on identical or similar goods or services, and hence there exists a likelihood of confusion on relevant consumers, each owner shall add an appropriate and distinguishing indication while using his/her own trademark. [507]

IV. Infringement

347. Infringement of a trademark right relates to the existence of the trademark right and the tortious act. The infringement of a trademark right is governed by the same law of its creation and protection, i.e., the *lex loci protectionis*. It is the state's

503. Trademark Act, Art. 35 para. 2.
504. Trademark Act, Art. 33.
505. Trademark Act, Art. 35 para. 1.
506. Trademark Act, Art. 42.
507. Trademark Act, Art. 43.

law under which the plaintiff asserted that the trademark right is conferred and protected, rather than the *lex fori*. It is also the law of closest connection with the tortious act of infringement, which governs the tort of infringement.[508]

348. Taiwan's Trademark Act stipulates the requirements of an infringement of a trademark right and the remedies for it. It states that any of the following act, in the course of trade and without consent of the owner of a trademark right, constitutes infringement of such trademark right: 1. using a trademark which is identical with the registered trademark in relation to goods or services which are identical with those for which it is registered; 2. using a trademark which is identical with the registered trademark and used in relation to goods or services similar to those for which the registered one is designated, and hence there exists a likelihood of confusion on relevant consumers; or 3. using a trademark which is similar to the registered trademark and used in relation to goods or services identical with or similar to those for which the registered one is designated, and hence there exists a likelihood of confusion on relevant consumers.[509]

349. Furthermore, it states that any of the following acts, without consent of the owner of a trademark right, shall be deemed infringement of such trademark right: 1. knowingly using a trademark which is identical with or similar to another person's well-known registered trademark, and hence there exists a likelihood of dilution of the distinctiveness or reputation of the said well-known trademark; 2. knowingly using words contained in another person's well-known registered trademark as the name of a company, business, group or domain or any other name that identifies a business entity, and hence there exists a likelihood of confusion on relevant consumers or a likelihood of dilution of the distinctiveness or reputation of the said well-known trademark; or 3. manufacturing, possessing, displaying, selling, exporting or importing labels, tags, packaging or containers that have not been applied in relation to goods or services, or articles that have not been applied in relation to services, knowing that such articles would likely infringe trademark rights as mentioned above. [510]

350. For remedies, it furtherly states that an owner of a trademark right is entitled to demand a person who infringes or is likely to infringe the trademark right to stop or prevent such infringement; when making such a demand, the owner is entitled to demand for destruction of infringing articles, materials and equipment used in infringing the trademark. However, the court may order other dispositions as it considers necessary after taking into account the need for proportionality between the seriousness of the infringement and the interests of third parties. The owner is entitled to demand the infringer who knowingly, or with reasonable grounds to know, infringed such a trademark right to pay damages. [511] Damages demanded by the owner of a trademark right may be calculated according to any of

508. Choice-of-law Act 2010, Art. 25.
509. Trademark Act, Art. 68.
510. Trademark Act, Art. 70.
511. Trademark Act, Art. 69.

the following: 1. the method provided in the Civil Code[512]; the owner is entitled to demand damages based on the amount of the balance derived by subtracting the profit earned through using the trademark after infringement from the profit normally expected through using the same trademark, if no method of proof can be furnished to prove the damage suffered; 2. the profit earned by the infringer as a result of the infringement of trademark right; if no proof on costs or necessary expenses can be furnished by the infringer, the total amount of income from selling the infringing goods shall be presumed to be the amount of profit; 3. the amount not more than 1,500 times of the unit retail price of the infringing goods; if over 1,500 pieces of infringing goods were found, the amount of damages shall be a lump sum of the market value of the infringing goods; or 4. the equivalent amount of royalty that may be collected from using the trademark under licensing. A court may, at its discretion, reduce the amount of the above damages if such amount is apparently inappropriate. [513]

§5. INDUSTRIAL DESIGNS

351. In addition to patent rights, copyrights, and trademark rights, some rights in industrial designs are also prescribed and recognized as intellectual property rights in Taiwan's legislations. For examples, the Integrated Circuit Layout Protection Act[514] provides protection of the two-dimensional or three-dimensional design of electronic components and interconnecting leads on an integrated circuit[515]; the Trade Secrets Act[516] protects trade secrets which include any method, technique, process, formula, program, design, or other information that may be used in the course of production, sales, or operations, and also meet the following requirements: 1. it is not known to persons generally involved in the information of this type; 2. it has economic value, actual or potential, due to its secretive nature; and 3. its owner has taken reasonable measures to maintain its secrecy. [517]

352. Article 42 of the Choice-of-law Act 2010 applies to all rights that may be characterized as 'a right in an intellectual property'. This open concept can include all the intellectual property rights to follow the principle of *lex loci protectionis* embodied in it. The problems of whether an integrated circuit layout, industrial design, or trade secret is legally protected, if yes, how it is protected, and what constitutes an infringement and its remedies, are therefore governed by the law for which protection is sought.

512. CC, Art. 216.
513. Trademark Act, Art. 71.
514. The Integrated Circuit Layout Protection Act (Ji-Ti Dian-Lu Bu-Ju Bao-Hu Fa, 積體電路電路布局保護法) was adopted in 1995 and last revised in 2002.
515. *Ibid.*, Art. 2 Item 2.
516. The Trade Secrets Act (Ying-Ye Mi-Mi Fa, 營業秘密法) was adopted in 1996 and last revised in 2020.
517. *Ibid.*, Art. 2.

Chapter 5. Family Law

§1. State Law – Religious Law

353. Religions and beliefs are safeguarded by the Constitution of the ROC. It provides that 'all citizens of the ROC, irrespective of sex, religion, race, class, or party affiliation, shall be equal before the law'[518]; 'the people shall have freedom of religious belief.' [519] However, the religious norms are not necessarily applicable to the legal relations between believers of the same religion or the internal affairs within the religion.

354. In Taiwan, state law prevails over religious law even in civil matters relating to religion. As the norms applicable to such matters are not specially stipulated, general principles shall be followed. According to Taiwan's Civil Code, all civil matters shall be governed by the law; if there is no applicable law for a civil case, the case shall be decided according to customs; if there is no such custom, the case shall be decided according to the principles of law.[520] Only those customs which are not against the public order or *boni mores* shall be applied to a civil case.[521] Apparently, there is no room for religious norms to govern the civil matters relating to religion. If the religious norms are qualified as customs, the applicability is limited by the existence of relevant law and the scrutiny of the public order or *boni mores*.

355. The religious norms may be asserted to be binding on the believers or the members of the particular religious group. If so, they are characterized as terms of agreement resulted from a juridical act. They may be void and non-binding because it is stated that a juridical act which violates an imperative or prohibitive provision of the act is void except voidance is not implied in the provision[522]; and a juridical act which is against the public order or *boni mores* is also void. [523]

356. The above provisions and principles can only apply to a civil matter involving foreign elements if Taiwanese law governs it. If it is governed by a foreign law, the criteria for applying religious law or norms shall be decided by the law of that foreign country. In other words, foreign religious law is not necessarily excluded due to its origin or formality. The Choice-of-law Act 2010 recognizes the personal law of a party may be the religious law and will thus govern the party's personal matters and family matters. It addresses that where reference is made by this Act to the national law of a party, but the national law of the party differs by reference to sub-national region or another factor, the applicable law is the law as indicated by the rules on choice of law of that national law; if the rules on choice of law of that

518. Constitution of the ROC, Art. 7.
519. Constitution of the ROC, Art. 13.
520. CC, Art. 1.
521. CC, Art. 2.
522. CC, Art. 71.
523. CC, Art. 72.

national law are unclear, the law with which the party is most closely connected, whether by region or by the other factor, is applied.[524]

§2. Marriage

I. Engagement

357. An engagement or betrothal is the legal relationship between two people who want to get married. Taiwan's Civil Code provides that an agreement to marry shall be made by the male and the female parties in their own concord[525]; a male or female who has not reached his or her seventeenth year of age may not make an agreement to marry (a female who has not reached her fifteenth year of age may not make an agreement to marry before 2023)[526]; no demand shall be made to force the performance of an agreement to marry[527]; where one of the betrothed parties is found in one of the prescribed conditions, the other party may dissolve the agreement to marry[528]; where an agreement to marry has been dissolved accordingly, the innocent party may claim compensation from the other party who is at fault for damage thus sustained[529]; one party to an agreement to marry, who breaks it without any of the prescribe grounds, shall be liable to compensate the other party for any damage thus sustained[530]; and one party may claim the other party for returning gift presented for betrothal when the agreement to marry is null and void, or dissolved, or annulled. [531]

358. The conflict of laws problems arise in the situation where an agreement to marry connects to laws of different countries which vary in the legal policy toward engagements or betrothals. The Choice-of-law Act 2010 hence states that: '(1) The formation of an engagement to marry is governed by the respective national law of each party. However, an engagement to marry is also effective if it satisfies the formal requisites of the national law of one of the parties or of the law of the place where the engagement is concluded. (2) The effect of an engagement to marry is governed by the national law common to the parties; in the absence of a common national law, by the law of the domicile common to them; in the absence of a common law of domicile, by the law most closely connected with them.'[532]

---

524. Choice-of-law Act 2010, Art. 5.
525. CC, Art. 972.
526. CC, Art. 973. The revised provisions will enter into force from January 1st 2023.
527. CC, Art. 975.
528. CC, Art. 976.
529. CC, Art. 977.
530. CC, Art. 978.
531. CC, Art. 979-1.
532. Choice-of-law Act 2010, Art. 45.

359. The above provision is a replication of the conflicts rule for marriage. The national laws of the parties are equally treated to designate the governing law.[533] The common national law, common law of domicile, and law of closest connection are applicable in sequence to decide the effects of an engagement to marry and the consequences of breaking it. [534] Such a cascade system does not alter the rigidness of applying the persons' common national law, the rule on *renvoi* in Article 6 of the Choice-of-law Act 2010 shall thus apply to achieve a more harmonious result.[535]

II. Heterosexual Marriage

360. Taiwan's Civil Code defines marriage as heterosexual marriage and states that a man or woman who has not reached his or her eighteenth year of age may not conclude a marriage (a woman who has not reached her sixteenth year of age may not conclude a marriage before 2023). [536] Without mentioning gender, sex, man/woman or male/female, 'marriage' in Article 46 of the Choice-of-law Act may be interpreted in a broader sense to include the same-sex legal relationship. But this room of interpretation is too advanced to be noticed, since the same-sex legal relationship was legalized by the Act for Implementing Interpretation 748[537] in 2019, long after the provision was enacted.

A. Form

361. Formal requisites are generally defined as the required external conducts of the parties or a third person, especially public officer or religious staff, necessary to the formation of a legally valid marriage. They are distinguished from the substantive requirements for validity of a marriage such as age, health, lineal relation, or presentation. In this respect, Taiwan's Civil Code stipulates that a marriage shall be effected in writing, which requires the signatures of at least two witnesses, and by the registration at the Household Administration Bureau. [538] If the formalities are not well conformed, the marriage is void. [539]

362. The formal and substantive requisites of a marriage are distinguished in the Choice-of-law Act 2010. It states: 'The formation of a marriage is governed by the national law of each party. However, a marriage is also effective if it satisfies the formal requisites prescribed either by the national law of one of the parties or by

533. The rule on *renvoi* in Act. 6 of the Choice-of-law Act 2010 shall thus apply. Liu & Chen, *supra* n. 12, at 535.
534. Liu & Chen, *supra* n. 12, at 412.
535. *Ibid.*, at 535.
536. CC, Art. 980. The revised provisions will enter into force from January 1st 2023.
537. The official title of this enactment is the 'Act for Implementation of J.Y. Interpretation No. 748' (Si-Fa-Yuan Shi-Zi Di Qi-Si-Ba-Hao Jie-Shi Shi-Xing Fa, 司法院釋字第七四八號解釋施行法). It was adopted on 22 May 2019.
538. CC, Art. 982.
539. CC, Art. 988 Item 1.

the law of the place of ceremony.'[540] In the first sentence, the 'formation' of a marriage covers mainly the substantive requisites, because the 'formal requisites' are particularly specified in the second sentence.

363. Apparently, the *locus regit actum* principle is not a compulsory rule for formal requisites of a marriage. Instead, to favour the formal validity of a marriage with foreign elements, the national law of any party is alternatively applicable. As recordation at the Household Administration Bureau is required for a domestic marriage, this conflicts policy opens the gate to welcome marriages with foreign elements, and thus undermines the marriage recordation system.

B. *Substance*

364. The substantive requisites to formation of a marriage include a wide range of questions. Taiwan's Civil Code states that a minor must have the consent of his statutory agent for concluding a marriage (before 2023)[541]; a person may not marry any of the prescribed relatives[542]; a guardian may not marry his ward during the continuance of guardianship, unless consent of the ward's parents has been obtained[543]; a person who has a spouse may not contract another marriage; and a person shall not marry with two or more persons simultaneously[544]. A marriage violating the above prohibition on marriage is either void[545] or may be applied for its annulment. [546] In addition, it also states that where one spouse is sexually impotent at the time of marriage and such incapacity is incurable, the other party may apply to the court for the annulment of the marriage[547]; where, at the time of marriage, one spouse is in a condition of absence of discernment or mental disorder, such spouse may within six months after he/she is restored to normal condition apply to the court for the annulment of such marriage[548]; and a person who has concluded a marriage by fraud or by duress may apply to the court for its annulment within six months after awareness of the fraud or after the cessation of the duress. [549]

365. In marriage cases with foreign elements, whether the above rules are applicable depends on whether any party to such marriage is a Taiwanese citizen. According to the Choice-of-law Act 2010, the intrinsic conditions or substantive requisites of a marriage are governed by the national law of each party.[550] Simply

540. Choice-of-law Act 2010, Art. 46.
541. CC, Art. 981. This Article will be revealed from January 1st 2023.
542. CC, Art. 983.
543. CC, Art. 984.
544. CC, Art. 985.
545. CC, Art. 988.
546. CC, Arts 989–991. Article 990 will be revealed from January 1st 2023.
547. CC, Art. 995.
548. CC, Art. 996.
549. CC, Art. 997.
550. Choice-of-law Act 2010, Art. 46 Sentence1.

speaking, they are governed by the respective national law of each party. Both their national laws are simultaneously or distributively applicable to their own part of substantive requisites. [551]

III. Same-Sex Marriage

366. As mentioned above, Taiwan's Civil Code defines marriage as a heterosexual marriage only and does not recognize the legal relation of same-sex couples. Such a legal structure and design was declared unconstitutional by Judicial Yuan's Interpretation 748 in 2017. The Act for Implementing Interpretation 748 was passed in 2019 to legalize the same-sex relation and to address the relevant rules.

367. The Act for Implementing Interpretation 748 does not include the same-sex relation in the concept of marriage. Instead, it addresses that 'two persons of the same sex may form a permanent union of intimate and exclusive nature for the purpose of living a common life'.[552] However, the requisites to formation of such a union are almost the same as of a marriage, except the gender requirement.

A. Form

368. The Choice-of-law Act 2010 does not address the conflicts problems of a same-sex union with foreign elements. Whether the rules on marriage are applicable depends on how the same-sex union is characterized. If it is characterized as a marriage in Article 46 of it, the marriage conflicts rules apply directly, if not, this author is of opinion that they may apply by analogy to a same-sex union.

369. The Act for Implementing Interpretation 748 states that a same-sex union shall be effected in writing, which requires the signatures of at least two witnesses, and by marriage registration at the Household Administration Bureau[553]; a union that does not conform to such formalities is void. [554] Such provisions apply only when Taiwanese law governs the same-sex union involving foreign elements. According to the Choice-of-law Act 2010, the formal requisites of a same-sex union is alternatively governed by the national law of any party to the union or the law of the place of ceremony.[555] It is valid in formality if it satisfies the formal requisites prescribed either by the national law of one of the parties or by the law of the place of ceremony. [556]

551. Liu & Chen, *supra* n. 12, at 417.
552. Act for Implementing Interpretation 748, Art. 2.
553. Act for Implementing Interpretation 748, Art. 4.
554. Act for Implementing Interpretation 748, Art. 8 para. 1 Item 1.
555. Choice-of-law Act 2010, Art. 46 Sentence 2.
556. Liu & Chen, *supra* n. 12, at 419.

B. Substance

370. The Act for Implementing Interpretation 748 states that persons under the age of eighteen may not form a same-sex union; a minor must have the consent of his statutory agent for forming such a union[557]; person of the same sex in the prescribed relation may not form such a union[558]; a guardian may not form such a union with the ward of the same sex during the continuance of guardianship, unless consent of the ward's parents has been obtained[559]; a person who has a spouse or formed a union may not contract another such union; a person shall not form such a union with two or more persons, or contract a marriage of the Civil Code and form such a union simultaneously; persons in such a union shall not contract a marriage of the Civil Code. [560] The effects of violating the prohibitions are also similar to the prescriptions of a marriage. [561]

371. The conflict of laws problems arise also out of the substantive requisites to formation of a same-sex union with foreign elements. As mentioned above, according to or by analogy to the Choice-of-law Act 2010, the intrinsic conditions or substantive requisites of a same-sex union are governed by the national law of each party.[562] Simply speaking, they are governed by the respective national law of each party. Both their national laws are simultaneously or distributively applicable to their own part of substantive requisites. The lack of any substantive requisite in the national law of any party may thus infect the validity of the same-sex union. It is noteworthy that the freedom of forming a same-sex union has been established as an integral part of Taiwan's *ordre public* under the Act for Implementing Interpretation 748. A foreign law that prohibits same-sex unions can be deemed contrary to the *ordre public* and excluded when it is otherwise applicable to the substantive requisites of a same-sex of which a citizen of Taiwan is a party. [563]

IV. Personal Effects of Marriage

372. A marriage results in personal effects and other effects on property. Taiwan's Civil Code prescribes that the husband and the wife should keep his or her own surname, unless one party shall prefix to his or her surname that of the spouse in writing at the household administration authority[564]; the husband and the wife are under mutual obligation to cohabit, unless for a good cause they cannot live together[565]; the domicile of the husband and the wife shall be agreed by mutual agreement; if it has not been agreed or cannot be agreed, it may depend on the court

557. Act for Implementing Interpretation 748, Art. 3.
558. Act for Implementing Interpretation 748, Art. 5.
559. Act for Implementing Interpretation 748, Art. 6.
560. Act for Implementing Interpretation 748, Art. 7.
561. Act for Implementing Interpretation 748, Arts 8–10.
562. Choice-of-law Act 2010, Art. 46 Sentence 1.
563. Taipei High Administrative Court' Judgment, Su 1805 of 2019. *See supra* n. 168.
564. CC, Art. 1000.
565. CC, Art. 1001.

by application[566]; in daily household matters, the husband and the wife act as agents for each other[567]; and the payment for living expenses of the household will be shared by the husband and the wife according to each party's economical ability, household labour or other conditions unless otherwise provided for by law or mutual agreement. [568]

373. As the laws of different countries vary in provisions of the personal effects of marriage, the conflict of laws problems arise. The Choice-of-law Act 2010 states: 'The effect of a marriage relationship is governed by the national law common to the spouses; in the absence of a common national law, by the law of the domicile common to them; in the absence of a common law of domicile, by the law of the place most closely connected with the marriage relationship.'[569] This provision first emphasizes on the spouses' common personal law (national law and law of domicile) rather than their common connecting factor (nationality and domicile), and then supplements with the closest connection test. It treats the spouses' personal law and connecting factors equally. As mentioned earlier, the rule on *renvoi* in Article 6 of the Choice-of-law Act 2010 shall apply to ease the rigidness of the *lex patriae*.[570]

V. Dissolution

A. Annulment

374. In Taiwan's Civil Code, annulment and divorce are both legal grounds for a court to dissolve a valid marriage. The effect of an annulment of marriage is not retroactive. [571] A party to a marriage who has sustained damage through nullity or annulment of the marriage may claim compensation from the other party. This, however, does not apply where the other party is not at fault. In such a case, the injured party who is not at fault may also claim an equitable compensation in money though there is no pecuniary loss. [572] The prescribed substantive effects of a divorce shall be applicable *mutatis mutandis* to an annulled marriage. [573]

375. In conflict of laws, the distinction between an annulment and a divorce may be obscure and problematic. Since nullity cannot be based on grounds other than those existing at the moment of the solemnization of the marriage, while divorce must have a cause either after the celebration or at least continuing during coverture, they are distinguishable in the law of conflicts. There is no specific provision

566. CC, Art. 1002.
567. CC, Art. 1003.
568. CC, Art. 1003-1.
569. Choice-of-law Act 2010, Art. 47.
570. Liu & Chen, *supra* n. 12, at 535.
571. CC, Art. 998.
572. CC, Art. 999.
573. CC, Art. 999-1.

on annulment in the Choice-of-law Act 2010. It is this author's opinion that annulment arises out of lacking a substantive requisite of the marriage so that the conflicts rule on substantive requisites shall apply directly.[574] This enables the parties to claim respectively on the grounds prescribed in their national law and protects the interested parties equally. The effects of an annulment are governed by the governing law of the substantive requisites to formation of a marriage.

B. Divorce

376. In Taiwan's Civil Code, a divorce can be made privately by mutual consent of the parties or decreed by a court's judgment. It recognizes a divorce by mutual consent and states that the husband and the wife may effect a divorce by themselves with their mutual consent. [575] However, some formal requisites are imposed on divorce by mutual consent. It shall be effected in writing which requires the signatures of at least two witnesses, and by the divorce registration at the household administration authority. [576]

377. It also addresses that where either the husband or the wife meets one of the following conditions, the other party may petition the court for a juridical decree of divorce: (1) where he or she has committed bigamy; (2) where he or she has consensual sexual intercourse with another person; (3) where he or she abuses the other party as to render common living intolerable; (4) where he or she abuses the lineal relative of the other party, or his or her lineal relative abuses the other party as to render common living intolerable; (5) where the other party has deserted him or her in bad faith and such desertion still continues; (6) where he or she is intent on murdering the other party; (7) where he or she has a loathsome disease which is incurable; (8) where he or she has a serious mental disease which is incurable; (9) where it has been uncertain for over three years whether he or she is alive or dead; or (10) where he or she has been sentenced to more than six months imprisonment for an intentional crime. [577] Either the husband or the wife may petition for a juridical decree of divorce upon the occurrence of any gross event other than the abovementioned that renders it difficult to maintain the marriage, except if either the husband or the wife is responsible for the event, only the other party may petition for the divorce. [578] Such provisions embody the spouse's freedom to divorce, and the foreign law that prohibits or restricts unfairly on a spouse's freedom who has close connection with Taiwan may thus be excluded on the ground that the results of its application are contradictory to the public order or *boni mores* of Taiwan.[579]

---

574. Liu & Chen, *supra* n. 12, at 418.
575. CC, Art. 1049. In the case of a minor, the consent of his or her statutory agent must be obtained before 2023.
576. CC, Art. 1050.
577. CC, Art. 1052 para. 1.
578. CC, Art. 1052 para. 2.
579. Rong-Chwan Chen, *Application of the Ordre Public Clause*, 1 Taiwan Law Review (月旦法學雜誌) 70 (May 1995).

378. The laws of divorce around the world are diverse in institutions, methods and contents. The recognition of a foreign divorce is as important as the choice of law in a divorce case involving foreign elements. The former is dealt with elsewhere with the general stipulation of recognizing the foreign courts' judgments, while the latter is provided in the Choice-of-law Act 2010. It states that divorce and the effect of divorce are governed by the national law common to the spouses; at the time they reach an agreement of divorce or when a suit is brought for the divorce; in the absence of a common national law, by their common law of domicile; in the absence of a common law of domicile, by the law of the place most closely connected with the marriage relationship.[580]

379. This provision evidently stipulates the conflicts problems of both the divorce by mutual consent and the divorce by a court decree.[581] Common national law and common law of domicile are designated as the governing law in order, and the closest connection test lies on the bottom to take care of the interests of the relevant parties equally.[582] As the connecting factor to designate the governing law may change from time to time, the decisive time is stipulated to be the time they reach an agreement of divorce or when a suit is brought for the divorce. The rule on *renvoi* in Article 6 of the Choice-of-law Act 2010 also applies to harmonize the *lex patriae* and the personal law designated by the conflicts rule in the otherwise applicable foreign national law.[583]

380. The effects of a divorce are mainly the personal effects between the spouses. But some effects with third person or property are also provided under the heading of divorce in Taiwan' Civil Code. For instance, it states that after the husband and the wife effect a divorce, one party or both parties of the parents will exercise the rights or assume the duties in regard to the minor child by mutual agreement; if the mutual agreement did not or could not be done, the court may decide by the application of the husband or the wife, the authorities concerned, the social welfare institution or any other interested person, or may decide by its authority; if the mutual agreement is unfavourable to the child, the court may change the agreement upon the application of the authority concerned, the social welfare institution or any other interested person or by its authority in regard to the interests of the minor child.[584]

381. When the party who should but could not exercise the rights and assume the duties in regard to the minor child or did not protect the interests of the minor child, the other party of the husband and the wife, the minor child, the authorities

580. Choice-of-law Act 2010, Art. 50.
581. Divorce by mutual consents was not addressed in the Choice-of-law Act 1953, the conflicts rule for divorce by court's decree applied by analogy to it. Rong-Chwan Chen, *Conflict of Laws of Divorce: Judicial Practice and Legislative Development of Taiwan*, in *Convergence and Divergence in Private International Law – Liber Amicorum Kurt Siehr* 193, 207 (Katharina Boele-Woelki et al. eds, Eleven International Publishing 2010).
582. Liu & Chen, *supra* n. 12, at 441.
583. Liu & Chen, *supra* n. 12, at 535.
584. CC, Art. 1055 paras 1–3.

concerned, the social welfare institution or any other interested person may apply the court to change the mutual agreement in regard to the interests of the minor child; the court may decide the way and period of meeting or communication with the minor child by the application of the party who could exercise the rights and assume the duties in regard to the minor child, or by its authority. When the meeting or communication affects the interests of the minor child, the court may change it by application or by its authority.[585]

382. It is noteworthy in conflicts law that custody of children or any other incident of parental relations is not a matter substantially ancillary to divorce, although the divorce court may have power to take care of these matters and a divorce is a seasonable occasion to adjust the legal relationship. The judicial practice erred in characterizing the custody of children after the parents' divorce as an effect of the divorce before the Choice-of-law Act was revised in 2010. It was suggested by this author to correct the established opinion and to characterize it as a separate question of parental power or parents-children relation.[586] The legislative explanation also echoes and mentions that the effects of a divorce are limited to the personal effects between the spouses and such judicial opinion shall no more be followed.[587]

C. Other

383. In addition to the annulment and divorce which are particularly prescribed in legislation, some disputes may be raised with regard to the invalidity of a marriage and non-existence of a marriage. The courts' jurisdiction over such matters are recognized and dealt with in Article 52 of the Act on Family Matters along with the annulment and divorce. Yet, their choice-of-law problems are not specifically prescribed.

384. The existence, validity and nullity of a marriage are determined by the court under the general rules of a juridical act. They concern the lack of element or requisite of a marriage, so they shall apply the conflicts rule for requisites of a marriage in the Choice-of-law Act 2010 and be governed by the national law of the relevant spouse.[588] Legal separation is not known in Taiwan's Civil Code, it is acceptable to characterize it as divorce in conflicts law. The conflicts rule for divorce[589] shall thus be applied directly, or otherwise by analogy, to ascertain the governing law of a legal separation.

585. CC, Art. 1055 para. 5.
586. Rong-Chwan Chen, *The Applicable Law to the Assigning and Reassigning Custodian for Children after Their Parents' Divorce: A Comment on the Supreme Court Judgment Tai-Shang 1888 of 1993*, (Part One), 24 Taiwan Law Review (月旦法學雜誌) 93 (April 1997); (Part Two), 25 Taiwan Law Review (月旦法學雜誌) 92 (May 1997); Rong-Chwan Chen, *The Characterization in Matters of Parental Power*, 32 Taiwan Jurist (月旦法學教室) 40 (June 2005).
587. The explanatory comment to Choice-of-law Act 2010, Art. 50.
588. Choice-of-law Act 2010, Art. 47.
589. Choice-of-law Act 2010, Art. 50.

§3. MATRIMONIAL PROPERTY

I. Choice of Law Agreement

385. The effects of marriage on property constitute a special system of matrimonial property. The differences of the laws on matrimonial property regimes around the world are obvious and far-reaching. Taiwan's Civil Code addresses that the spouses and their properties are subject to the statutory matrimonial property regime unless they choose a contractual one. The husband and the wife may, before or after getting married, adopt by contract one of the contractual regimes provided by this Code as their matrimonial property regime. [590] Where the husband and the wife have not chosen a matrimonial property regime by contract, unless otherwise provided by this Code, the statutory regime shall be applied. [591] The conclusion, modification or termination of a contract for the matrimonial property regime must be done in writing. [592] The conclusion, modification or termination of a contract for the holding of matrimonial property may not be a valid defence against any third party unless it has been registered. [593] During the continuance of the marriage, the husband and the wife may, by contract, terminate their contract for the matrimonial property regime, or adopt any other contractual regime. [594]

386. Corresponding to the limited freedom of choice in substantive law, the Choice-of-law Act 2010 takes party autonomy into account in determining the law applicable to a matrimonial property regime. '(1) Where the spouses have agreed in writing that either the national law or the law of domicile of one of them shall apply to their matrimonial property regime, the law agreed-upon governs. (2) Where there is no agreement or where their agreement is void under the applicable law of the preceding paragraph, the matrimonial property regime of the spouses is governed by the national law common to them; in the absence of a common national law, by the law of domicile common to them; in the absence of a common law of domicile, by the law of residence common to them; in the absence of a common law of residence, by the law of the place most closely connected with their marriage relationship. (3) With respect to the immovable property of the spouses, if the property is subject to special provisions under the law of the place where it is located, the preceding two paragraphs do not apply.'[595]

387. According to Paragraph 1 above, the spouses' chosen law can be the governing law of matrimonial property regime in the first priority, if the choice is among the national law and the law of domicile of the parties and is validly written by the spouses. In case there is no agreement or where their agreement is void, Paragraph 2 above applies. It stipulates that the following laws govern in order: their

590. CC, Art. 1004.
591. CC, Art. 1005.
592. CC, Art. 1007.
593. CC, Art. 1008.
594. CC, Art. 1012.
595. Choice-of-law Act 2010, Art. 48.

common national law, their common law of domicile, their common law of residence, and the law of the place most closely connected with the marriage relationship.

388. Paragraph 3 above addresses particularly the immovable property of the spouses. The matrimonial law creates an estate of the spouses to cover all assets that belong to them and the debts they owe. According to the unity principle adopted in the Choice-of-law Act 2010, immovable property is not subject to a special conflicts rule for matrimonial property regime. To balance the interests of the conflicts policy of the place where it is situated, Paragraph 3 yields Paragraphs 1 and 2 to the special conflicts rule there. This is a correction to the unitary conflicts principle.

389. It is noteworthy that the conflicts rule for rights *in rem* over an immovable property overrides the conflicts rule for matrimonial property regime to protect the creditors and *bona fide* purchasers in such place. The Choice-of-law Act 2010 thus furtherly provides: 'where the applicable law to a matrimonial property regime is a foreign law, but where the spouses have undertaken a juridical act with a third person acting in good faith concerning a property located in the ROC, the effect of the matrimonial property regime on the third person is governed by the law of the ROC.'[596] This provision enables the *lex situs* to override the foreign governing law with respect to the effects of the matrimonial property regime which is governed by such foreign law. This constitutes another correction to the unitary conflicts principle.

II. Relationship to Succession Law

390. It is quite problematic to draw a proper line between the matrimonial property law and succession law. The scope of conflicts rules on matrimonial property regime and succession is thus difficult to define. If one of the spouses passes away, the other spouse may claim under the municipal law the share of the matrimonial property or to distribute the estate that the deceased left upon death. If such a case involves foreign elements, the court will encounter the problems of characterization and adjustment.

391. Judicial practice in Taiwan has identified the respective functions of matrimonial property law and succession law and recognized the living spouse's claim simultaneously in both fields. In other words, the living may claim to distribute the estate of the deceased one after claiming his/her own share under the matrimonial property law.[597] Taiwan's Civil Code stipulates that upon dissolution of the statutory marital property regime, the remainder of the property acquired by the husband or wife in marriage, after deducting the debts incurred during the continuance of the marriage relationship, if any, shall be equally distributed to the husband and the wife, except property listed as follows: 1. property acquired from succession or as

596. Choice-of-law Act 2010, Art. 49.
597. Supreme Court's Civil Judgment, Tai-Shang 941 of 2012.

a gift; and 2. solatium. The court shall adjust or waive the share of distribution provided that equal distribution is obviously unfair. [598] The share of the deceased spouse and other properties left behind constitute the estate to be inherited by all the heirs. The living spouse stands in the first place to inherit the estate with other heirs. [599]

392. The conflicts rules for both matrimonial property regime and succession on death are provided in the Choice-of-law Act 2010. However, the relationship between matrimonial law and succession law is not dealt with. Following the way of thinking in Taiwan's Civil Code, this author is of opinion that characterization is not necessarily a problem, because it depends on the factual and legal grounds that the plaintiff asserts in the suit. The two legal relations are basically separate and independent,[600] the governing laws of them shall thus be ascertained under the conflicts rules for them respectively.

393. It is noteworthy that in applying the governing law of succession on death, the living spouse's share of the matrimonial property is not part of the estate left by the deceased which is inherited by all the heirs. If foreign elements are involved, the claims that the living spouse may have at the time the other spouse passes away are separate and are subject respectively to the conflicts rules for matrimonial property regime and succession on death. The governing law of the matrimonial property regime applies firstly to ascertain the living spouse's share of matrimonial property. The governing law of succession on death then applies to ascertain the properties within the estate and individual shares of the heirs, including the living spouse.

§4. Registered Partnership – Partnership / Civil Unions

394. As mentioned above, Taiwan's Civil Code defines marriage as heterosexual marriage and the Act for Implementing Interpretation 748 stipulates the same-sex union. The Choice-of-law Act 2010 addresses governing laws of marriage only without mentioning any registered partnership. In light of recent legal trends and comparative law, registered partnership and civil unions are alternatives to heterosexual marriage and may be included in the concept of marriage in a broader sense. This author is therefore of opinion that they may all be characterized as a marriage in conflicts law and apply the marriage conflicts rules directly. Otherwise, we have to acknowledge the gap of the conflicts rules on registered partnership or civil unions, and to apply the marriage conflicts rules to them by analogy.

598. CC, Art. 1030-1.
599. CC, Art. 1038.
600. Supreme Court's Civil Judgment, Tai-Shang 773 of 2015.

I. Personal Effects

395. The personal effects of a valid same-sex union are similar to that of a marriage. The Act for Implementing Interpretation 748 states that parties of a same-sex union are under mutual obligation to cohabit, unless for a good cause[601]; the domicile of parties of a same-sex union shall be decided through mutual agreement; if it has not been agreed or cannot be agreed, it may be decided by the court by application[602]; parties of a same-sex union act as agents for each other with regard to the daily household matters; where one of the parties abuses the aforesaid right of agency, the other party may restrict it, but such restriction shall not be set up against any *bona fide* third party[603]; the payment for living expenses of the household shall be shared by parties of a same-sex union, according to each party's economical ability, household labour or other conditions unless otherwise provided for by law or mutual agreement; parties of a same-sex union will be jointly liable for debts incurred by the living expenses. [604]

396. The conflicts rule for effect of a same-sex union is not specifically provided in the Choice-of-law Act 2010. The conflicts rule for the effect of a marriage applies directly or by analogy to the effect of a same-sex union.[605] Hence, the effect of a same-sex union is governed by the national law common to the spouses; in the absence of a common national law, by the law of the domicile common to them; in the absence of a common law of domicile, by the law of the place most closely connected with the same-sex union.

II. Dissolution

397. The dissolution of a valid same-sex union is similar to that of a marriage. The Act for Implementing Interpretation 748 prescribes annulment and determination of it. It adopts the methodology of legislative reference to the provisions of marriage and states that the relevant provisions of the Civil Code concerning the legal requirements and effects of annulment[606] shall apply *mutatis mutandis* to a same-sex union; in the event where a same-sex union has been nullified or annulled, the provisions of Article 999 and Article 999-1 of the Civil Code concerning the determination of child custody and guardianship, damages, alimony and recovery of property shall apply *mutatis mutandis*. [607]

398. It also states that a same-sex union can be terminated by mutual agreement of the parties; but a minor must obtain the consent of his statutory agent for termination; such termination shall be effected in writing, requiring the signatures of at

601. Act for Implementing Interpretation 748, Art. 11.
602. Act for Implementing Interpretation 748, Art. 12.
603. Act for Implementing Interpretation 748, Art. 13.
604. Act for Implementing Interpretation 748, Art. 14.
605. Choice-of-law Act 2010, Art. 47.
606. CC, Arts 996–998.
607. Act for Implementing Interpretation 748, Art. 10.

least two witnesses and by registering termination at the Household Administration Bureau. [608] Where either party of the same-sex union meets one of the prescribed conditions, the other party may petition the court for a juridical decree of termination; either party to the union may petition for a juridical decree of termination upon the occurrence of any gross event other than the prescribed ones that renders it difficult to maintain the union. [609] In the event where a same-sex union has been terminated, the relevant provisions of the Civil Code concerning the determination of child custody and guardianship, damages, alimony and recovery of property[610] shall apply *mutatis mutandis*.

399. The conflicts rule for dissolution of a same-sex union is not provided specifically in the Choice-of-law Act 2010. The annulment is the consequence of lacking substantive requisites. Its governing law shall be ascertained by applying the conflicts rule for requisites of marriage[611] directly or by analogy. The annulment of a same-sex union is thus governed by the national law of the spouse whose requisites to it was asserted to be lacking.

400. Termination of a same-sex union is similar to a divorce. Therefore, the conflicts rule for divorce[612] shall be applied directly or by analogy to ascertain the law applicable to it. Termination of a same-sex union and the effect of it are thus governed by the national law common to the spouses at the time they reach an agreement of termination or when a suit is brought for the termination; in the absence of a common national law, by their common law of domicile; in the absence of a common law of domicile, by the law of the place most closely connected with the same-sex union.

III. Property

401. The effects of a same-sex union on property are similar to that of a marriage. Legislative reference is adopted to transform the matrimonial property regime to a property regime for same-sex spouses. The Act for Implementing Interpretation 748 stipulates that provisions of matrimonial property regimes in Taiwan's Civil Code shall apply *mutatis mutandis* to parties of a same-sex union. [613]

402. The Choice-of-law Act 2010 does not address on the conflicts rule for property regime for same-sex spouses. The conflicts rules for matrimonial property regime[614] shall be applied directly or by analogy to the property regime of same-sex spouses. The following rules therefore form the foundation to ascertain the governing law of the property regime of the same-sex spouses: (1) Where the spouses

608. Act for Implementing Interpretation 748, Art. 16.
609. Act for Implementing Interpretation 748, Art. 17.
610. CC, Arts 1055–1055-2 and 1056–1058.
611. Choice-of-law Act 2010, Art. 47.
612. Choice-of-law Act 2010, Art. 50.
613. Act for Implementing Interpretation 748, Art. 15.
614. Choice-of-law Act 2010, Arts 48 & 49.

have agreed in writing that either the national law or the law of domicile of one of them shall apply to their property regime for same-sex spouses, the law agreed-upon governs. (2) Where there is no agreement or where their agreement is void under the applicable law so agreed, the property regime for same-sex spouses is governed by the national law common to them; in the absence of a common national law, by their common law of domicile; in the absence of a common law of domicile, by the law of residence common to them; in the absence of a common law of residence, by the law of the place most closely connected with their same-sex union. (3) With respect to the immovable property of the spouses, if the property is subject to special provisions under the law of the place where it is located, such special provisions shall be applied. (4) Where the applicable law to a property regime of same-sex spouses is a foreign law, but where the spouses have undertaken a juridical act with a third person acting in good faith concerning a property located in the ROC, the effect of the property regime for same-sex spouses on the third person is governed by the law of the ROC.

§5. Extra-Marital Cohabitation

403. Cohabitation of the spouses of a marriage or a same-sex union is legalized and stipulated in the Taiwan's Civil Code[615] or the Act for Implementing Interpretation 748. [616] It is protected as one of the personal effects of marriage or same-sex union. Any spouse may request the other to cohabitate under such provisions unless there is a legitimate cause. Extra-marital cohabitation is not legalized and recognized as a legal relation in Taiwanese law. The parties to it are not protected as spouses. Their promise to cohabitate is deemed to be contradictory to the public order or *boni mores* and is void and unenforceable. Therefore, an extra-marital cohabitation is treated in Taiwan as a fact and results in no personal effect on the cohabitees or right on their properties.

404. The Choice-of-law Act 2010 does not address the non-marital cohabitation. As the laws on non-marital cohabitation and the parties' agreement on cohabitation are different in the world, a non-marital cohabitation involving foreign elements is still in need of applying private international law to ascertain its governing law. Given the fact that non-marital cohabitation is not legalized under Taiwanese law, the gap of conflicts rule on agreement of non-marital cohabitation deserves acknowledgment. It is this author's opinion that the conflicts rules on marriage [617] shall be applied by analogy to fill the gap.

405. As a result of applying by analogy the conflicts rule for validity of a marriage[618] to the validity of an agreement non-marital cohabitation, the formation of an agreement of non-marital cohabitation is governed by the national law of each

615. CC, Art. 1001.
616. Act for Implementing Interpretation 748, Art. 11.
617. Choice-of-law Act 2010, Arts 46 & 47.
618. Choice-of-law Act 2010, Art. 46.

party. However, an agreement of non-marital cohabitation is valid if it satisfies the formal requisites prescribed either by the national law of one of the parties or by the law of the place of juridical act.

I. Personal Effects

406. The conflicts rule for personal effects of an agreement of non-marital cohabitation is not provided in the Choice-of-law Act 2010. The conflicts rule for the effects of a marriage[619] applies by analogy to that of an agreement of non-marital cohabitation. Hence, the effect of an agreement of non-marital cohabitation is governed by the national law common to the cohabitees; in the absence of a common national law, by their common law of the domicile; in the absence of a common law of domicile, by the law of the place most closely connected with the non-marital cohabitation.

II. Dissolution

407. Termination of an agreement non-marital cohabitation is similar to a divorce. Therefore, conflicts rule for divorce[620] shall be applied by analogy to it to ascertain its governing law. Therefore, termination of an agreement non-marital cohabitation and the effect of it are governed by the national law common to the parties at the time they reach an agreement of termination or when a suit is brought for the termination; in the absence of a common national law, by their common law of domicile; in the absence of a common law of domicile, by the law of the place most closely connected with the of non-marital cohabitation.

III. Property

408. The effects of an agreement non-marital cohabitation on property are similar to that of a marriage. Conflicts rules for matrimonial property regime[621] shall be applied by analogy to the property regime for the cohabitees. The following rules therefore form the foundation to ascertain the governing law of the property regime for cohabitees: (1) Where the parties have agreed in writing that either the national law or the law of domicile of one of them shall apply to their property regime for cohabitees, the law agreed-upon governs. (2) Where there is no agreement or where their agreement is void under the applicable law so agreed, the property regime for cohabitees is governed by the national law common to them; in the absence of a common national law, by their common law of domicile; in the absence of a common law of domicile, by the law of residence common to them; in the absence of a common law of residence, by the law of the place most closely connected with

619. Choice-of-law Act 2010, Art. 47.
620. Choice-of-law Act 2010, Art. 50.
621. Choice-of-law Act 2010, Arts 48 & 49.

their non-marital cohabitation. (3) With respect to the immovable property of the spouses, if the property is subject to special provisions under the law of the place where it is located, such special provisions shall be applied. (4) Where the applicable law to a property regime for cohabitees is a foreign law, but where the parties have undertaken a juridical act with a third person acting in good faith concerning a property located in the ROC, the effect of the property regime for cohabitees on the third person is governed by the law of the ROC.

§6. Maintenance Law

409. Taiwan's Civil Code deals with the maintenance obligations in a separate chapter among the chapters of domestic relations. It addresses broadly the creditors and obligors. The following relatives are under a mutual obligation to maintain one another: 1. lineal relatives by blood; 2. one of the husband and the wife and the parents of the other party living in the same household; 3. brothers and sisters; and 4. the head and the members of a house. [622] Persons entitled to maintenance shall be limited to those who cannot support the living and are unable to earn the living. The limitation in respect of inability to earn a living shall not apply to the case of the elder lineal relatives by blood. [623] If a person who can no longer support his/her own living if he/she assumes the obligation of furnishing maintenance to another, he/she may be exempted from such an obligation, but his/her obligation could only be relieved if the person entitled to receive maintenance is the elder lineal relatives by blood or the spouse. [624] The extent of furnishing maintenance shall be determined according to the needs of the person entitled to maintenance, and the economic ability and social status of the person bound to furnish it. [625]

410. The conflict of laws problems arise in maintenance because laws on maintenance vary from country to country. The Choice-of-law Act 2010 hence provides that maintenance is governed by the national law of the person entitled to maintenance.[626] This general conflicts rule on maintenance yields to special rules on maintenance resulting from specific legal relations such as marriage and parental responsibility. It applies only to the maintenance that is not included in the effect of a legal relation that is subject to a special conflicts rule.

I. Spousal Maintenance

411. Taiwan's Civil Code provides that the husband and the wife are under a mutual obligation to maintain each other, the order in which they are to perform such obligation is the same with the younger lineal relatives by blood, and the order

622. CC, Art. 1114.
623. CC, Art. 1117.
624. CC, Art. 1118.
625. CC, Art. 1119.
626. Choice-of-law Act 2010, Art. 57. The rule on *renvoi* in Act. 6 of the Choice-of-law Act 2010 shall thus apply. Liu & Chen, *supra* n. 12, at 535.

in which they are entitled to receive maintenance is the same with the elder lineal relatives by blood. [627] This spousal maintenance is supplemented by the provisions for payment of living expenses in the matrimonial property law. It also states that the payment for living expenses of the household will be shared by the husband and the wife according to each party's economical ability, household labour or other conditions unless otherwise provided for by law or mutual agreement. The husband and the wife will be jointly liable for debts incurred by such expenses. [628]

412. The conflict of laws problem of spousal maintenance pertains to both the conflicts rules on maintenance and effects of marriage. As mentioned above, it is suggested to be governed by the governing law of the effects of marriage. It is therefore governed by the national law common to the spouses; in the absence of a common national law, by their common law of the domicile; in the absence of a common law of domicile, by the law of the place most closely connected with the marriage relationship.[629]

II. Partnership Maintenance

413. The partnership maintenance is addressed in the Act for Implementing Interpretation 748. The payment for living expenses of the household shall be shared by parties of a same-sex union, according to each party's economical ability, household labour or other conditions unless otherwise provided for by law or mutual agreement. They will be jointly liable for debts incurred by the living expenses.[630] They are under a mutual obligation to maintain each other. The provisions of spousal maintenance in Taiwan's Civil Code shall apply *mutatis mutandis* to a same-sex union. [631]

414. This author suggests that the partnership maintenance shall be governed by the governing law of the effects of the same-sex union. By analogy or according to the conflicts rule for effects of a marriage[632], it is therefore governed by the national law common to the spouses; in the absence of a common national law, by their common law of domicile; in the absence of a common law of domicile, by the law of the place most closely connected with the same-sex union.

627. CC, Art. 1116-1.
628. CC, Art. 1003-1.
629. Choice-of-law Act 2010, Art. 47.
630. Act for Implementing Interpretation 748, Art. 14.
631. Act for Implementing Interpretation 748, Art. 22.
632. Choice-of-law Act 2010, Art. 47.

III. Maintenance of Cohabitees

415. Maintenance of cohabitees is not stipulated in Taiwan's municipal law. This author suggests that the governing law of it shall be ascertained by applying the conflicts rule for effects of a marriage[633] by analogy. It is therefore governed by the national law common to the cohabitees; in the absence of a common national law, by their common law of domicile; in the absence of a common law of domicile, by the law of the place most closely connected with the extra-marital cohabitation.

§7. Child Law

416. Taiwan's Civil Code addresses a lot of legal relationships in the chapter of 'Parents and Children'. The Choice-of-law Act 2010 stipulates that the legal relationship between parents and their children is governed by the national law of the children.[634] This law applies without doubt to the questions addressed in that chapter such as the child's surname and domicile[635], which are governed by the child's personal law.

417. The following legal relationships specified in Taiwan's Civil Code are not specifically addressed in the Choice-of-law Act 2010. Children shall be filial to and respect their parents. Parents have the rights and the duties to protect, educate and maintain their minor children.[636] Parents may, within the limit of necessity, inflict punishment upon their children. [637] Parents are the statutory agents of their minor children. [638] Such civil matters pertain to both the parents' responsibility and the child's interests. They are governed by the child's national law.

I. Determination of Parenthood

418. In traditional view about the birth of a child, the motherhood is not legally problematic because it can be determined by the fact of the mother's conception and giving birth. Taiwan's Civil Code thus addresses only the question of fatherhood. A legitimate child is the child who is born with the conception during the marriage relationship. [639] Where the wife conceives during the continuance of a marriage relationship, a child so born is presumed to be legitimate. In regard to such presumption of legitimacy, either the husband, the wife, or the child may bring an action for disavowal if he or she can prove that the child was born out of wedlock.

633. Choice-of-law Act 2010, Art. 47.
634. Choice-of-law Act 2010, Art. 55.
635. CC, Arts 1059, 1059-1 & 1060.
636. CC, Art. 1084.
637. CC, Art. 1085.
638. CC, Art. 1086.
639. CC, Art. 1061.

[640] The period of conception is presumed to be from the one hundred and eighty-first day to the three hundred and second day, both inclusive, traced back from the day of the birth of a child. [641]

419. As the fatherhood is presumed by the marriage of the mother, it results in conflict of laws problems. The Choice-of-law Act 2010 adopts a conflicts policy to favour the child's legitimacy and the husband's fatherhood. It states that a child is a legitimate child if he/she was a legitimate child at the time of birth under the national law of the child, of his/her mother, or of the husband of his/her mother; however, where the marriage relationship between the parents has ended before a child was born, the child is a legitimate child if he/she was a legitimate child under his/her national law when born or under the national law of his/her mother or of the husband of his/her mother at the time the marriage relationship ended.[642]

420. Under such conflicts rules, the legitimacy of a child to his/her mother's husband is governed by alternatively his/her national law, his/her mother's national law, or the national law of his/her mother's husband.[643] The time factor to ascertain the relevant parties' nationality or national law is stipulated under two different circumstances. It is either the time of the child's birth or the time when his/her mother's marriage relationship ended if it has ended before the child was born.

421. Legitimization of an illegitimate child can also be the basis of his/her legitimacy under Taiwan's Civil Code. A child born out of wedlock whose natural father and mother have concluded a marriage to each other is deemed to be legitimate. [644] A child born out of wedlock who has been acknowledged by the natural father is deemed to be legitimate; where he has been maintained by the natural father, acknowledgment is deemed to have been established. In the relation to his/her mother, a child born out of wedlock is deemed to be legitimate and no acknowledgment is necessary. [645] Where there is a fact sufficient to prove that the person is the natural father of the child born out of wedlock, the child born out of wedlock, or the mother, or other statutory agent, may claim acknowledgement from the natural father. Such a claim can be filed after the death of the natural father against the father's successors or the social welfare authority if the natural father does not have successors. [646]

422. The laws around the world vary with regard to legitimization of an illegitimate child. The problems of conflict of laws thus arise out of it. Two separate conflicts rules are formulated to deal with legitimization by the parents' marriage and the father's acknowledgement in the Choice-of-law Act 2010.

640. CC, Art. 1063.
641. CC, Art. 1062.
642. Choice-of-law Act 2010, Art. 51.
643. The rule on *renvoi* in Act. 6 of the Choice-of-law Act 2010 shall thus apply. Liu & Chen, *supra* n. 12, at 535.
644. CC, Art. 1064.
645. CC, Art. 1065.
646. CC, Art. 1067.

423. It firstly provides that where the natural father and natural mother of a child born out of wedlock become married, the status of the child is governed by the law applicable to the effects of the marriage.[647] This provision emphasizes that the legitimization of an illegitimate child is part of the effects of the marriage and is governed by the same applicable law which is ascertained according to conflicts rule for the effects of the mother's marriage.[648] But the legitimacy of a child is at the centre of the relevant interests. It is this author's opinion that the conflicts rule for legitimacy[649] can also be applied here by analogy to establish the child's legitimacy. Therefore, an illegitimate child is legitimized either under the governing law of the parents' marriage, the national law of the child, of his/her mother, or of his/her natural father at the time of their marriage.

424. Secondly, it addresses the conflicts problem of an acknowledgement. '(1) An acknowledgement of paternity is effective if, at the time it is made or an action concerning paternity is filed, it is effective under the national law of either the acknowledging person or the acknowledged person. (2) If, under the preceding paragraph, the acknowledged person is a foetus, the national law of the mother is the national law of the foetus. (3) The effect of an acknowledgement of paternity is governed by the national law of the acknowledging person.'[650]

425. Paragraph 1 above adopts the methodology of alternative application of the parties' national laws. The decisive time is the time of the act to acknowledge or of the filing of action for acknowledgment. Paragraph 2 addresses the case in which a foetus is acknowledged. Paragraph 3 specifies that the effects of the acknowledgment such as the retroactive effect and irrevocability that are provided in Taiwan's Civil Code[651] are governed by the national law of the natural father.

II. Custody and Contact

426. Custody is a typical matter of parental power and responsibility, and is a mixture of parental right and duty. According to Taiwan's Civil Code, the parents shall jointly exercise their rights and assume their duties in regard to their minor child, unless otherwise provided by law. If one of them cannot exercise such rights, the rights shall be exercised by the other party. If the parents cannot assume the duties jointly, the duties shall be assumed by the parent who has the ability to do so. If there is inconsistency between the parents in the exercise of the rights in regard to the grave events of the minor child, they may apply to the court for the decision in accordance with the best interests of the child. [652] Where one of the parents has abused his or her rights over their children, the court can suspend all or part of his

647. Choice-of-law Act 2010, Art. 52.
648. Choice-of-law Act 2010, Art. 47.
649. Choice-of-law Act 2010, Art. 51.
650. Choice-of-law Act 2010, Art. 53.
651. CC, Arts 1069 & 1970.
652. CC, Art. 1089.

or her rights to the children based upon its discretion or petition of the other party, minor children, administrative authority, social welfare institution or other interested person. [653]

427. The parents' exercise of rights and assumption of duties in regard to their minor child mentioned above are custody of children in nature. Article 55 of the Choice-of-law Act 2010 phrases in its first part 'the legal relationship between the parents and children'. This includes the parents' obligation to maintain the minor children and other matters. They are all governed by the national law of the children.

428. The custody of minor children after the parents' divorce or separation results in conflict of conflicts rules on parental responsibility and divorce. Taiwan's Civil Code provides that after the parents' divorce, the parents will exercise the rights or assume the duties in regard to the minor child by mutual agreement; if the mutual agreement did not or could not be done, the court may decide by the applications of any parent, the authorities concerned, the social welfare institution or any other interested person, or may decide by its authority. If the mutual agreement is unfavourable to the child, the court may change it for the interests of the minor child. [654] Where the parents do not continue their cohabitation for more than six months, exercise of the rights or assumption of duties to the minor in case of divorce applies *mutatis mutandis*. [655] They also apply *mutatis mutandis* to the rights and duties of the child born out of wedlock and have been acknowledged by his/her natural father. [656] It is this author's opinion to characterize them as the parents' rights and duties rather than the effect of divorce or separation. They are thus governed by the child's national law.

III. Guardianship

429. In Taiwan's Civil Code, guardianship over minors is distinguished from parents' rights and duties to their children. A guardian shall be appointed for a minor when he has no parent or when both the parents cannot exercise the rights nor assume the duties in regard to the minor child. But this does not apply where the minor has been married. [657] In regard to a minor child, parents may authorize, in a written form, another person to perform the function of a guardian for specific matters and within a fixed period. [658] The parent who exercises and takes rights and responsibilities to the minor may appoint a guardian by will. [659]

653. CC, Art. 1090.
654. CC, Art. 1055.
655. CC, Art. 1089-1.
656. CC, Art. 1069-1.
657. CC, Art. 1091.
658. CC, Art. 1092.
659. CC, Art. 1093.

430. The laws on guardianship differ from country to country, the conflict of laws problems hence arise. The Choice-of-law Act 2010 states that a guardianship is governed by the national law of the ward; however, if an alien ward has a domicile or residence within the ROC, and under his/her national law a guardian should have been appointed for him/her, but there is no person performing the office of a guardian, his/her guardianship is governed by the law of the ROC.[660] Such provisions emphasize on applying the national law of the ward to protect him/her.[661] And the law of the ROC applies in the second tier to provide protection of interests of the ward within its territory.

IV. Adoption

431. Adoption is an institution that creates the legal relation of parent and child between the persons that are not parent and child in nature or blood. With diverse purposes, the pictures of laws on adoption in different countries vary significantly. In Taiwan's Civil Code, adoption is designed to protect mainly the interests of adopted children. Adoption shall be effected in writing and petitioned for the court's approval. The court shall not approve the adoption where the adoption is based on a ground that it is void, may be annulled, or violates other laws. [662] The court shall approve the adoption of the minor based upon the best interest of the adoptive child. [663]

432. Some substantive requisites to adoption are stipulated in Taiwan's Civil Code. The adopter shall be at least twenty years older than the person to be adopted. [664] None of the following relatives may be adopted as an adopted child: 1. lineal relatives by blood; 2. lineal relatives by marriage, except adoption of the other party's child by either the husband or the wife; or 3. collateral relatives by blood or marriage of a different rank, except where the former is within the sixth degree of relationship and the latter is within the fifth degree of relationship. [665] Except when being adopted by a husband and wife, a person shall not be simultaneously adopted by two persons. [666] A minor of younger than seven years of age shall make the declaration of intention and accept the declaration of intention through his/her statutory agent when he/she is to be adopted. A minor older than seven years of age shall obtain the consent of his/her statutory agent when he is to be adopted. [667]

660. Choice-of-law Act 2010, Art. 56 para. 1.
661. The rule on *renvoi* in Act. 6 of the Choice-of-law Act 2010 shall thus apply. Liu & Chen, *supra* n. 12, at 535.
662. CC, Art. 1079.
663. CC, Art. 1079-1.
664. CC, Art. 1073.
665. CC, Art. 1073-1.
666. CC, Art. 1075.
667. CC, Art. 1076-1.

433. According to Taiwan's Civil Code, the relationship between an adopted child and his adoptive parents may be terminated by mutual agreement of the parties. The termination of adoption shall be made in writing. Where the adoptive child is a minor, the termination shall be petitioned to the court. The court's approval of the termination of adoption must be based on the best interest of the child. Where the adoptive child is a minor, termination of the adoption is effective at the time when the court's approval of the termination is finalized. [668] After the death of the adopted parents, the adopted child may petition the court for approval to terminate the adoption. [669]

434. In light of the differences in the laws on adoption around the world, the Choice-of-law Act 2010 states that the formation and termination of an adoption of a child are governed for the adoptive parent and for the adopted child by their respective national laws.[670] It adopts the methodology of distributive or simultaneous application of the national laws of the adoptive parent and for the adopted child. The requisites will be thus distributed to respectively for the adoptive parent or the adopted child and governed by the national law of the relevant party.

435. The effects of adoption and its termination are stipulated in Taiwan's Civil Code. The relationship between an adopted child and his adoptive parents and their relatives is the same as that between a legitimate child and his parents, unless otherwise provided by law. The rights and duties between an adopted child and his/her natural parents and their relatives is suspended during the period of adoption, except where one party of the husband and the wife adopts the other party's child, the other party's rights and duties to the child are not affected by the adoption. [671] An adopted child may assume the surname of the adopter or maintain the original surname. [672] The effect of the adoption is retroactive as from the time that the court's admission was finalized to the time when the contract of adoption was formed. Except, where the rights obtained by the third party are not affected. [673] Where the adoptive relationship has been terminated by the judgment, and the innocent party is thereby reduced to difficulties in livelihood, he may demand payment of an equitable sum of money from the other party. [674] From the time of the termination of the adoption, the adoptive child and his or her lineal relative by blood who is affected by the adoption shall resume use of his or her surname, and the rights and duties to his or her natural parents and relatives. However, the rights obtained by the third party are not affected. [675]

668. CC, Art. 1080.
669. CC, Art. 1080-1.
670. Choice-of-law Act 2010, Art. 54 para. 1.
671. CC, Art. 1077.
672. CC, Art. 1078.
673. CC, Art. 1079-3.
674. CC, Art. 1078.
675. CC, Art. 1083.

436. The Choice-of-law Act 2010 states that the effect of an adoption is governed by the national law of the adoptive parent.[676] The scope of this provision is restraint to the direct effects resulting from adoption. Some effects such as custody of the adopted child and the adoptive parents' responsibility are included in the legal relationship between parents and children are governed by the national law of the adopted child.[677] It is also noteworthy that the nationality of the adopted child may change due to the adoption, hence the national law of the adopted child may be the same as of the adoptive parent.

V. Artificial Insemination, Surrogacy

437. In contrast to a natural reproduction that has been discussed earlier, an assisted reproduction refers to the use of assisted means not involving sexual intercourse to achieve conception and birth with assistance from reproductive medicine. Artificial insemination and surrogacy are two of its types. Taiwan passed the Assisted Reproduction Act[678] in 2007 to foster assisted reproduction, to protect the rights and interests of infertile couples, children conceived through assisted reproduction, and donors, and to preserve social ethics and health. It defines the recipient couple as a husband and a wife receiving assisted reproduction, where the wife's uterus can carry a foetus and give birth to a child. Under such terms, artificial insemination can be employed to assist reproduction, while surrogacy is not yet permitted by the Taiwanese law.[679]

438. The Assisted Reproduction Act set up some conditions to employ assisted reproduction. 'An assisted reproduction institution shall not accept reproductive cells donation unless the donor meets the following criteria: 1. men at least 20 and less than 50 years of age; women at least 20 and less than 40 years of age; 2. the results of testing and assessment as prescribed in the proceeding article confirm the suitability of the donor; 3. the donor agrees to donate without compensation; and 4. the donor has never donated sperm or oocytes before, or the donor's previously donated reproductive cells never helped any recipient couple complete live birth and were not stored.'[680] In conflict of laws, this relates only to the contract concluded between the institution and the recipient couple, and is not in the focus of family relationship.

439. Status of children conceived through assisted reproduction is the point that needs to be analysed in conflict of laws. Taiwan's Assisted Reproduction Act states some basic substantive rules that are different from rules of natural reproduction. Such variation includes the presumption of legitimacy to the mother's husband, the

676. Choice-of-law Act 2010, Art. 54 para. 2.
677. Choice-of-law Act 2010, Art. 55.
678. The Assisted Reproduction Act (Ren-Gong Sheng-Zhi Fa, 人工生殖法) was adopted in 2007 and last revised in 2018.
679. Assisted Reproduction Act, Art. 2 Item 3.
680. Assisted Reproduction Act, Art. 8 para. 1.

acknowledgment of a child born out of wedlock by his natural father, and the relevant provisions for natural reproduction are inapplicable to assisted reproduction.

440. So, any child born to a married woman and conceived through the use of donated sperm with the consent of her husband shall be considered a child born in wedlock. Where the husband can prove that such consent was obtained by fraud or coercion, he may bring a lawsuit for denial of paternity not later than six months after the fraud or coercion has ceased. [681] Any child born to a married woman and conceived through the use of her husband's sperm and donated oocytes with her consent shall be considered a child born in wedlock. Where the wife can prove that such consent was obtained by fraud or coercion, she may bring a lawsuit for denial of her parental status not later than six months after the fraud or coercion has ceased. [682] If a marriage is annulled or found to be invalid after a wife has conceived, a child or children born to that wife shall be considered a child or children born to the recipient couple in wedlock. [683]

441. There is no provision for assisted reproduction in the Choice-of-law Act 2010. As Taiwan's Assisted Reproduction Act has pointed above, the conflicts rules for natural reproduction are not necessarily appropriate for assisted reproduction. There is necessarily a new question of characterization as to whether the reproduction is a natural one or an assisted one. For assisted reproduction, conflicts problem of its motherhood is new and has no conflicts rule to refer to, while its fatherhood shall look to some fresh conflicts rules to reflect its nature. But one thing is for sure: the interests of the child shall be protected to the extent as much as the legal methodology can reach.

442. It is this author's opinion that the juridical act to arrange the assisted reproduction and the status of the child born and conceived out of it shall be dealt with separately. The formation and effect of the juridical act to arrange the assisted reproduction relate closely to the place where the assisted reproduction is to be performed, while it is an obligatory juridical act of which governing law shall be ascertained under the conflicts rule of it.[684] Nonetheless, the foreign governing law will be excluded if its application results in an effect that is contradictory to the public order or *boni mores* of Taiwan.

443. The motherhood in assisted reproduction is no more a mere question of fact as in natural reproduction. It is a legal question whether the woman to whom a child was born is the mother. This author suggests that the national law of the child governs. This law also governs whether the man who donated sperm is the legal father. Apparently, the validity of the arrangement to perform the assisted reproduction lies in the premises to those problems.

681. Assisted Reproduction Act, Art. 23.
682. Assisted Reproduction Act, Art. 24.
683. Assisted Reproduction Act, Art. 25.
684. Choice-of-law Act 2010, Art. 20.

444. As to the child's legitimacy to the mother and her husband, in light of the policy embodied in the above provisions of Taiwan's Assisted Reproduction Act, this author suggests applying the conflicts rule of natural reproduction[685] by analogy to favour the child's legitimacy in assisted reproduction. Therefore, a child born to a married woman and conceived through the use of donated sperm with the consent of her husband, or born to a married woman and conceived through the use of her husband's sperm and donated oocytes with her consent, is a legitimate child to the recipient couple if he/she was a legitimate child at the time of birth under the national law of the child, of his/her mother, or of the husband of his/her mother. However, where the marriage relationship between the recipient couple has ended before a child was born, the child is a legitimate child if he/she was a legitimate child under his/her national law when born or under the national law of his/her mother or of the husband of his/her mother at the time the marriage relationship ended.

445. As surrogacy is not yet legal in Taiwan, it seems too early to address its conflicts problems. Given the fact that a child born through arrangements of surrogacy or other assisted reproduction is innocent and deserves parental love and legal protection, once its status has been established in the recipient couple's by birth, legitimation or adoption, it is this author's suggestion to recognize it as far as possible.

VI. Child Support

446. Child support is an integral part of the parents' parental responsibility and maintenance obligation in Taiwan's Civil Code. The obligation of the parents to maintain their minor child shall not be affected by the annulment of the marriage or the divorce.[686] This obligation may not be mitigated by the court even if it would be grossly inequitable for any parent. [687] In divorce proceedings, where both the parents are not suitable for exercising their parental rights or power, the court shall consider all relevant circumstances and the best interest of the minor child, appoint a guardian and the methods of guardianship, and order the parents to assume the duties for supporting the minor child. [688]

447. As mentioned above, the governing law of child support ascertained by the Choice-of-law Act 2010 is the national law of the child, according to the conflicts

685. Choice-of-law Act 2010, Art. 51.
686. CC, Art. 1116-2.
687. CC, Art. 1118-2.
688. CC, Art. 1055-2.

rule either for the legal relationship between parents and their children[689] or the relationship of maintenance.[690] This author prefers the former than the latter to reflect the nature of parental responsibility and its characterization.[691]

VII. Child Abduction

448. Child abduction is a tortious act that infringes a parent's custodial rights. International abduction removes the child from a country to another and creates a changed situation in the new country. The abductor often applies to the court in the new country to review the change of circumstances and to designate a new custodian to replace the old one in the original country. It usually disconnects the former relevant fact and relationship. It also leaves the old court decree rendered by the court of the original country untouched while new circumstances are considered.

449. Before the Choice-of-law Act was revised in 2010, according to Article 15 Paragraph 1 of that time, if the divorced wife is a Citizen of the ROC, the effect of the divorce is governed by the ROC law. When the divorced mother removed a child from the home of her ex-husband abroad and asked the ROC court for appointing her as the new custodian to replace the old one, the court applied the ROC law as the governing law of the effect of divorce accordingly. This author urged the court to focus on the fact of child abduction and characterize it as the legal relationship between the parents and children.[692]

450. The effective scheme of international judicial co-operation to discourage child abduction is built on international convention as its umbrella of co-operative relationship with foreign nations. As Article 55 of the Choice-of-law Act 2010 clearly states that the legal relationship between parents and their children is governed by the national law of the children and mentions intentionally in its explanatory comments that the change of custodian sometime after the old custodian was designated by a court decree shall be characterized as a problem of the legal relationship between parents and their children,[693] it is hoped that such international judicial co-operation can be established to yield Taiwanese courts' jurisdiction over the litigation of such disputes involving international child abduction to the courts' jurisdiction of the original country.

---

689. Choice-of-law Act 2010, Art. 55.

690. Choice-of-law Act 2010, Art. 57.

691. *See also* Hua-Kai Tsai, *Recent Developments in Taiwan's Private International Law on Family Matters*, in Basedow & Pissler (eds.), *supra* n. 7, 281, at 299–300.

692. *See* Rong-Chwan Chen, *supra* n. 125.

693. Legislative explanatory comments for Article 50 of the Choice-of-law Act 2010.

§8. Protection of Adults

451. As a principle, adults are mature and capable of taking risks and responsibility resulting from their juridical acts. But some adults are in special need of protection from the effects of juridical acts against them. Taiwan's Civil Code thus provides the institutions of guardianship and assistantship (curatorship) over adults.

452. With respect to any person who is not able to make declaration of intention, receive declaration of intention, or who lacks the ability to discern the outcome of the declaration of intention due to mental disability, the court may order the commencement of guardianship at the request of the person in question, his/her spouse, any relative within the fourth degree of kinship, a prosecutor, a competent authority, an organization of social welfare, an assistant, an agent of adult guardianship by agreement or any other interested person. When the cause of guardianship ceases to exist, the court must revoke the order of the commencement of guardianship at the request of the above applicants.[694]

453. It is noteworthy that an adult may select a potential guardian before the court proceedings by mutual agreement. The parties may agree on a guardianship over adults by agreement whereby one agrees to appoint the other as his/her guardian when he/she becomes subject to the order of commencement of guardianship, and the latter agrees to do so. The parties may agree on one or several guardians; unless otherwise agreed upon by the parties, the guardianship shall be jointly managed by all the guardians. [695] The conclusion, modification of an adult guardianship agreement shall be made in the notarization made by the notary public. The notary public shall give a written notice to the court for the place of the domicile of the ward within seven days after the agreement notarized. An adult guardianship agreement becomes effective from the date of the declaration of commencement of guardianship. [696]

454. With respect to any person who has insufficient capacity to make declaration of intention, receive declaration of intention, or who lacks the ability to discern the outcome of the declaration of intention due to mental disability, the court may order the commencement of assistance at the request of the person in question, his/her spouse, any relative within the fourth degree of kinship, a prosecutor, a competent authority or an organization of social welfare. When the cause of assistance ceases to exist, the court must revoke the order of the commencement of guardianship at the request of the above applicants. [697]

694. CC, Art. 14.
695. CC, Art. 1113-2.
696. CC, Art. 1113-3.
697. CC, Art. 15-1.

455. A person who has become subject to the order of the commencement of guardianship has no capacity to perform any juristic act. [698] A person under assistance must obtain the consent of his/her assistant if he/she intends to perform any of the following acts; provided, however, that, this shall not apply to any act relating to pure legal benefit or the necessity based on the person's age, status, and daily life: 1. being a responsible person of a sole proprietorship, of a partnership company, or of a juristic person; 2. making loans for consumption, consumption deposit, a guaranty, a gift, or a trust; 3. taking any procedural action; 4. agreeing to compromise, conciliation, adjustment, or signing arbitration contract; 5. performing any act with the purpose of obtaining or relinquishing any right regarding real estate, vessels, aircrafts, vehicles, or other valuable property; 6. performing partition of the inheritance, legacy, waiving the right to inheritance, or any other related right; and 7. performing any other act, at the request of the person or his/her assistant, appointed by the court. [699]

456. The conflict of laws problems of guardianship and assistantship are dealt with in the Choice-of-law Act 2010. It states that 'where there is a valid ground to declare guardianship or assistantship (curatorship) in respect of an alien under both his/her national law and the law of the ROC, a declaration of guardianship or assistantship (curatorship) may be decreed if he/she has a domicile or residence within the ROC.'[700] Apparently the legal grounds for a ROC court to declare guardianship or assistantship (curatorship) over a foreign adult are governed cumulatively by his/her national law and the law of the ROC. The formation and effect of an adult guardianship agreement are not specifically addressed in the above provision, it is this author's opinion that they shall be treated as personal matters and governed by the national law of the adult in question.

457. The effect of a declaration of guardianship or assistantship (curatorship) decreed over a foreign adult is stated to be governed by the law of the ROC.[701] It makes sense that the main purpose of the said declaration is to protect the interests of the adult and the public order of transactions in which he/she is involved.

458. After the court decrees the declaration of guardianship or assistantship (curatorship) over the protected adult, conflict of laws problems arise in the legal relationship between the protected adult and the guardian or assistant. The Choice-of-law Act 2010 hence sets forth the conflicts rule for guardianship and states that a guardianship is governed by the national law of the ward; however, the guardianship of a ward who is an alien, who has a domicile or residence within the ROC, and who satisfies one of the following circumstances is governed by the law of the ROC: 1. where, under the national law of the ward, a guardian should have been

698. CC, Art. 15.
699. CC, Art. 15-2.
700. Choice-of-law Act 2010, Art. 12 para. 1.
701. Choice-of-law Act 2010, Art. 12 para. 2.

appointed for him/her, but there is no person performing the office of a guardian; and 2. where the ward is the subject of a declaration of guardianship in the ROC.[702]

459. It also states that the conflicts rule of a guardianship applies *mutatis mutandis* to an assistantship (curatorship). [703] So, an assistantship is governed by the national law of the protected adult. However, the assistantship over a foreign adult who has a domicile or residence within the ROC, and who satisfies one of the following circumstances is governed by the law of the ROC: 1. where, under the national law of the protected adult, an assistant should have been appointed for him/her, but there is no person performing the office of an assistant; and 2. where the protected adult is the subject of a declaration of assistantship in the ROC.

702. Choice-of-law Act 2010, Art. 56 para. 1.
703. Choice-of-law Act 2010, Art. 56 para. 2.

Chapter 6. Succession Law

§1. *Lex Successionis*

460. Succession upon death refers to the transfer of the deceased's properties to the heirs upon death by operation of law. Two conflicts systems are adopted around the world. Plurality of succession in principle divides the properties inherited in nature and refers the immovable properties to the *lex situs* while movables to the *lex domicilii*. Unity of succession puts all the properties together into an estate and refers to the personal law of the deceased.

461. The Choice-of-law Act 2010 states: 'A succession upon death is governed by the national law of the decedent. However, if a national of the ROC is an heir under the law of the ROC, he/she is entitled to inherit that part of the estate which is located within the ROC.' [704] In sight of the first sentence, it is generally accepted that unity of succession is adopted and the unitary governing law is the decedent's national law.[705] But this author finds that the second sentence establishes an exception to the national law of the decedent, and states that the domestic properties are governed by the *lex situs* under the condition that a national of the ROC is an heir under the law of the ROC.

§2. Scope of Application

462. The scope of application of the *lex successionis* covers two basic parts that are stipulated in Taiwan's Civil Code. The first part relates to the heirs to the properties or estate. [706] The second part concerns the effects or the heirs' succession to properties. [707]

463. In the first part, Taiwan's Civil Code stipulates that heirs to property other than the spouse come in the following order: 1. lineal descendants by blood; 2. parents; 3. brothers and sisters; and 4. grandparents. [708] Among the lineal descendants by blood, the person nearest in degree of relationship comes first as the heir. [709] Where an heir of lineal descendants by blood has died or lost the right to inheritance before the opening of the succession, his/her lineal descendants shall inherit his/her entitled portion in his/her place. [710] Where there are several heirs of the same order, they inherit in equal shares as per capita, unless it is otherwise provided by law. [711] Each spouse has the right to inherit the property of the other, and his or her

704. Choice-of-law Act 2010, Art. 58.
705. The rule on *renvoi* in Act. 6 of the Choice-of-law Act 2010 shall thus apply. Liu & Chen, *supra* n. 12, at 535.
706. CC, Arts 1138–1146.
707. CC, Arts 1147–1185.
708. CC, Art. 1138.
709. CC, Art. 1139.
710. CC, Art. 1140.
711. CC, Art. 1141.

entitled portion is determined according to whom he/she inherits concurrently with. [712] In addition, the forfeiture of a person's right to inherit[713] and the infringement of a person's right to inherit[714] are also addressed.

464. In the second part, it states that succession opens with the death of the deceased. [715] An heir principally assumes all the rights and obligations pertaining to the estate of the decedent at the time of the commencement of the succession, except those rights and obligations which exclusively belong to the decedent. An heir's obligations to the debts of the decedent are limited to the extent of the property acquired from the estate. [716] Where there are several heirs, the whole of the deceased's property is, owned in common by the heirs before partitioning. [717] An heir may waive his or her right to an inheritance. Such waiver must be asserted by a written declaration to the court within three months after becoming aware of his or her right to the inheritance. [718] Waiver of inheritance takes effect retroactively at the opening of the succession. [719]

465. The subjects covered in the above provisions are within the scope of the *lex successionis*. Such provisions can be applied as long as the Taiwanese law governs the succession with foreign elements. It is evident that the question who may be heir to the estate is governed by the national law of the decedent, if there is no one qualified to be the heir to succession, the disposal or belonging of the properties or estate will be governed by the same law. Yet, there might arise conflict of the national law of the decedent and the governing law of the rights *in rem* over the properties, the *lex rei situs*.

466. The Choice-of-law Act 2010 adopts a realistic way and states that where an alien dies leaving property within the ROC, if under the applicable law aforementioned, no person is entitled to take the property by descent, such property is dealt with in accordance with the law of the ROC.[720] According to Taiwan's Civil Code, where no one acknowledges as the heir to succession, on the expiration of the period prescribed accordingly, the remained property of the decedent after the settlement of claims and the delivery of legacies accrues to the Treasury. [721]

712. CC, Art. 1144.
713. CC, Art. 1145.
714. CC, Art. 1146.
715. CC, Art. 1147.
716. CC, Art. 1148.
717. CC, Art. 1151.
718. CC, Art. 1174.
719. CC, Art. 1175.
720. Choice-of-law Act 2010, Art. 59.
721. CC, Art. 1185.

§3. TESTAMENTARY DISPOSITION

467. Testamentary disposition refers to a decedent's juridical act to dispose of property upon death. It may be a last will or other acts. Taiwan's Civil Code addresses just the last will and legacy. It varies quite a lot with the laws of foreign countries.

I. Legal Capacity

468. Legal capacity is specially stipulated for making a last will in Taiwan's Civil Code. It generally states for juridical acts that majority is attained upon reaching the eighteenth (or twentieth before 2023) year of age; [722] the minor, who has not reached their seventh year of age, has no capacity to make juridical acts; the minor, who is over seven years of age, has a limited capacity to make juridical acts; and the married minor has the capacity to make juridical acts. [723] For making a last will, it states that a person without capacity to make juridical acts may not make a last will; a person with a limited capacity to make juridical acts may make a last will without obtaining the approval of his statutory agent in advance; a person who has not completed his sixteen years of age may not make a last will. [724]

469. The conflict of laws on legal capacity for testamentary disposition or making a last will is not particularly addressed in the Choice-of-law Act 2010. Its governing law shall be ascertained according to the conflicts rule on capacity to act.[725] Hence, the capacity of a person to make a last will is governed by his/her national law; the capacity of a person to make a last will is not lost or limited because of a change of nationality by him/her. The juridical act of testamentary disposition takes effect at the time of death of the testator, while legal capacity is required at the time of act. It is this author's opinion that the decisive nationality to ascertain the national law is basically nationality at the time of making last will, although the *lex successionis* is the national law at the time of death.

II. Choice of Law

470. Testamentary disposition is an institution to recognize a certain freedom to dispose of one's own properties upon death. The testator may change his/her nationality or domicile at will so to change the governing law of succession and effects of last will. However, the restraint on the freedom by the governing law of succession makes it different from the juridical acts that are embraced by the principle of party autonomy. Although the nature of a testamentary disposition may be obligatory, it is

722. CC, Art. 12. This Article was revised in 2021 to lower the age of majority to eighteen. The revised provisions are set to come into effect from January 1st 2023.
723. CC, Art. 13.
724. CC, Art. 1186.
725. Choice-of-law Act 2010, Art. 10.

not within the scope of conflicts rule for obligatory juridical acts[726]. Instead, it is governed by the national law of the testator. The choice of law by the party or parties is thus not allowed.

III. Compulsory Portion

471. The freedom of testation and the protection of the heir's expectation to receive value of property are balanced in Taiwan's Civil Code by adopting rules of compulsory portion. The range of persons entitled to a compulsory portion is quite wide. It states that the compulsory portion of an heir is determined as follows: 1. for a lineal descendant by blood, the compulsory portion is one half of his/her entitled portion; 2. for a parent, the compulsory portion is one half of his/her entitled portion; 3. for a spouse, the compulsory portion is one half of his/her entitled portion; 4. for a brother or a sister, the compulsory portion is one-third of his or her entitled portion; and 5. for a grandparent, the compulsory portion is one-third of his/her entitled portion. [727] A compulsory portion is determined by deducting the amount of debts from the property of the succession. [728]

472. A testator may freely dispose of his/her property by a will so far as it does not contravene the provisions in regard to compulsory portions. [729] The compulsory portion is a personal claim by the deceased's heir against other heirs or legatees to receive the value of his/her portion. It is not a proprietary share over any property of the estate.[730] A person entitled to a compulsory portion may have the amount of the deficit deducted from the property of a legacy, if the amount of his compulsory portion becomes deficient on account of the legacy made by the testator. If there are several legatees, deductions must be made in proportion to the value of the legacies they severally receive. [731] Once the right of deduction is exercised, the compulsory portion is restored to be effective over the deceased's estate.[732]

473. In conflict of laws, the question of compulsory portion is an integral part of succession upon death, and is governed by the personal law of the deceased. However, Taiwan's law on the protection of an heir's compulsory portion relates closely to its citizens, it is hence stipulated in the Choice-of-law Act 2010 that the Taiwanese law governs to protect his/her compulsory portion. It is stated that if a national of the ROC is an heir under the law of the ROC, he/she is entitled to inherit that part of the estate which is located within the ROC.[733] It applies to the case that the deceased was a foreigner at the time of death, part of the estate is located in Taiwan, and a Taiwanese citizen is an heir under Taiwanese law. Obviously, Taiwanese

726. Choice-of-law Act 2010, Art. 20.
727. CC, Art. 1223.
728. CC, Art. 1224.
729. CC, Art. 1187.
730. Supreme Court's Civil Judgment, Tai-Shang 2193 of 2020.
731. CC, Art. 1225.
732. Supreme Court's Civil Judgment, Tai-Shang 2071 of 2014.
733. Choice-of-law Act 2010, Art. 58 Sentence 2.

and the national law of the deceased govern simultaneously and distributively.[734] The Taiwanese heir's compulsory portion is thus only effective over the estate within Taiwan.

IV. Interpretation

474. Interpretation of a testamentary disposition relates to the approach and criteria to find real intent of the testator. Taiwan's Civil Code states that in the interpretation of an expression of intent, the real intention of the parties rather than the literal meaning of the words must be sought.[735] The criteria of interpretation is embodied in the Civil Code as a substantive rule and is subject to the conflicts rule on relevant acts. Therefore, this author's opinion is that the criteria of interpreting a testamentary disposition is governed by the national law of the deceased, while the procedural problems of evidence are governed by the *lex fori*.

V. Last Will

475. Taiwan's Civil Code treats a last will as one of the fundamental approaches for estate planning. The laws on last wills vary greatly especially with regard to its forms in different countries. To cope with the unity conflicts principle of succession, the engendered conflicts problems of last wills are not categorized as wills for movable properties and wills for immovable properties. Yet, their formal validity and substantive validity are dealt with respectively.

A. *Formal Validity*

476. Taiwan's Civil Code accepts five forms of a last will: 1. a holographic of self-written will; 2. a notarial will; 3. a sealed will; 4. a ghost-written or dictated will; and 5. an oral or nuncupative will. [736] Oral or nuncupative wills are only allowed in extraordinary emergency situations and are subject to review of their genuineness. It is stated that where a testator by reason of imminent danger of death or other exceptional circumstances is unable to make a will in any other form, he/she may make it orally in one of the two prescribed forms. [737] In case the testator is able to make a will in another way, an oral will shall be invalid after three months accordingly. [738] An oral will must be brought up by one of the witnesses or an interested person, within three months after the death of the testator, for decision

---

734. Rong-Chwan Chen, *Succession to the Property Left by a Deceased Foreigner in Taiwan*, 5 Taiwan Law Review (月旦法學雜誌) 63–64 (September 1995).
735. CC, Art. 98.
736. CC, Art. 1189.
737. CC, Art. 1195.
738. CC, Art. 1196.

by the family council as to its genuineness. Where objections arise regarding the decision of the family council, application may be made to the court for a judgment. [739]

477. Taiwan's Choice-of-law Act 1953 did not specifically address the conflicts issue of formality of a last will. It might fall into the category of its validity which is governed by the national law of the testator at the time of executing it.[740] As a juridical act with foreign elements, its formality can also be subject to the general conflicts rule for juridical acts, which states that the formal requisites of a juridical act are governed by the law applicable to the act, but a juridical act that conforms to the formal requisites provided for in the law of the place where the act was undertaken is also effective.[741] In judicial practice, when the testator was a Taiwanese national at the time of execution, even though he/she had lost almost all other close connection with Taiwan, the courts ruled that the Taiwanese law governs the form of his/her last wills.[742]

478. Moreover, a last will notarized according to the law of a foreign country where the Taiwanese testator lived and it was executed is deemed to be invalid because it was not notarized according to the national law of the testator, i.e., the Taiwanese law. Taiwan's Civil Code provides that for making a notarial will, the testator must designate at least two witnesses and make an oral statement of his testamentary wishes before a public notary; the statement must be written down, read over and explained by the public notary, and, after the testator has given approval, signed by him together with the witnesses and the testator, stating the year, month and day; the functions of a public notary may be exercised by a court clerk in a place where there is no public notary, or by a Taiwanese consul when an overseas citizen makes a will in the place where such consul resides. [743] This author advocated that such provisions apply only to the notarial last wills notarized by Taiwanese public notaries. To favour the formal validity of a last will with foreign elements, the conflicts rule for formality of a juridical act[744] shall apply to the form of a last will executed abroad by an overseas Taiwanese.[745]

479. To cure the pitfall, the Choice-of-law 2010 specifically addresses the conflicts problem of formal requisites of a last will. It adopts the methodology of alternative application and states that in addition to the applicable law of the substantive requisites of a last will, a last will is also effectively made or revoked by following the formal requisites as provided in any one of the following laws: 1. the law of the place where the last will was made; 2. the law of the place in which the testator was

739. CC, Art. 1197.
740. Choice-of-law Act 1953, Art. 24.
741. Choice-of-law Act 1953, Art. 5.
742. Taiwan High Court's Civil Judgment, Shang 789 of 1999; Supreme Courts' Civil Judgment, Tai-Shang 172 of 2001.
743. CC, Art. 1191.
744. Choice-of-law Act 1953, Art. 5.
745. Rong-Chwan Chen, *The Last Will of an Overseas Taiwanese Notarized Abroad*, 29 Taiwan Jurist (月旦法學教室) 40 (March 2005).

domiciled at the time of death; and 3. where the will concerns immovable property, the law of the place where the immovable property is located.[746]

B. Substantive Validity

480. The Choice-of-law Act 2010 addresses the execution and revocation of a last will. '(1) The execution and effect of a last will are governed by the national law of the testator at the time of execution. (2) The revocation of a will is governed by the national law of the testator at the time of revocation.'[747] In light of the conflicts rule for formal requisites[748] mentioned earlier, Paragraph 1 deals with the law applicable to substantive requirements and effects of a last will.

481. The substantive requirements of a last will includes almost other requisites than its form. Although a last will is different from other juridical acts to freely dispose of one's property, the governing law of the capacity to make a last will is subject to the same conflicts rule prescribed for all juridical acts. [749] The national law of the testator at the time of execution governs his/her capacity.

482. The other substantive requisites concern basically the testator's expression of intent to make the last will. The intrinsic requirements of the testator's intent and the quality of expression are governed by the national law of the testator at the time of execution. If there is lack of intent, error, fraud, duress, undue influence, immorality, illegality or other failure to comply with the substantive requisites, the technical effects, namely, nullity, relative nullity, voidability by action, collateral attack, are also subject to the provisions specified in the same law. The causes of restraints on the testator's power of disposal relate closely to protection of the heirs' legitimate shares and are governed by the governing law of succession to property.

483. It deserves mentioning that the effects of a last will are different from that of other juridical acts. Taiwan's Civil Code states that a last will takes effect from the time of the death of the testator[750], but a testator may at any time withdraw the whole or a part of his/her last will in one of the forms prescribed for making a will. [751] If a will of an earlier date and a will of a later date conflict, the former is deemed to have been withdrawn as regards the conflicting parts. [752] Where acts done by the testator after having made a will conflict with such will, the will is deemed to have

746. Choice-of-law Act 2010, Art. 61.
747. Choice-of-law Act 2010, Art. 60.
748. Choice-of-law Act 2010, Art. 61.
749. Choice-of-law Act 2010, Art. 10.
750. CC, Art. 1199.
751. CC, Art. 1219.
752. CC, Art. 1220.

been withdrawn as regards the conflicting parts. [753] Where the testator has intentionally destroyed or repealed a will, or stated in the will his/her intention of annulling it, the will is deemed to have been withdrawn. [754] Such provisions apply only to the law wills of which effects are governed by the Taiwanese law.

484. It is noteworthy that when the testator's national law is applicable to the substantive requisites or effects of his/her last will, the rules of *renvoi* applies accordingly. The conflicts rule for such issue in that person's national law shall be applied to consider its further reference to other law. The rigidness of the nationality as a connecting factor can thus be softened.[755]

VI. Legacy

485. Taiwan's Civil Code treats a legacy as an exercise of the testator's freedom to testamentary disposal of the estate within the restraints by law. The relevant provisions are grouped under the heading of 'effects' of a last will. The Choice-of-law Act 2010 does not address legacies specifically. Their conflicts problems shall be determined according to the nature of the issues.

A. *Formal Validity*

486. A legacy is created by clauses in a testamentary deed. Its formal validity relies on the formal requirements for such a testamentary deed. For the legacy created by a last will, its formal requisites are governed by the governing law of the formal requisites of the last will.[756] It is valid in form by complying with the formal requisites provided in the applicable law of the substantive requisites of the last will, the law of the place where the last will was made, the law of the place in which the testator was domiciled at the time of death, or the law of the place where the concerned immovable property is located.

B. *Substantive Validity*

487. A legacy touches the core of succession to property on death. The substantive requisites of it rest partly on the substantive validity of the adhered last will and the law governing the succession. The governing law of the intrinsic requirements of a legacy is the same as of a last will. The requisites, validity and effects of lack

753. CC, Art. 1221.
754. CC, Art. 1222.
755. Liu & Chen, *supra* n. 12, at 535.
756. Choice-of-law 2010, Art. 61.

of intent, error, fraud, duress, undue influence, immorality, and illegality are governed by the law of the last will[757], i.e., the national law of the testator at the time when the last will was executed.

488. Taiwan's Civil Code states particularly some rules on a legacy. The provisions concerning the forfeiture of an heir's right to inheritance apply to a legatee *mutatis mutandis*.[758] When a legacy provided in a will is subject to a preliminary condition, it takes effect from the time when such condition is fulfilled. [759] If the legatee dies before the will becomes effective, the legacy does not take effect. [760] If certain properties are made the subject of legacy by the testator and, at the time of the opening of the succession, part of the properties does not belong to the property of the deceased, such part of the legacy is invalid. If all the properties do not belong to the deceased, the whole legacy is invalid. [761] A legatee may waive a legacy after the death of the testator. The waiver of a legacy takes effect retroactively as from the time of the death of the testator. [762] Where a legacy is invalid or waived, the property of the legacy remains part of the property of the deceased. [763]

489. The above special provisions on validity and effects of a legacy are beyond the scope of a last will. The issues fall into the succession to property on death and shall be governed by the law designated accordingly.[764] It is noteworthy that under Taiwan's Civil Code a legacy creates the legatees' obligatory claims against the estate. The legacy by vindication which makes the property under the legacy transferred immediately after the legacy takes effect is contradictory to the property law of Taiwan. However, such a legacy shall be recognized in Taiwan as a vested right that has been created under a foreign law. It may be adapted to a legacy in Taiwanese law.

VII. Testamentary Contract

490. Taiwan's Civil Code adopts the policy of compulsory portion to protect the heirs' legitimate shares under the law on succession. A last will is the sole mode that has been provided in it. The juridical act to make a last will is unilateral in nature and is not subject to the rules for contracts. The testamentary trust created by a last will under Taiwan's Trust Act[765] thus faces the problem of the trustee's acceptance. [766] Theoretically, a testator cannot create a contract with somebody simply by his/her last will.

757. Choice-of-law Act 2010, Art. 60.
758. CC, Art. 1188.
759. CC, Art. 1200.
760. CC, Art. 1201.
761. CC, Art. 1202.
762. CC, Art. 1206.
763. CC, Art. 1208.
764. Choice-of-law Act 2010, Art. 58.
765. Trust Act, Art. 2.
766. Trust Act, Art. 46.

491. In judicial practice, a contract conditioned on death is seriously distinguished from a legacy or other testamentary disposal of property.[767] A *donatio causa mortis* or a gift in prospect of death is an *inter vivos* contract to which the law on gift contracts is applicable. A legacy, in contrast, follows the law on succession and the law on a last will.

492. In short, the concept of a testamentary contract is not recognized in Taiwan's Civil Code. The Supreme Court has ruled the enforceability of a contract between a mother who announced the child who promised to take care of her would get the house she lived in and the daughter who promised and actually took care of her.[768] It is noteworthy that an institution similar to the testamentary contract with a consideration is adopted in Taiwan's Civil Code. Where the legacy is burdened with an obligation, the legatee is responsible for the performance only to the extent of the benefit received from the legacy. [769] The relationship is divided into two as one remains as a legacy and the other is the adhered burden to enjoy the legacy.

493. Since there is no conflicts rule on testamentary contracts in the Choice-of-law Act 2010, it is unlikely that any legal relation will be characterized as a testamentary contract in Taiwan. Yet, a testamentary contract validly created under a foreign law shall not be ignored. This author's opinion is that a foreign testamentary contract may be adapted to a legacy with burden and applies the conflicts rules on succession and on a last will.

A. *Formal Validity*

494. A testamentary contract is created by clauses in a last will. Like a legacy, its formal validity is governed by the laws designated accordingly.[770] It is valid in form by complying with the formal requisites provided in the applicable law of the substantive requisites of the last will, the law of the place where the last will was made, the law of the place in which the testator was domiciled at the time of death, or the law of the place where the concerned immovable property is located.

B. *Substantive Validity*

495. Evidenced by clauses in a last will, the testamentary contract constitutes a testamentary disposal of property. As a contract, it requires two parties, an offer, an acceptance, and a consideration. The capacity of the two parties is governed respectively by their own national law. The intrinsic requisites, validity and effects of lack

767. Supreme Court's Civil Judgment, Tai-Shang 2731 of 2017.
768. Supreme Court's Civil Judgment, Tai-Shang 612 of 2015.
769. CC, Art. 1205.
770. Choice-of-law 2010, Art. 61.

of intent, error, fraud, duress, undue influence, immorality, and illegality are governed by the same law that governs the last will. It is the national law of the testator at the time when the last will was executed.[771]

§4. INHERITANCE AND LIABILITY

496. Law of succession deals with how and when the rights and liabilities of the deceased transfer to the heirs. Taiwan's Civil Code provides that unless it is otherwise provided for in this Code, an heir assumes all the rights and obligations pertaining to the estate of the decedent at the time of the commencement of the succession, except those rights and obligations which exclusively belong to the decedent; an heir's obligations to the debts of the decedent are limited to the extent of the property acquired from the estate. [772] If an heir receives gifts in property (assets) from the decedent within two years prior to the opening of succession, the assets shall be deemed as estate. [773] Where there are several heirs, the whole of the deceased's property before partitioning is owned in common by the heirs. [774]

497. Liability is an integral part of a deceased's estate. Heirs shall be jointly liable for the debts of the decedent but liabilities are limited to the extent of the property acquired from the estate; among the heirs, each heir is liable for the decedent's debts based upon their relative share of the total estate, unless otherwise provided by law or agreed upon by the heirs. [775] Expenses relating to the management and partition of the deceased's property and the execution of the will are to be paid out of that property except those that have been incurred by the faults of the heir.[776]

498. Taiwan's Choice-of-law Act 2010 simply states in Article 58 'succession' to cover the issues governed by the law applicable to succession. The above issues stipulated under the heading of succession are basically included. Therefore, the following issues are governed by the *lex successionis*: the inheritance of rights and properties, the imposition of liability on particular persons, and the nature of the imposed liability, i.e., whether it is unlimited, or limited to the assets composing the estate, or to their value, and what steps are needed for any limitation.[777] If the properties composed in the estate scatter among several countries, the administration of properties is inevitably governed by the *lex situs*, and such administration shall be recognized by the *lex successionis*.

771. Choice-of-law 2010, Art. 60.
772. CC, Art. 1148.
773. CC, Art. 1148-1.
774. CC, Art. 1151.
775. CC, Art. 1153.
776. CC, Art. 1150.
777. Liu & Chen, *supra* n. 12, at 498.

Part III. International Civil Procedure

Chapter 1. Sources of International Civil Procedure

499. The international civil procedure relates to the proceedings that courts will follow when hearing cases with cross-border or international elements. The law on it covers international jurisdiction in civil cases, the civil procedural status of foreign citizens, enterprises, and organizations, the subjection of a foreign state and its diplomatic representatives to jurisdiction, service of documents abroad, taking evidence abroad, recognizing and enforcing courts rendered by foreign judgments, and other procedural problems. It is in theory a special section of private international law.

500. The issues raised in international civil procedure are dealt with by the national courts of a country. Like other sections of private international law, national legislature responds with certain efforts in codifying rules for the procedural needs. Considerable efforts have been madc to unify these rules and to simplify the formalities with a view to a rapid and simple system both on the international and regional level. However, due to its geographic location and the situation mentioned earlier, the international instruments like Hague Conventions and the relevant EU Regulations for some countries are not legal sources of Taiwan's international civil procedure.

501. In Taiwan, there is neither statute specifically aiming at prescribing rules on international civil procedure, nor court specifically established and responsible for civil matters involving foreign elements. All courts are under a duty to apply and interpret the relevant rules on international civil procedure *ex officio*. The Choice-of-law Act 2010 applies to all the problems of 'choice of law' to civil matters involving foreign elements, while its Article 1 states the scope covers all civil matters involving foreign elements. 'Civil matters' refer to commercial, family and other civil matters which are neither criminal nor administrative in nature. Procedural matters are within its scope. All elements that can possibly be grounded on for the law of a foreign country to apply in such civil matters are 'foreign elements'. They include, *inter alia*, personal elements such as foreign nationalities, domiciles, residences, and factual elements such as places in foreign countries.

502. The international civil procedure is considered as a civil matter with foreign elements in a broader sense. Its sources are considered as an integral part of private international law and shall be dealt with by the national legislature and the courts. In addition to the numbered bilateral treaties between Taiwan and other countries, the international civil procedural issues are fragmentarily and insufficiently stipulated in some legislations on civil procedure. The provisions will respectively be discussed later in relevant chapters.

Chapter 2. The Principle of *Lex Fori*

503. The questions of procedure in a civil litigation or a non-contentious matter with foreign elements shall be governed by the law of the forum. This principle of *lex fori* is fundamental and essential both in private international law and procedural law. The Choice-of-law Act 2010 does not address expressly on this principle, while according to Article 1, such questions shall be governed by other legislations of Taiwan and the legal principles in the relevant fields.

504. Taiwan's CCP takes it as granted without stating anything because it is undoubted that the policy of such code is to apply to all procedural questions the Taiwanese courts encounter in practice. The Enforcement Act of the CCP[778] stipulates directly the conflict of the Amended Code and the Previous Code on the basis that the civil procedure is governed by Taiwanese law. Unlike this approach, Article 1 of the Act on Non-contentious Matters[779] declares the legislative policy and provides that unless otherwise provided, all non-contentious matters under the Taiwanese courts' competence shall be governed by this Act.

505. Provided or not, the principle of *lex fori* is inherent in private international law and applies to the procedural questions. The governing law to substantive problems with foreign elements shall be determined and ascertained in accordance with the provisions in the Choice-of-law Act 2010. In practice, some disputes might be raised as to the distinction between the procedural and substantive questions or whether the problem at issue is substantive and is within its scope.

778. Enforcement Act of the Code of Civil Procedure (Min-Shi Su-Song Fa Shi-Xing Fa) was adopted in 1932 and last revised in 2018.
779. The Act on Non-contentious Matters (Fei-Song Shi-Jian Fa, 非訟事件法) was adopted in 1964 and last revised in 2018.

Chapter 3. National Jurisdiction

506. When a state established a system of courts to exercise its adjudicatory power and resolve the disputes between the parties, it is fundamental and essential to allocate every case to a certain court within the system. It is thus the first aim of Taiwan's CCP to deal with this problem. The problems of national jurisdiction are basic and preliminary for the court to resolve a dispute or enforce a legal provision.

§1. General Principles

507. For allocating jurisdictions to the courts in Taiwan, the CCP sets some basic rules. It adopts the traditional jurisdictional rules in civil law. Jurisdiction *in personam* and jurisdiction *in rem* are not legislatively differentiated and deployed to decide on the court's jurisdiction. A court's jurisdiction shall be determined according to the standards existing at the time of the initiation of the action.[780] A court, upon determining a lack of jurisdiction over the action in whole or in part, will transfer the action to a court with jurisdiction either by ruling on the plaintiff's motion or on its own initiative.[781]

508. The court's jurisdiction over the case at the time legal action was initiated shall not be affected by the changes of facts or of legal status that occurred after the case was filed. If a case is already pending with a court of another jurisdiction, the case in question shall not be reinitiated with another civil court.[782] When a civil court determines that it has jurisdiction over a case, and delivers a final and binding ruling, other courts are bound by such ruling. If a civil court determines that it does not have jurisdiction over a case, the court shall rule to transfer the case *ex officio* to the court with jurisdiction. If the party of a case is disputing whether the civil court has jurisdiction over the case, the civil court should adjudicate that dispute as its first priority.[783]

509. The CCP follows the Latin maxim '*Potior est conditio defendentis*,' and states that a defendant may be sued in the court for the place of the defendant. It focuses on an individual defendant's domicile and residence. 'A defendant may be sued in the court for the place of the defendant's domicile or, when that court cannot exercise jurisdiction, in the court for the place of defendant's residence. A defendant may also be sued in the court for the place of defendant's residence for a claim arising from transactions or occurrences taking place within the jurisdiction of that court.'[784] For a legal person that is established in pursuance with laws of a country, the CCP deploys its principal office or principal place of business as the connecting factors for a court to exercise adjudicatory jurisdiction. A public juridical person

780. CCP, Art. 27.
781. CCP, Art. 28 para. 1.
782. CCP, Art. 31-1.
783. CCP, Art. 31-2.
784. CCP, Art. 1 para. 1.

may be sued in the court where its principal office is located. A central or local government agency may be sued in the court for the jurisdiction where such office is located.[785] A private juridical person or unincorporated association that has the capacity to be a party to an action may be sued in the court for the location of its principal office or principal place of business.[786]

§2. Rules for Particular Matters

I. Matters Relating to Proprietary Rights

510. In Taiwan, the rights arising from civil matters are divided into proprietary rights (Cai-Chan Quan, 財產權) and non-proprietary rights. The proprietary rights include obligatory rights, rights *in rem*, quasi rights *in rem*, and intangible rights. The CCP addresses several jurisdictional rules for actions on proprietary rights. For examples, an action may be initiated against an apprentice, an employee, or any other sojourners in the court for the sojourning place of such person;[787] an action may be initiated against a soldier or seaman in the court for the location of the principal office or where the warship or ship is registered.[788]

511. In matters relating to proprietary rights, an action may be initiated against a defendant who either does not have a place of domicile in the ROC or whose domicile is unknown, in the court for the location of the defendant's attachable property or the subject matter of the claim. Where the defendant's attachable property or the subject matter of a claim is a creditor's right, either the place of the debtor's domicile or the location of the subject matter of a security shall be deemed to be the location of the defendant's attachable property or the subject matter of the claim.[789]

II. Matters Relating to Rights *in Rem*

512. Matters relating to rights *in rem* are not necessarily subject to exclusive jurisdiction of certain courts. In matters relating to rights *in rem*, partition, or demarcation of real property, exclusive jurisdiction resides in court for the place where the real property is located; in other matters relating to real property, an action may be initiated in the court for the place where the real property is located.[790] In matters relating to debts or rights in rem of any real property provided as a security for such debt, an action may be initiated against the same defendant in the court for the place where the real property is located.[791]

785. CCP, Art. 2 para. 1.
786. CCP, Art. 2 para. 2.
787. CCP, Art. 4.
788. CCP, Art. 5.
789. CCP, Art. 3.
790. CCP, Art. 10.
791. CCP, Art. 11.

III. Matters Relating to Businesses and Commerce

513. In matters relating to the business of a person's office or place of business, an action may be initiated against such person in the court for the location of its office or place of business.[792] In matters relating to a ship or its voyage, an action may be initiated against the owner or user of the ship in the court for the place of registration of the ship.[793] In matters relating to a debt arising from or secured by a ship, an action may be initiated in the court for the location of the ship.[794] In matters relating to claims arising from its membership, an action may be initiated by a corporation or any association, or its creditor or member, against a member in the court for the location of the association's principal office or principal place of business.[795] In registration matters, an action may be initiated in the court for the location where the registration is administered.[796]

IV. Matters Relating to Contractual Obligations

514. In contract matters, an action may be initiated in the court for the place agreed to by the parties as the place of performance of the contract.[797] In matters relating to negotiable instruments, an action may be initiated in the court for the location where the instruments are to be honoured.[798] In matters relating to claims arising from the management of property, an action may be initiated in the court for the location where the property is to be managed.[799] In salvage matters, an action may be initiated in the court for the location where the salvage took place, or where the salvaged ship first arrived.[800]

V. Matters Relating to Torts

515. In matters relating to torts, an action may be initiated in the court for the location where the tortious act occurred. In matters relating to claims for damages arising from a collision of ships or other accidents at sea, an action may be initiated in the court for the location where the damaged ship first arrived, or where the ship inflicting damages is seized or registered. In matters relating to claims for damages arising from the crash of aircraft or other aviation accidents, an action may be initiated in the court for the location where the damaged aircraft first arrived, or where the aircraft inflicting damages is seized.[801]

792. CCP, Art. 6.
793. CCP, Art. 7.
794. CCP, Art. 8.
795. CCP, Art. 9 para. 1.
796. CCP, Art. 17.
797. CCP, Art. 12.
798. CCP, Art. 13.
799. CCP, Art. 14.
800. CCP, Art. 16.
801. CCP, Art. 15.

VI. Matters Relating to Death of a Person

516. In matters concerning acts effective upon the death of a natural person, an action may be initiated in the court of jurisdiction at the location of the decedent's domicile at the time of death. When such court of jurisdiction cannot exercise its authority or the occurrences giving rise to the lawsuit took place at the natural person's place of residence, or the natural person was a ROC citizen and either did not have a domicile in the ROC or the natural person's domicile is unknown at the time of death, then the court of the decedent's residence, of the decedent's last domicile in the ROC, or of the place where the ROC's central government is located, has jurisdiction by applying Article 1 of the CCP *mutatis mutandis*.[802] In matters relating to an encumbrance upon an inheritance, an action may be initiated in such court of jurisdiction provided that the inheritance is in whole or in part located within the jurisdiction of that court.[803]

§3. Conflict of Jurisdiction

517. There conflict of jurisdiction of different courts over a single case is inevitable. The CCP adopts the inclusive approach to enable all the potential courts to exercise jurisdiction. The court for the location of a co-defendant's domicile has jurisdiction over all co-defendants, except where a court can obtain jurisdiction over the action in accordance with the rules mentioned above.[804] When the defendant's domicile, or the locus of real property, or the locus of the tort, or any other *loci* determinative of the court that has jurisdiction crosses or spreads over the jurisdictional boundaries of several courts, any such court may have jurisdiction over the action.[805] When several courts may have jurisdiction over an action, a plaintiff may choose to initiate the action in any one of those courts.[806]

518. To resolve the conflict of jurisdiction, the CCP provides that the immediate superior court shall, on motion or the request of the court in which the action is pending, designate a court to exercise jurisdiction in case of any of the following: 1. when the court with jurisdiction cannot exercise jurisdiction due to legal or actual impediments, or when special circumstances suggest that by exercising jurisdiction such court may affect the public order or the fairness of the proceeding; and 2. when a court with jurisdiction cannot be determined because the jurisdictional boundaries are unascertainable.[807] When the immediate superior court cannot exercise such authority, the designation shall be made by the court superior to the immediate superior court.[808]

802. CCP, Art. 18.
803. CCP, Art. 19.
804. CCP, Art. 20.
805. CCP, Art. 21.
806. CCP, Art. 22.
807. CCP, Art. 23 para. 1.
808. CCP, Art. 23 para. 2.

§4. Choice of Jurisdiction

519. Limited freedom of choice of court lies in the inherent policy of the CCP. It is in conformity with the idea of party autonomy and protection of the parties' procedural options. It stipulates that the parties may, by agreement, designate a court of first instance to exercise jurisdiction, provided that such agreement relates to a particular legal relation. Such agreement shall be evidenced in writing.[809] A court obtains jurisdiction over an action where the defendant proceeds orally on the merits without contesting lack of jurisdiction.[810] However, the above rules do not apply to an action that is subject to another court's exclusive jurisdiction.[811]

520. Besides, the CCP sets an additional rule to reflect the need to control the choice of court clause in a standard contract. Before proceeding orally on the merits, a party may move the court to transfer the action to another court with jurisdiction when the court in which the action is pending obtains jurisdiction an agreement accordingly and such agreement is part of a standard contract prepared by the opposing party which is either a juridical person or a merchant, and the contract is manifestly unfair under the circumstances. However, where both parties are either judicial persons or merchants, their choice of jurisdiction in a standard contract is not excluded.[812]

§5. Family Matters

521. The Act on Family Matters (AFM) addresses the allocation of national jurisdiction and international jurisdiction over a case relating to marriage simultaneously. It states that a matter seeking the nullification or revocation of a marriage or a divorce, or seeking a declaratory judgment confirming the existence or nonexistence of a marriage, is subject to the exclusive jurisdiction of the following courts: 1. the court of the husband's and wife's common domicile; 2. the court of the husband's and wife's common habitual residence, or 3. the court at the place where the husband or the wife resides and the grounds or occurrences giving rise to the action took place. However, the parties may choose the competent court in writing. If the husband or wife who is party to such a matter has died, the proceedings are subject exclusively to the jurisdiction of the court of the husband's or wife's domicile at the time of death. If no court can be found to be competent in this way, the court of the defendant's domicile or residence has jurisdiction. If the defendant's domicile or residence cannot be established, the matter is then subject to the court at location of the central government.[813] The above rules apply also *mutatis mutandis* to other family matters in accordance with the relevant provisions in the AFM.

---

809. CCP, Art. 24.
810. CCP, Art. 25.
811. CCP, Art. 26.
812. CCP, Art. 28 para. 2.
813. AFM, Art. 52.

522. Beside marriage matters, the jurisdiction over parent-child matters is also dealt with in the AFM. The jurisdiction to hear the proceedings exclusively belongs to the following courts: 1. the court for the place of the domicile of the child or the adopted child; and 2. the court for the place of the father, the mother, the adoptive father or the adoptive mother.[814] However, where a minor child or an adopted child is listed among the defendants in any matter mentioned above, the court for the domicile of such a child shall have the exclusive jurisdiction to hear the proceedings.[815] The rules of national jurisdiction and international jurisdiction over marriage matters apply, *mutatis mutandis*, to the parent-child matters.[816]

523. Some rules on jurisdiction over non-contentious matters of parent-child relation are set in the AFM. The following matters are subject exclusively to the jurisdiction of the court for the place of the domicile or habitual residence of the child; in case that the said child does not have a domicile or a habitual residence, to the court for the place where the child currently resides, if the court considers appropriate: 1. matters concerning the minor child's claim of maintenance, petition for determination, change, or modification of the parental rights and obligations, or petition for determination of exercising rights with regard to important matters of the minor child; 2. matters concerning the change of the surname of the minor child; 3. matters concerning the cessation of parental power; 4. matters concerning the designation of a special agent for the minor child; 5. matters concerning the handing over of a child; and 6. other matters concerning parent-child relations.[817]

524. Adoption shall be effected in writing and petitioned for the court's approval.[818] The relationship between an adopted child and the adoptive parents may be terminated by mutual agreement in writing of the parties. Where the adoptive child is a minor, the termination shall be petitioned to the court.[819] The court's proceeding for approval of the adoption or its termination is a non-contentious matter. The decisions must be based on the best interest of the minor child. The court's jurisdiction also needs to be in convenience of properly considering the child's best interest. The AFM thus deals with the adoption matters and its termination matters separately. The matter on approving the adoption of a child is exclusively subject to jurisdiction of the court for the place of the domicile of the adopter or the adoptee; if the adoptee has no domicile within Taiwan, then subject to jurisdiction of the court for the place of the domicile of the adopter.[820] The matter concerning acknowledgement of the termination of adoption, approval of the termination of adoption, or declaration of the termination of adoption, is subject exclusively to the

814. AFM, Art. 61 para. 1.
815. AFM, Art. 61 para. 2.
816. AFM, Art. 69.
817. AFM, Art. 104 para. 1.
818. CC, Art. 1079 para. 1.
819. CC, Art. 1080 para. 2.
820. AFM, Art. 114 para. 1.

jurisdiction for the place of the domicile of the adoptee.[821] It is apparent that Taiwanese courts have international jurisdiction over the matters involving foreign elements where the said domicile of the adopter or adoptee is located within Taiwan.

525. Some non-contentious matters of other nature are also provided for in the AFM. The following matters concerning guardianship of minors are subject exclusively to the jurisdiction for the place of the domicile or the residence of the minor concerned; where the said minor has no domicile or residence, then subject to the jurisdiction for the place where the minor is currently present, if the court considers appropriate: 1. matters concerning designation, re-designation, or changing of a guardian for a minor; 2. matters concerning reporting of or submissions by the guardian; 3. matters concerning the resignation of a guardian; 4. matters concerning the determination of the rights exercised by a guardian; 5. matters concerning the determination of the remuneration of a guardian; 6. matters concerning the designation of a special agent for the ward; 7. matters concerning the authorization of an action taken by the guardian; 8. matters concerning the handing over of a child; 9. matters concerning damages out of guardianship; and 10. other matters concerning guardianship of minors.[822] The following matters concerning maintenance are subject exclusively to the jurisdiction for the place of the domicile or the residence of the person who is entitled to maintenance: 1. matters concerning claims for maintenance; 2. matters concerning claims for reduction or waive of maintenance obligation; 3. matters concerning claims for modifying the extent or manner of furnishing maintenance on grounds or change of circumstances; and 4. other matters concerning maintenance.[823]

526. For non-contentious matters of parent-child relation, if two or more minor children are involved in a single matter, and their domiciles or residences do not locate in a single jurisdiction, the court for jurisdiction of any minor children's domicile or residence has jurisdiction.[824] Such rules applies *mutatis mutandis* to the above two groups of matters. They may also be applied by analogy to ascertain Taiwanese courts' international jurisdiction. Hence, if the minor child has a domicile or residence within Taiwan, then, Taiwanese courts have jurisdiction over the non-contentious matter of parent-child relationship.

§6. Labour Matters

527. The Act on Labour Matters[825] 2018 stipulates the allocation of national jurisdiction within Taiwan. For labour cases with plaintiff workers, the court of the region where the defendant's domicile, residence, main business, or main office is located, or where the plaintiff provides labour service, shall have the jurisdiction

821. AFM, Art. 114 para. 2.
822. AFM, Art. 120 para. 1.
823. AFM, Art. 125 para. 1.
824. AFM, Art. 104 para. 2.
825. Lao-Dong-Shi-Jian-Fa (勞動事件法, aka Labour Incident Act) was adopted in 2018.

over the case. For labour cases with plaintiff employers, the court of the region where the defendant's domicile or residence is located, or where current or the last labour service is/was provided, shall have the jurisdiction over the case. For cases with plaintiff employers, as described above, the worker involved in the case may petition to transfer the case to the jurisdictional court of his choice before the beginning of oral arguments. However, such rules do not apply to the cases which continue after the parties fail to reach an agreement in labour mediation.[826]

528. Concerning the jurisdictional agreement for the first instance in labour cases, if one of the parties is a worker, and the agreement is clearly unfair, the worker may initiate an action directly in other courts that has jurisdiction. If the worker is the defendant, the worker may petition to transfer the case to other jurisdictional court of his/her selection prior to the start of the oral arguments of the trial; however, such rules do not apply to the cases which continue after the parties fail to reach an agreement in labour mediation.[827]

826. *Ibid.*, Art. 6.
827. *Ibid.*, Art. 7.

Chapter 4. International Jurisdiction

§1. Statutory Forums

I. General Principles

529. International jurisdiction raises problems of private international law in two perspectives. One is the domestic court's direct international jurisdiction to adjudicate the case, the other is the foreign court's indirect international jurisdiction to have the judgment thus rendered to be qualified for recognition and enforcement. The jurisdiction discussed in this chapter is direct international jurisdiction. The provisions of the CCP and the Act on Non-contentious Matters on indirect international jurisdiction for recognizing foreign judgments[828] will be discussed later in relevant parts.

530. Before any Taiwanese court chooses the law applicable to the civil matter involving foreign elements accordingly, it is often asked to answer whether it is competent to decide the matter before it or whether it is the right court to exercise jurisdiction over such a case. The questions asked can be problems of international jurisdiction or national jurisdiction. But theoretically, the courts have to resolve problems of international jurisdiction before problems of national jurisdiction.

531. The problem of courts' national jurisdiction, as mentioned earlier, is well stipulated in the CCP, the AFM, the Act on Non-contentious Matters, and the Act on Labour Matters. The provisions in those legislations are basically rules on national jurisdiction, with very few exceptions on international jurisdiction.[829] No legislation has been enacted to comprehensively deal with the ROC courts' international jurisdiction over cases involving foreign elements. International jurisdictional problems seem too complex to be codified comprehensively. It is undisputed that the allocation of jurisdiction over domestic cases among the different ROC courts has been dealt with by the legislature fragmentarily.

532. The enactments mentioned above deal basically with ROC courts' national jurisdiction. It seems acceptable that once a ROC court is entrusted with the power to exercise its national jurisdiction over a specific case, its international jurisdiction over the same case is inherent and beyond doubt. This way of thinking presumes that the international jurisdiction of the ROC courts exists before any one ROC court is confirmed to have national jurisdiction over the case. Such a 'reverse presumption' makes it easy to confirm the international jurisdiction of the ROC courts. But it overlooks the need to consider the ROC courts' international jurisdiction over a particular case.[830]

---

828. CCP, Art. 402; Act on Non-contentious Matters, Art. 49.
829. Liu & Chen, *supra* n. 12, at 626.
830. Liu & Chen, *supra* n. 12, at 627.

533. The prevailing academic opinion and judicial practice in Taiwan subscribes to the idea that the problem of international jurisdiction needs to be answered in accordance with legislative provisions or underlying principles. It is established that in order to fill the loopholes in the ROC courts' international jurisdiction in the ROC law, the provisions in the Code of Civil Procedure and other procedural enactments concerning national jurisdiction, e.g. the AFM and the Act on Non-contentious Matters, must be applied by analogy.[831] The special factors framed and categorized in such enactments enable not only the specific Taiwanese court to hear the case, but also interpret the reason why Taiwanese courts have jurisdiction.

534. It has been established that the ROC courts have to address whether they have international and national jurisdiction before discussing the case on its merits. The Taiwan High Court's Civil Judgment Jia-Shang 130 of 2007 on an international divorce decree is illustrative as a judicial model.[832]

535. This judgment composed of a special part entitled 'Choice of Applicable Law in Civil Matters Involving Foreign Elements' and the following four steps were addressed to discuss the problems of private international law:

1. The Foreign Elements in this Case: This action was brought by the appellee against the appellant who is a Vietnamese citizen. A foreigner is involved in this case, and it is obviously a civil matter involving foreign elements.
2. International Jurisdiction: The appellant, a Vietnamese citizen, participated in the preparatory procedure and admitted that she lived and worked in Shin-Chu County of Taiwan. The place of her main economic activity is within the ROC. She can also be served by the court with notice of the proceedings. This is in conformity with the principle of the strongest protection of the defendant as it would be the most convenient for her to litigate in the ROC courts. The ROC court's judgment will be the most effective and enforceable in the future. The ROC courts have jurisdiction over this case under the principle of effectiveness and the related need for a plaintiff to initiate the action in a court whose jurisdiction the defendant is subject to.
3. Domestic Jurisdiction: It is provided in Article 1 Paragraph 1 of the Code of Civil Procedure that a defendant may be sued in the court of the place of the defendant's domicile. Paragraph 2 provides that where a defendant has no place of domicile in the ROC, or where the defendant's place of domicile is unknown, then the defendant's place of residence in the ROC shall be deemed to be the defendant's place of domicile. The residence of the appellant in this case is located in Shin-Chu County which is within the jurisdiction of Shin-Chu District Court; therefore such Court has jurisdiction over the case according to the above provisions.

---

831. Supreme Court's Civil Decision, Tai-Kang 185 of 2008. *See* also Liu & Chen, *supra* n. 12, at 627; Fuldien Li & Rong-Chwan Chen, *Taiwan*, in *Direct Jurisdiction: Asian Perspectives* chap. 4 (Anselmo Reyes & Wilson Lui eds, Hart Publishing 2021).
832. Rong-Chwan Chen, *Jurisdiction, Choice of Law and the Recognition of Foreign Judgments in Taiwan*, in Basedow & Pissler (eds.), *supra* n. 7, at 26.

4. Law Applicable to this Case: Article 14 of the Choice-of-law Act 1953 provides: 'A divorce may be decreed if the factual basis is considered to be a ground for divorce under both the national law of the husband and the law of the ROC at the time when the action is instituted thereof. However, if any one of the spouses is a citizen of the ROC, the law of the ROC shall be applied.' In this case, the appellee is a citizen of the ROC and the appellant is a citizen of Vietnam, so that the law applicable to the divorce in this case shall be ROC law.[833]

II. Fragmentary Rules on International Jurisdiction

536. Some fragmentary rules on international jurisdiction are provided for in the Choice-of-law Act 2010, the AFM, and the Act on Non-contentious Matters[834].

A. *Choice-of-Law Act*

537. In a civil case containing foreign elements, after confirming its jurisdiction over an international case, a Taiwanese court will face the problem of determining the law applicable to the case. The Supreme Court distinguishes in practice between the jurisdictional rules and the choice-of-law provisions in the Choice-of-law Act.[835] It is noteworthy that the Choice-of-law Act 1953 basically addressed merely the choice-of-law problems or laws applicable to civil legal relations involving foreign elements. The Choice-of-law Act 2010 follows this pattern and provides exceptionally the conditions for the ROC courts to exercise jurisdiction over the declaration of a foreigner's guardianship and death.[836]

538. Where an alien having a domicile or residence within the ROC has disappeared, a declaration of death of that alien may be decreed with respect to his property located within the ROC or with respect to those legal relations affecting him that are required to be determined by reference to the law of the ROC. A declaration of death of an alien may be decreed in accordance with the law of the ROC and without regard to the limitations mentioned in the preceding paragraph, upon the application of the spouse or a lineal relative by blood of the disappeared alien if the spouse or lineal relative is a national of the ROC and has a domicile or residence within the ROC.[837]

833. Civil Judgment (Taiwan High Court), Jia-Shang 130 of 2007.
834. The Act on Non-contentious Matters (Fei-Song Shi-Jian Fa) was adopted in 1964 and last revised in 2018.
835. Civil Decision (Supreme Court), Tai-Kang 165 of 2005.
836. Choice-of-law Act 2010, Art. 11 para. 1 and Art. 12 para. 1.
837. Choice-of-law Act 2010, Art. 11 para. 1 & para. 2.

539. Where there is a valid ground to declare guardianship or curatorship in respect of an alien under both his/her national law and the law of the ROC, a declaration of guardianship or curatorship may be decreed if he/she has a domicile or residence within the ROC.[838]

B. Code of Civil Procedure

540. Most jurisdictional provisions in the CCP deal with the allocation of jurisdiction among the various ROC courts. Yet, some basic provisions in the CCP have significance in international jurisdiction as well. Article 1 provides that a court has national jurisdiction over a case if the individual defendant has domicile or residence within its jurisdiction; the defendant's residence or last domicile can in some circumstances be deemed to be the defendant's domicile in order to confer international jurisdiction to the ROC courts; and the ROC courts have jurisdiction over its citizen who enjoys immunity from the jurisdiction of courts of foreign nations.[839] If a foreign juridical person or unincorporated association has its domicile abroad, the ROC courts may not exercise national or international jurisdiction by connecting with its domicile, but it may be sued in the court for the location of its principal office or principal place of business in the ROC.[840] Those provisions state indirectly that the ROC courts have international jurisdiction.

C. Act on Family Matters

541. The AFM demonstrates a different approach by simultaneously providing both rules on national jurisdiction and international jurisdiction. It addresses the allocation of jurisdiction over a case relating to marriage to different ROC courts in Article 52. Furthermore, it states the conditions on which the ROC courts are empowered to exercise their international jurisdiction over the cases with international elements. The ROC courts are competent to exercise jurisdiction over and to rule on marital matters where any of the following four conditions exists: 1. the husband or the wife is a ROC citizen; 2. neither the husband nor wife is a ROC citizen, but they are domiciled or have had common residence within the ROC for over one year; 3. the husband or wife is stateless and has habitual residence within the ROC; or 4. the husband or wife has had habitual residence within the ROC for over one year.[841] Jurisdictional competence exists unless ROC court judgments or decisions are clearly unlikely to be recognized by the state of the husband's or wife's nationality. If it is apparently inconvenient for the defendant to litigate within the ROC, the ROC court is to dismiss the case on the basis of the forum *non conveniens* principle. There is no legislative definition of 'habitual residence'. Whether a residence is habitual is to be decided by the court on a case-by-case basis.

838. Choice-of-law Act 2010, Art. 12 para. 1.
839. CCP, Art. 1 para. 3.
840. CCP, Art. 2 para. 3.
841. AFM, Art. 53 para. 1.

542. Taiwan's Civil Code defines a marriage as a legal relation between a man and a woman and establishes its relevant rules.[842] The Act for Implementing Interpretation 748 stipulated that two persons of the same sex may form a permanent union of intimate and exclusive nature for the purpose of living a common life,[843] and that a dispute arising within such a union are considered as a family matter, which is subject to the provisions of the AFM.

543. Article 53 of the AFM applies directly to litigation matters on marriage. It also applies, *mutatis mutandis*, to the court's jurisdiction over the non-contentious matters on marriage.[844] Among them are matters concerning mutual obligation of cohabitation between spouses, designation of the domicile for a spouse by a court, mutual obligation between the spouses to inform each other of the condition of his or her property acquired in marriage, payment for living expenses of the household, for expenses of maintenance, for alimony, or court order of the application of the separation of property regime for matrimonial property. The Supreme Court ruled that such rules of jurisdiction apply to a Taiwanese court's provisional measures to secure enforcement of a US court's future judgment.[845]

544. The rules of international jurisdiction over marriage matters apply, *mutatis mutandis*, to parent-child matters.[846]

D. Maritime Act

545. The issues of national jurisdiction over maritime matters are addressed broadly in the CCP. The provisions cover matters relating to proprietary rights initiated against a seaman[847], matters relating to a ship or its voyage[848], matters relating to a debt arising from or secured by a ship[849], matters relating to claims for damages arising from a collision of ships or other accidents at sea [850], and salvage matters[851]. Those provisions can be applied by way of analogy to problems of international jurisdiction. However, the Maritime Act stipulates issues of international jurisdiction over cases relating to a bill of lading in two provisions.

546. The Maritime Act states that 'the action about any dispute arising out of a bill of lading on which a ROC port is described as the port of loading or port of discharge is subject to the jurisdiction of the court at the place where the port of loading or port of discharge is located or other ROC court which has jurisdiction

842. CC, Arts 980, 1000-1003-1.
843. Act for Implementing Interpretation 748, Art. 2.
844. AFM, Art. 98.
845. Supreme Court's Civil Decision, Tai-Kang 1020 of 2014.
846. AFM, Art. 69.
847. CCP, Art. 5.
848. CCP, Art. 7.
849. CCP, Art. 8.
850. CCP, Art. 15.
851. CCP, Art. 16.

according to the law.'[852] A ROC court has both international and domestic jurisdiction under such a provision over the initiated action.

547. The same methodology was adopted for the action about a collision of ships. 'The action about a collision of ships is subject to the following courts: 1. the court at the place where the defendant's domicile or principal place of business is located, 2. the court at the place where the collision had occurred, 3. the court at the port of registry of the defendant ship, 4. the court at the place where the ship is placed under arrest, and 5. the court at the place where the parties agreed to litigate.'[853]

548. Logically speaking, the special jurisdiction of 'a particular court of a country' over a case is based upon the premise that the 'courts of that country' have international and general jurisdiction over it. So, as soon as one particular ROC court is legally conferred with jurisdiction over an international case, the international jurisdiction of the ROC courts as a whole is beyond doubt. The above provisions are thus construed to be significant in confirming the international jurisdiction of the ROC courts.

E. Act on Labour Matters

549. Before the Act on Labour Matters addresses the ROC courts' national jurisdiction in Articles 6 and 7, it stipulates in Article 5 the conditions for the ROC courts to exercise their international jurisdiction. It puts international jurisdiction in the first place, following by rules of national jurisdiction. This procedural sequence conforms to the logical order of problems that a court shall deal with in a practical case.

550. For labour cases with plaintiff workers, if the location where the labour service is provided, or the location of the defendant's domicile, residence, office, or business, is within the territory of the ROC, the case falls under the jurisdiction of the ROC.[854] The jurisdiction is conferred to protect the workers' freedom to access to the ROC courts, so the parties' choice of jurisdiction is accordingly limited. If any jurisdiction agreement of labour cases infringes the worker's freedom to access to the ROC courts, he/she is not bound by such agreement.[855] In other words, the worker can still initiate an action in the competent ROC court in spite of the facts that there was an effective agreement to subject the dispute to the courts of a foreign country.

852. Maritime Act, Art. 78 para. 1.
853. Maritime Act, Art. 101.
854. Act on Labour Matters, Art. 5 para. 1.
855. Act on Labour Matters, Art. 5 para. 2.

F. Analogy to the Statutory Provisions

1. General Picture

551. By analogy to the provisions of national jurisdiction in the CCP, the ROC courts may exceptionally be granted international exclusive jurisdiction over the matters relating to rights *in rem*, partition, or demarcation of real property, where such real property is located in the ROC.[856] They are also granted general international jurisdiction over the following matters: 1. matters relating to proprietary rights, if (i) the defendant's attachable property or the subject matter of the claim is located in the ROC[857], or (ii) the temporary residence of a defendant's apprentice, employee or any other visitor is located in the ROC[858]; 2. matters relating to the business of a defendant's office or place of business which is located in the ROC[859]; 3. matters relating to contractual obligations which the parties have agreed to perform in the ROC[860]; 4. matters relating to a negotiable instrument which is to be honoured in the ROC[861]; 5. matters relating to claims arising from the management of property which is to be managed in the ROC[862]; 6. matters relating to torts where the tortious act occurred in the ROC[863]; 7. registration matters which are administered in the ROC[864]; and 8. matters relating to succession, partition or compulsory share of an inheritance, or a legacy, or any other act that is to take effect upon death, if the deceased resided in the ROC at the time of death[865].

2. Matters on Torts

552. When Article 15 Paragraph 1 of the CCP is applied by analogy to international jurisdiction over a tort case, the key issue is whether Taiwan is the location where the tortious act occurred. The Supreme Court interpreted the connecting factor 'location where the tortious act occurred' as to compose of locations where any part of the tortious act was committed and where any part of consequence resulted from such act took place.[866] Claims for damages arising from a collision of ships or other accidents at sea are subject to jurisdiction of the court for the location where the damaged ship first arrived or where the ship inflicting damages is seized or registered, while claims for damages arising from the crash of aircraft or other aviation

856. CCP, Art. 10.
857. CCP, Art. 3.
858. CCP, Art. 4.
859. CCP, Art. 6.
860. CCP, Art. 10.
861. CCP, Art. 13.
862. CCP, Art. 14.
863. CCP, Art. 15.
864. CCP, Art. 17.
865. CCP, Art. 18.
866. Supreme Court's Civil Decision, Tai-Kang 369 of 1967.

accidents are subject to jurisdiction of the court for the location where the damaged aircraft first arrived, or where the aircraft inflicting damages is seized.[867]

553. It seems that the above rules apply to all cases involving foreign elements. But the Supreme Court clearly stated that the Taiwanese courts' international jurisdiction over a foreigner's claim for damages of torts was not stipulated in the Choice-of-law Act, and Article 1 Paragraph 1, Article 15 Paragraph 1 and Article 22 of the CCP shall apply by analogy to it.[868] Therefore, both the Taiwanese courts of locations where the defendant is domiciled and where the tortious act occurred have jurisdiction over it.

554. In cases of which the plaintiff contracted with the defendant for licensing and claimed damages for breach of contract, it is quite common that the defendant committed a tortious act infringing the plaintiff's licensed right. It is notable that the victim may claim on the basis of tort or breach of contract. However, different grounds support different claims and actions in practice. The Supreme Court ruled in a case of 2005 that a claim of tort is separate from a claim of contract, and they are subject to different court's jurisdiction under respective rules; the jurisdiction of a Taiwanese court is thus not bound by the choice of court clause in the licensing contract.[869] The Taiwanese courts of locations where the defendant is domiciled or where the tortious act occurred have jurisdiction over it. It is convenient for the defendant to appear in the court of jurisdiction decided under the rule. The decision is not contradictory to the principle that the defendant shall be better protected. The court's jurisdiction is not excluded by the choice of Japanese law and a Japanese court in the licensing contract.[870]

3. Jurisdiction by Voluntary Submission

555. The CCP provides that 'a court obtains jurisdiction over an action where the defendant proceeds orally on the merits without contesting lack of jurisdiction.'[871] By analogy, if the defendant proceeded to argue the merits of the case without contesting the court's lack of jurisdiction in an international case, the ROC courts could consequently have international jurisdiction over the matter. In a case where the defendant did initially object to the Court's exercising jurisdiction over the matter, but proceeded to litigate on the merits and participated in oral arguments without re-asserting a jurisdictional challenge, the Taipei District Court ruled that under such circumstances, the ROC Courts shall have international jurisdiction over this civil matter having foreign elements.[872]

---

867. CCP, Art. 15 paras 2 & 3.
868. Supreme Court's Civil Decision, Tai-Kang 185 of 2008.
869. Supreme Court's Civil Decision, Tai-Kang 164 of 2005.
870. Supreme Court's Civil Decision, Tai-Kang 164 of 2005.
871. CCP, Art. 25.
872. Taipei District Court's Civil Judgment, Guo-Mao 12 of 1999.

4. Matters on Succession to Property

556. A case before a Taiwanese court on succession to property might be a litigation or a non-contentious matter. The CCP stipulates generally that the Taiwanese court at the location where the decedent resided at the time of death has jurisdiction over the disputes on an act effective upon the decedent's death; if such court cannot exercise its authority, or the occurrences giving rise to the lawsuit took place at the decedent's place of residence, or the decedent was an ROC citizen but did not have either a domicile in the ROC or a known domicile at the time of death, then the Taiwanese court at the decedent's residence or last domicile in the ROC has jurisdiction. [873] If the legal relation at issue relates to an encumbrance upon the decedent's estate, the Taiwanese court at the place where the whole estate or any part of it locates has jurisdiction. [874] Therefore, if the decedent had personal connection of citizenship, domicile, or residence with Taiwan, or any part of the decedent's estate is located within the territory of Taiwan, Taiwanese courts have jurisdiction over the relevant disputes.

557. In the AFM, matters on inheritance or succession to property are divided into the litigation matters and non-contentious matters. The litigation matters include claims for the restitution of inheritance, partition of estate, forced shares, bequeath, probate of will, and other claims on succession among inheritors. The following courts have jurisdiction over them: 1. the Taiwanese court for the place of the domicile of the successor at the opening of the succession; 2. the Taiwanese court for the place of the primary property of the deceased. [875]

558. The non-contentious matters on succession to property are subject to the exclusive jurisdiction of the Taiwanese court at the domicile of the decedent when the succession commenced. They include matters concerning: 1. submission of a list of the decedent's estate to the court; 2. a creditor's petition for ordering the inheritors to submit a list of the decedent's estate to the court; 3. waiver of inheritance; 4. unacknowledged succession; 5. preservation of the decedent's estate; 6. designation or re-designation of an executor of a will; and 7. other matters concerning succession.[876] Over matters on preservation of the decedent's estate, the Taiwanese court at the place where any part of the estate locates can also exercise its jurisdiction. [877] In addition, as Article 52 Paragraph 4 of the AFM shall apply, *mutatis mutandis*, to such matters[878], the Taiwanese court at the place where the defendant has domicile or residence can exercise its jurisdiction as well.

559. The legal relation of inheritance results in some non-ligation matters on family council as well. The court jurisdiction over them are also addressed in the

873. CCP, Art. 18.
874. CCP, Art. 19.
875. AFM, Art. 70.
876. AFM, Art. 127 para. 1.
877. AFM, Art. 127 para. 2.
878. AFM, Art. 127 para. 3.

AFM. A petition for designating members of the family council for the estate is exclusively subject to the jurisdiction for the place of the domicile of the successor at the opening of the succession.[879] A petition to court for the following matters that are required to be dealt with by the family council is exclusively subject to the jurisdiction for the place of the domicile or the residence of the heir: 1. matters concerning giving a portion of the estate to a person; 2. matters concerning supervising the manager of the estate; 3. matters concerning determining the remuneration of a manager of the estate; 4. matters concerning determining the authenticity of an oral will; 5. matters concerning tendering of a will; 6. matters concerning opening and viewing a sealed will; and 7. other matters that shall be dealt with by the family council. [880]

5. Matters on Intellectual Property and Commercial Cases

560. There are several enactments on intellectual property in Taiwan. Among them are the Copyright Act, Trademark Act, Patent Act, Integrated Circuit Layout Protection Act, and Trade Secrets Act. To adjudicate disputes systematically, the Intellectual Property and Commercial Court enjoys prevailing jurisdiction to adjudicate all cases concerning intellectual property rights in Taiwan, in pursuance with Article 2 and Article 3 of the Intellectual Property and Commercial Court Organization Act[881] and Article 7 of the Intellectual Property Case Adjudication Act.[882] The above rule is in the nature of subject matter jurisdiction rather than territorial jurisdiction. It cannot apply to international jurisdiction either directly or by analogy. So, even though an international case about intellectual property rights is within the exclusive jurisdiction of the Intellectual Property and Commercial Court in Taiwan, it is not necessarily the situation that Taiwanese courts' jurisdiction can exclude courts of other countries from exercising their jurisdiction over the same case.

561. Since no special provision for international jurisdiction on any issue concerning intellectual property is provided, Taiwanese courts' jurisdiction over actions about intellectual property is to be decided by analogy to the rules on other actions about property as mentioned above. Unlike the disputes on rights *in rem* over immovable properties, all issues of intellectual property are not subject to exclusive jurisdiction of any single country's courts, even though the validity of a registered intellectual property is so stipulated in some foreign legal systems.

---

879. AFM, Art. 180 para. 2.

880. AFM, Art. 180 para. 5.

881. The Intellectual Property and Commercial Court Organization Act (Zhi-Hui Cai-Chan Ji Shang-Ye Fa-Yuan Zu-Zhi Fa, 智慧財產及商業法院組織法) was adopted in 2007 as the Intellectual Property Court Organization Act (Zhi-Hui Cai-Chan Fa-Yuan Zu-Zhi Fa, 智慧財產法院組織法), and was last revised and changed to the current name in 2020. The new Act comes into effect from July 1st 2021.

882. The Intellectual Property Case Adjudication Act (Zhi-Hui Cai-Chan An-Jian Shen-Li Fa, 智慧財產案件審理法) was adopted in 2007 and last revised in 2014.

562. In practice, most cases of intellectual property rights are international in nature and relate to their infringement. It is quite common that a foreign company sues a Taiwanese company or individual for infringing its patent in a Taiwanese court. The basis for Taiwanese courts' jurisdiction are normally personal connecting factors such as Taiwanese nationality, domicile and residence.

563. In a civil decision of 2015, the Supreme Court ruled on a dispute on a domain name (tvbs.com) registered in the US registry. [883] After the issue had been decided by the Asian Domain Name Dispute Resolution Center (ADNDRC) in Hong Kong against its Taiwanese owner, the owner initiated an action in Taiwan to seek for a judicial declaration that the domain name registration did not infringe the right on the trademark of 'TVBS' combination. The court of first instance ruled that Taiwanese courts had no jurisdiction. The court of second instance reversed it and claimed Taiwanese courts' jurisdiction. The latter decision was upheld by the Supreme Court. According to the Supreme Court's decision, the ground to support Taiwanese courts' jurisdiction is the link that the trademark at issue is registered and protected under Taiwanese Trademark Act. The problem is that the dispute had been decided by the ADNDRC in accordance with Uniform Domain-Name Dispute-Resolution Policy (UDRP) established by the Internet Corporation for Assigned Names and Numbers (ICANN). This dispute relates to the conflict of legal systems of the cyber world and the real world. A deeper and thorough re-consideration has been called for the future development.[884]

564. In addition to traditional transactions, e-commerce also resulted in some novel problems for the transactions in the digital era. In a recent case, the Taiwanese plaintiff sued the Japanese defendant company in a Taiwanese court asserting that some counterfeits (made in China) were sold in the defendant's store in Japan and on the defendant's website which can be accessed from Taiwan via internet while announcing abroad purchase orders will not be processed. The court of first instance ruled that Taiwanese courts have no jurisdiction over such a foreign defendant and such an e-commercial transaction. The court of second instance reversed it and ruled that Taiwanese courts have jurisdiction. The Supreme Court upheld such decision and stated that the Taiwanese courts' jurisdiction is fundamentally based on the fact that the consequence of such infringement occurred in Taiwan.[885] Quite clearly, Article 15 Paragraph 1 of the CCP was applied by analogy to this case. In light of the ubiquity of the internet and the fact that the website was established for online purchasing within Japan, it is suggested that Taiwanese courts' jurisdiction can base on the principle of intellectual right's territoriality.[886] The Taiwanese courts are in the appropriate place to handle the case on the infringed right of trademark which was characterized as a Taiwanese intellectual right.

---

883. Supreme Court's Civil Decision, Tai-Kang 1004 of 2015.

884. Rong-Chwan Chen, *International Jurisdiction over Disputes of a Foreign Domain Names: An Analytical Study on the Supreme Court's Decision Tai-Kang 1004 of 2015*, 351 Taiwan Law Journal (台灣法學雜誌) 7–33 (14 Sep. 2018).

885. Supreme Court's Civil Decision, Tai-Kang 256 of 2019.

886. Rong-Chwan Chen, *Territoriality and International Jurisdiction over Copyrights*, 207 Taiwan Jurist (月旦法學教室) 29–31 (January 2020).

565. The commercial cases which include commercial litigation cases and commercial non-litigation or non-contentious cases, fall exclusively under the jurisdiction of the Commercial Court, according to Article 3 Paragraph 2 of the Commercial Case Adjudication Act. [887] Like the provisions on matters on intellectual property, the problem of international jurisdiction is not addressed in this Act. The relevant provisions of the CCP shall thus be applied by analogy to decide whether the Commercial Court can exercise its international jurisdiction over a commercial case.

§2. Choice of Forum Agreement

I. Legislative Provisions

566. As a part of the right of procedural option, the parties' freedom to contract about jurisdiction is explicitly recognized and stipulated in the CCP. It states that '(1) parties may, by agreement, designate a court of first instance to exercise jurisdiction, provided that such agreement relates to a particular legal relation;' and '(2) the agreement provided in the preceding paragraph shall be evidenced in writing.'[888]

II. Limits to the Freedom of Choice of Forum Agreement

567. Under the above provisions, the parties' freedom to agree upon jurisdiction of a court is limited in the following respects:

(1) The agreement is required to be explicitly concluded. The defendant's implicit consent or the parties' implied agreement about jurisdiction is unenforceable if no other additional explicit legal prescription is provided to grant the chosen court jurisdiction. If an action was brought before a court which has no statutory jurisdiction, and the defendant proceeds orally on the merits without contesting lack of jurisdiction, such procedural facts indicate that the defendant agreed not to raise any jurisdictional issues and rather to proceed to the merits of the dispute. Article 25 of the CCP provides that the court thereby obtains jurisdiction over such action. This jurisdiction relates somehow to the defendant's fictional or implied consent to resolve the parties' dispute in such court. This is an exception to the principle of explicitness embodied in Article 24 of the CCP.
(2) The agreement is required to confer jurisdiction on a court of first instance. Courts of appeal are not within the scope of the parties' choice. The agreement shall therefore be concluded before the lawsuit is initiated. Once a court

887. The Commercial Case Adjudication Act (Shang-Ye Shi-Jian Shen-Li Fa, 商業事件審理法) was adopted in 2020 and comes into effect from July 1st 2021.
888. CCP, Art. 24.

is seized with the dispute, according to the rule established in judicial practice[889], the parties can only follow or enforce the previous agreement, no further choice or alteration to it is permitted. Such freedom is obviously limited by the time element.

(3) The agreement is required to relate to a particular legal relation. The explanatory comment for the CCP mentioned in 1936 that the scope of choice shall basically be defined and limited to 'a particular legal relation' such as a contract of sale or a contract of gift. The designated court is competent to decide disputes relating to damages for breach of contracts. The freedom of choice is thus limited in terms of contents as it requires the specification of definite scope of subject matters covered by the parties' choice. The disputes arising from the prescribed legal relation are all subject to the jurisdiction of the designated court. A general agreement on a court to exercise jurisdiction over all future disputes between the parties is unenforceable, as is an agreement on jurisdiction over disputes about unidentified legal relations.

(4) The agreement is limited to actions not subject to a Taiwanese court's exclusive jurisdiction. The provisions on choice of court do not apply to an action that is subject to another court's exclusive jurisdiction under the CCP.[890] The underlying principle is that the public interest to grant a court statutory exclusive jurisdiction shall not be infringed by the parties' exercise of procedural right of disposition.

(5) It is noteworthy that the weaker party to a standard contract is favoured in the CCP to neglect the validity of its choice of court clause. 'Before proceeding orally on the merits, a party may move the court to transfer the action to another court with jurisdiction when the court in which the action is pending obtains jurisdiction in accordance with the provision of Article 24 and such agreement is one part of a standard contract prepared by the opposing party which is either a juridical person or a merchant, and the contract is manifestly unfair under the circumstances, provided however, that this provision will not apply where both parties are either judicial persons or merchants.'[891] Consumers and employees are often referred to as the legally weaker parties. As mentioned earlier, the Act on Labour Matters states that if any jurisdiction agreement of labour cases infringes the worker's freedom to access to the ROC courts, he/she is not bound by such agreement. Beside the inequality of the bargaining power in negotiating the choice of court clause, it is also required that such clause is 'manifestly unfair under the circumstances' to invalidate it.[892] The court of the place where the ROC court can otherwise exercise its jurisdiction over the relevant disputes.

889. Supreme Court's Civil Decision, Kang 16 of 1930.
890. CCP, Art. 26.
891. CCP, Art. 28 para. 2.
892. Act on Labour Matters, Art. 5 para. 2.

III. The Form of Writing

568. Whether the choice of court agreement is required to be in writing is not beyond scholarly debate. The root of this problem is that the phrase adopted in Article 24 Paragraph 2 of the CCP is 'evidenced in writing' instead of 'concluded in writing'. No matter what view is taken, the relevant 'writing' is required in the court proceedings. With regard to the meaning or forms of 'writing', Taiwan's Civil Code provides that when a juridical act is required by law to be in 'writing', it is not necessary that it was written by the person himself, but it must be signed by him; if the person uses a seal instead of his signature, the affixing of such seal has the same effect as his signature.[893] Such a flexible attitude toward interpretation had easily adapted to the circumstances when the CCP was promulgated, but it has been superseded as the science and technology of information has created new forms to conclude contracts.

569. A signature is characterized as evidence of a party's consent. Two signatures are required to prove the mutual consent of the offeror and offeree to conclude a bilateral contract. However, there is no signature on an electronic contract which has been accepted by both parties, and only one signature exists on a ticket or waybill. A standard contract or contract of adhesion is usually the evidence of unilateral promise of its preparer. The other party's signature sometimes is found to be just evidence of accepting some portion of that contract while leaving other portions untouched. To cope with the evolution of communication technology, the requirement of 'writing' shall be flexibly interpreted so as to include agreements evidenced by telegraph, fax, email or other electronic records.

IV. The Applicable Law

570. According to Article 24 Paragraph 1 of the CCP, the parties 'may, by agreement, designate a court of first instance to exercise jurisdiction'. This consensual designation of court applies to both exclusive and optional choice of court agreements. No provisions on the effects of exclusive or optional choice of court agreements are prescribed in the CCP. The questions are left to the judicial practice.

571. The Choice-of-law Act deals basically with substantive international legal relationships, rather than procedural questions. Characterization of the legal relation at issue is necessary to identify the relevant conflicts rule to determine the law applicable to it. The standard of characterization is left to allow the courts to decide on a case-by-case basis. In such process, the nature of a choice of court agreement is essential in finding a principle to fill the gap. The effects of a choice of court agreement are that the designated court can thereby exercise its optional or exclusive jurisdiction over the prescribed dispute and the domestic court's jurisdiction under the domestic rules is thus co-shared or excluded. These effects indicate that

893. CC, Art. 3.

such an agreement is procedural in nature. It is a general principle in private international law that procedural problems are governed by the *lex fori*, and no conflicts rule is necessary to determine the law applicable to them. But a choice of court agreement is different from other purely procedural activity at court in many respects. Besides the procedural effects, it is similar to an obligatory contract.

572. This author is thus of the opinion that a choice of court agreement is a non-obligatory contract which does not fall into the category of 'obligatory acts' prescribed in Article 20 of the Choice-of-law Act 2010, yet the applicable law for its validity shall be decided under the 'legal rationale' of conflict of laws. It is thus reasonable to apply Article 20 by analogy to this question.[894] It can resort first to the parties' express intention and then to the law of the place which is most closely connected with the choice of court agreement.

573. The Intellectual Property Court ruled in a case of 2008 that although the parties agreed in their licensing contract that their disputes should be subject to the jurisdiction of the Netherlands courts, the courts of the Netherlands did not enjoy exclusive jurisdiction unless it was so explicitly agreed upon.[895] Supreme Court's Civil Decision Tai-Kang 268 of 2002 was cited in this case in interpreting the parties' expression as an agreement on non-exclusive jurisdiction which could coexist with jurisdiction being vested in other courts. The original jurisdiction that Taiwan courts could exercise was thereby not affected.

574. In a case of 2005, a Japanese company and a Taiwan company agreed in their 'contract of development, manufacture and sales' that 'all the litigations related to this contract or litigations of disputes incidental to it shall be subject to the exclusive jurisdiction of Osaka District Court in Japan for their first instance trials,' and that 'Japanese Law is the law applicable to this contract and its interpretation.' The Japanese company sued the Taiwanese company for its infringement of copyrights after the contract was terminated. The Supreme Court ruled that the problem of jurisdiction should be decided separately because the case at issue may stand beyond the scope of that contract.[896]

V. Construction of a Choice of Court Agreement

575. The characterization of a choice of court agreement relates to exploration of the parties' real intent - whether to grant jurisdiction exclusively to the designated court or just nominate it as one of the jurisdictionally competent courts. This can be categorized as construction of the parties' expressed intent. The construction of the choice of court agreement sometimes was treated as the ascertainment of facts about the agreement. The *lex fori* is thus applicable to its construction either under

894. Rong-Chwan Chen, *The Law Applicable to the Jurisdictional Agreement with foreign Elements*, 7 Taiwan Law Review (月旦法學雜誌) 39–40 (November 1995).
895. Intellectual Property Court's Civil Judgment, Ming-Zhuan-Shang 14 of 2008.
896. Supreme Court's Civil Decision, Tai-Kang 165 of 2005.

the idea that it is within the scope of the court's fact-finding authority or that such a procedural agreement is governed by the *lex fori*. The law of the designated forum competes with the law of the seized forum when the action is initiated in a court other than the chosen or designated court. The problem which forum law shall be decisive to the construction of the parties' intent remains to be solved.

576. It is apparent that the law of the designated court is more closely connected with the choice of court agreement than the law of the court seized, for deciding the validity and construction of the parties' agreement. A case of 2012 illustrated the related problems.[897] X (a Taiwanese company) and Y (a Japanese company) signed a patent license contract in which the following jurisdictional clause was included: 'Any United States District Court will have jurisdiction over any claim or controversy arising under or in relation to this Agreement.' X terminated the contract and stopped paying the licensing fee. Y first filed a lawsuit claiming damages for breach of contract in the US District Court for the Northern District of California. Then, Y withdrew this claim, and filed on the same day for the same purpose in the Superior Court of the State of California, County of San Francisco. A ruling against Y was granted after X contended that the US court is a forum *non conveniens* and an alternative Taiwanese court is appropriate to determine the dispute. X filed a lawsuit in the Taiwanese Court of Intellectual Property (of first instance). Y contended that Taiwanese courts' jurisdiction was excluded by the choice of court agreement.

577. In this case, the Taiwanese courts of three instances addressed their opinions in relation to several questions relating to the effect of the jurisdictional agreement. They all agreed that it is well established that the provisions of jurisdiction in the CCP shall be applicable by analogy to the choice of court agreement at issue. The enforceability of such an agreement was confirmed, while the three levels of court reached different conclusions about its nature and effects. With regard to the optional or exclusive nature of such agreement, their opinions differed in an interesting way. The Court of First Instance referred to the Hague Convention on Choice of Court Agreements 2005 and the Principles for Conflict of Laws in Intellectual Property 2010 (CLIP) and ruled that it is an exclusive agreement by which the Taiwanese court's jurisdiction was excluded. The Taiwan High Court looked into the wording of the choice of court clause and ruled that it is an optional agreement so that the Taiwanese courts can exercise their statutory jurisdiction. The Supreme Court upheld the lower court's ruling and stated that an agreement shall be presumed to be optional unless it has been proved to be exclusive. [898]

578. The Supreme Court reiterated some principles in this Decision. [899] The court stated in the first place that if the designated court has no jurisdiction over such international litigation, unless otherwise provided by the *lex fori*, the choice of court agreement is not necessarily binding on such designated court. As there is no rule on international transfer of jurisdiction in legislation or judicial practice, the

897. Supreme Court's Civil Decision, Tai-Kang 259 of 2012.
898. Supreme Court's Civil Decision, Tai-Kang 259 of 2012.
899. Supreme Court's Civil Decision, Tai-Kang 259 of 2012.

effects of choice of court agreements are not necessarily exclusive. The judgment went on to say that the disputes on international jurisdiction by agreement shall be settled by contract construction case by case. The elements that shall be taken into account include the factual background, usage of trade, economic purpose, reasonable and objective notice of common society, principles of experience, and the effects intended by the parties when they expressed their willingness. The result of construction shall be reviewed by weighing the above elements in order to pursue fairness and justice.

579. The Supreme Court ruled that the parties' agreement on court jurisdiction, if any, is only valid in relation to disputes about patent infringements, noting that this action on non-existence of obligation has nothing to do with patent. There is no federal element or federal interest in it, so it is not under jurisdiction of the US federal courts. The agreement on jurisdiction over patent infringements is therefore unenforceable over this action. Since this action is not covered by the parties' agreement on jurisdiction, the jurisdiction of the ROC courts over it, if any, is not excluded by it. The Supreme Court held that, by applying Article 3 Paragraph 1 of the CCP in analogy to this case,[900] the ROC courts' jurisdiction over this action should be confirmed.

580. In this Decision, the law of the designated court was taken into account to evaluate the effects on jurisdiction of the court in which the action was initiated. The Supreme Court characterized the agreement as an optional choice of court without mentioning the applicable law in this case. Apparently the standards adopted to construe and characterize the agreement are some criteria evolved from the practice in the domestic courts. It seems a two-tier method underlies in this judicial thinking: the validity is governed by the law of the designated court, and the construction or characterization is governed by the forum law. The Supreme Court ruled in this decision that a choice of court agreement is characterized as optional if the parties' intentions are not established as exclusive. The fact that the word 'shall' or 'must' is used in the forum selection clause is not sufficient to indicate the exclusiveness of the selection.[901]

581. When a choice of court agreement is characterized as exclusive, the Taiwanese courts often interpret its words so as to limit its scope of application. The Supreme Court's Civil Decision Tai-Shang 592 of 1989 illustrates this attitude. In this decision, the Supreme Court ruled that the Taiwanese courts are jurisdictionally competent to decide the dispute between a Swiss corporation and the manager of its Taiwanese branch who is a Swiss citizen. The Taiwanese branch sued the Swiss manager in Shi-Lin District Court where he had a residence provided by the former

900. CCP, Art. 3 para. 1 provides: 'In matters relating to proprietary rights, an action may be initiated against a defendant who either does not have a place of domicile in the ROC or whose domicile is unknown, in the court for the location of the defendant's attachable property or the subject matter of the claim.'

901. Rong-Chwan Chen, *Legislation and Practice on Choice of Court Agreements in Taiwan*, in, *Optional Choice of Court Agreements in Private International Law* 395 (Mary Keyes ed., Springer 2020).

at the time the lawsuit commenced. The Swiss manager contended that Taiwanese courts have no jurisdiction because it was prescribed in the employment contract that the related disputes should be subject to the jurisdiction of the court at Zurich. The Supreme Court ruled that Taiwanese courts are jurisdictionally competent according to Article 1 Paragraphs 1 & 2 of the CCP. The legal relationships that the Taiwan branch asserted are based on the tortious act and unjust enrichment which occurred after the employment contract was terminated, which the court said were beyond the scope of the choice of court clause.[902] Therefore, the Taiwanese courts' jurisdiction was not affected by the choice of court agreement in favour of a foreign court at Zurich.

582. It is noteworthy that exclusive jurisdictional agreement is effective in principle. A recent case relates to the parties' dispute on the following jurisdictional clause: 'all claims and actions arising between the Carrier and the Merchant in relation with the contract of Carriage evidenced by this Bill of Lading shall exclusively be brought before the Tribunal de Commerce de Marseille and no other Court shall have jurisdiction with regards to any such claim or action'. The Supreme Court ruled that the parties' agreement to subject their disputes exclusively to a foreign court and thus to exclude the jurisdiction of Taiwanese courts is effective, unless the case is within the statutory exclusive jurisdiction of the Taiwanese courts, or the jurisdictional clause is a standard clause prepared by the party who is a legal person or merchant for the same kind of contracts and is obviously unfair to the other ordinary party under the circumstances. [903]

§3. Procedural Requirements

I. Basic Provisions

583. Procedural requirements for an action involving foreign elements are basically the same as for a domestic action. Seven circumstances of lacking requirements are stipulated in Article 249 Paragraph 1 of the CCP. They are as follows: 1. where the civil court does not have jurisdiction over the case, and the case cannot be forwarded in accordance with the provisions of the second paragraph of Article 31-2; 2. where the court in which the action is pending does not have jurisdiction over the action and cannot issue a ruling provided in Article 28; 3. where the plaintiff or defendant lacks the capacity to be a party; 4. where the plaintiff or defendant lacks the capacity to litigate and is not legally represented by his/her statutory agent; 5. where an advocate initiates the action and the advocate lacks authority; 6. where the action is not initiated in accordance with the prescribed formality, or lacks other requirements; and 7. where the action is initiated in violation of either the provisions of the second paragraph of Article 31-1, Article 253 or the second paragraph of Article 263, or its claim has been adjudicated by a final judgment with binding effect.

902. Supreme Court's Civil Decision, Tai-Shang 592 of 1989.
903. Supreme Court's Civil Decision, Tai-Kang 273 of 2020.

584. In case of any of the circumstances mentioned above, the court shall dismiss the plaintiff's action by a ruling, but where the defect is rectifiable, the presiding judge shall order the plaintiff to rectify within a designated period of time.[904] Where the plaintiff's claim, given the facts that he/she alleges, is manifestly without legal grounds, the court may, without oral argument, issue a judgment dismissing the action with prejudice. [905] Some of the requirements have special significance in private international law and deserve more thoughtful consideration.

II. Capacity to Litigate and Capacity to Be Parties

585. The CCP borrows the substantive concept of capacity to juridical acts to establish the procedural concept of capacity to litigate. It states that any person who has the capacity to undertake obligations through independent juridical acts has the capacity to litigate.[906] The 'capacity to undertake obligations through independent juridical acts' is tantamount to 'the capacity to act' in Taiwan's Civil Code[907] which was discussed earlier.

586. Under Choice-of-law Act 2010, a person's capacity to act is also governed by his/her national law, while the capacity of a person to act is not lost or limited because of a change of nationality by him/her. In order to protect the third parties and the public order in the forum state, where an alien of no or limited capacity to act under his/her national law is of full capacity to act under the law of the ROC, he/she is deemed to be of full capacity to act with respect to his juridical acts undertaken within the ROC.[908] The CCP follows this line and states specifically for the foreign plaintiff or defendant. A foreign national who does not have the capacity to litigate under his/her national law but who has the capacity to litigate under the ROC law will be deemed to have the capacity to litigate.[909]

587. Similarly, the CCP borrows the concept of legal capacity (capacity to enjoy rights and to be liable for duties) to build up the capacity to be parties. Any person who has legal capacity has the capacity to be a party; a foetus has the capacity to be a party in an action concerning the entitlement of its interests; an unincorporated association with a representative or an administrator has the capacity to be a party; and a central or local government agency has the capacity to be a party.[910] The legal capacity of a person to enjoy rights is governed by his/her national law. [911] A foreign plaintiff or defendant's capacity to be a party relies thus on the provisions on legal capacity in his/her national law.

904. CCP, Art. 249 para. 1.
905. CCP, Art. 249 para. 2.
906. CCP, Art. 45.
907. CC, Art. 13.
908. Choice-of-law Act 2010, Art. 10 paras 1 & 2.
909. CCP, Art. 46.
910. CCP, Art. 40.
911. Choice-of-law Act 2010, Art. 9.

588. Under the Enforcement Act of the Par of General Principles of the Civil Code, a foreign legal person recognized by the ROC has the same legal capacity as a ROC legal person of the same kind, and are equally subject to the ROC laws.[912] The Supreme Court established several rules in practice: an unrecognized foreign person is not a legal person in Taiwan, it is rather an unincorporated association; it has the capacity to be a party if it has a representative or an administrator; the question whether it has an office or place of business in Taiwan is beyond the scope of consideration.[913]

589. In a case of 2018, the Supreme Court affirmed the lower court's ruling that although GE Limited, Thomson (Bermuda) Limited, and Technicolor are registered in the United States, Bermuda and France respectively and have not been approved as a registered foreign company in Taiwan, they may be sued in Taiwan's courts since they are unincorporated associations with their own legal representatives and are granted standing to be a party to a civil proceeding.[914]

590. Article 13 of the Choice-of-law Act 2010 adopted the principle of incorporation theory and stated that a foreign legal person's national law is the law under which it was established without mentioning its recognition by the ROC government. Taiwan's Company Act replaced the system of recognizing foreign companies with a new system of establishing and registering a branch in Taiwan in 2018. The legal capacity of an unrecognized foreign organization shall be governed by its national law. It is likely that the basis for an unrecognized foreign legal person's standing to be a party will shift from an 'unincorporated association' to a 'legal person'. In other words, it will have the capacity to be a party in pursuance with Article 40 Paragraph 1 of the CCP as a 'person'

III. *Lis Alibi Pendens*

591. According to the CCP, when the decision, in whole or in part, is premised upon certain legal relations to be determined in another action, the court may stay the proceeding until that other action is concluded.[915] In cases where a party has initiated an action with regard to a subject matter for which an action is pending in a foreign court, if reasons exist for the court reasonably to believe that the foreign court's judgment on the action may be recognized in the ROC, and it is not substantially inconvenient for the defendant to litigate in such foreign country, then the court by a ruling may stay the proceeding until the entry of a final and binding judgment on the action in that foreign country, except where the parties have otherwise consented to have the subject matter adjudicated by the ROC court. [916]

912. Enforcement Act of the Part of General Principles of the Civil Code, Art. 12.
913. Supreme Court's Civil Decision, Tai-Shang 1898 of 1961.
914. Supreme Court's Civil Judgment, Tai-Shang 267 of 2018.
915. CCP, Art. 182.
916. CCP, Art. 182-2 para. 1.

592. The Taiwan High Court once was faced with a situation where it has to determine whether the guarantor liability at issue was premised upon the decision pending from the High Court of Malaysia on the parties' primary liability under Malaysian law. To prevent any contradictory conclusion, it ruled that such domestic proceedings shall stay until the High Court of Malaysia concludes its case on the primary liability issue.[917]

§4. International Service

I. Service of Process Outside of the Territory

593. Unlike jurisdictional requirements in some common law jurisdiction, jurisdiction of the Taiwanese court cannot be assumed by personal service in Taiwan. It is not surprising that service of process within and outside of Taiwan is comprehensively stipulated in the CCP in addition to other relevant provisions on jurisdiction.

594. Personal service by parties is not acceptable under the CCP. Service of process is administered by the court clerk on his/her own authority.[918] Service of process shall be effectuated by an execution officer or post office delegated by the court clerk.[919] Service is deemed effectuated when the court clerk delivers the paper to be served to the person in the courthouse.[920] In an action regarding a business, service may be effectuated upon the manager.[921] However, in case the manager is a prisoner, service upon the manager shall be effectuated by the chief officer in charge of the prison who is to serve the documents as requested by the court.[922]

595. For service of process to be conducted in a foreign country, notwithstanding that the CCP does not provide separate subchapter for such purpose, special rules on service of process on foreigners are provided for the Taiwanese courts. Where service is to be effectuated in the domicile or residence or office of a person who enjoys immunity, the Ministry of Foreign Affairs may be requested to effect service.[923] Where service is to be made in a foreign country, it shall be effectuated by the competent authorities of such country, or the relevant ROC ambassador/minister envoy/consul, or other authorized institutes or organizations in that country. Where service cannot be effectuated in accordance with the provisions of the preceding paragraph, it may be effectuated by dispatching the documents to be served by registered and receipt requested mail.[924] However, if the foreign legal person or unincorporated association has set up an office or a place of business in the

917. Taiwan High Court's Civil Decision, Kang 1293 of 2000.
918. CCP, Art. 123.
919. CCP, Art. 124.
920. CCP, Art. 126.
921. CCP, Art. 131.
922. CCP, Art. 130.
923. CCP, Art. 144.
924. CCP, Art. 145.

ROC, service upon that place shall be effectuated on its representative or administrator in the ROC.[925] Service upon a ROC ambassador/minister envoy/consul, or any other staff stationed in a foreign country shall be effectuated by the Ministry of Foreign Affairs being requested to do so.[926]

596. It is noteworthy that the exceptional constructive notice (public notice) can be applied to service of process outside of Taiwan under some circumstances. The court in which the action is pending may, on motion, permit service upon a party to be effectuated by constructive notice under the following circumstances: 1. where the place service shall be made is unknown; 2. where service effectuated in the domicile or residence or office of a person who enjoys immunity is ineffective; and 3. where service in a foreign country cannot be effectuated accordingly, or it is foreseeable to be futile even if it has been so effectuated. When no person moves for service by constructive notice in the cases prescribed above, the court in which the action is pending may on its own initiative order service to be effectuated by constructive notice if it considers necessary for avoidance of delay. Where the plaintiff or the defendant who has been served previously fails to notify the court in which the action is pending of the change of place where he/she can be served, and such failure results in the above situation, the court may, on its own initiative, order service to be effectuated by constructive notice.[927]

597. Service by constructive notice shall take effect twenty days after the date of posting the notice or summons on the court's bulletin board or the court's website, and in case of publication in an official gazette or newspaper, from the last day of such publication. Where service should be effectuated in a foreign country by constructive notice, such service shall take effect sixty days thereafter.[928] When service by constructive notice is effectuated, the court clerk shall make a report, indicating the fact and date, and include it in the record.[929] Any litigation paper may be transmitted by telefax or by any other technological device, and such transmission shall render service effectuated when: 1. the person to be served notifies the court that he/she has received the documents served by telefax or by other technological device; or 2. a person interested in the action moves for transmission of a specific litigation paper.[930]

II. Service of Foreign Proceedings Within the Territory

598. Documents of foreign proceedings are basically served under the relevant laws of such foreign country. Unless required by the effective bilateral treaties or

925. CCP, Art. 128.
926. CCP, Art. 146.
927. CCP, Art. 149.
928. CCP, Art. 152.
929. CCP, Art. 153.
930. CCP, Art. 153-1.

multilateral conventions to which Taiwan and the foreign country are signatory parties, and the parties to the legal proceedings are nationals of those signatories, Taiwanese courts will have rare role to play in the procedure.

599. The Act on Supporting Foreign Courts on Consigned Cases[931] was promulgated to pave the way for potential support. It mainly provides rules for Taiwanese courts when they are consigned by a foreign court to assist with foreign civil or criminal cases.[932] A court, when consigned by a foreign court to assist with foreign civil or criminal cases, shall not act in conflict with the laws of the ROC.[933] The consigned cases shall be conveyed in writing through foreign affairs authorities.[934] The country of the consigning foreign court shall declare reciprocal support to the ROC courts when similar situations arise.[935] The documents of civil or criminal cases for which a court is consigned by a foreign court to for assistance shall be duly served in accordance with the document service provisions under ROC's Code of Civil Procedure or the Code of Criminal Procedure. The service document shall expressly state the name, nationality, domicile, address or office of the party to be served.[936]

600. If consigned by a foreign court, a Taiwanese court shall follow the provisions of the CCP mentioned above to support it in service of process. Given the fact that the number of foreign countries with which Taiwan has established official relations and reciprocal arrangements of mutual judicial assistance are very limited, it has been heard that several foreign courts have directly applied their own procedural rules to service of process in Taiwan without requesting support from the local courts.

§5. Rules of Evidence

I. General Rules

601. The CCP comprehensively formulates rules on evidence for the courts. The provisions apply to both national and international procedure. It provides in the first place that a party bears the burden of proof with regard to the facts which he/she alleges in his/her favour, except either where the law provides otherwise or where the circumstances render it manifestly unfair.[937] A fact need not be proved if it is alleged by a party and admitted by the opposing party in the preparatory pleadings, in the oral-argument sessions, or before the commissioned judge or the assigned judge. Where a party makes an addition to or limitation on his/her admission, the

931. The Act on Supporting Foreign Courts on Consigned Cases (Wai-Guo Fa-Yuan Wei-Tuo Shi-Jian Xie-Zhu Fa, 外國法院委託事件協助法) was adopted in 1963.
932. *Ibid.*, Art. 1.
933. *Ibid.*, Art. 2.
934. *Ibid.*, Art. 3.
935. *Ibid.*, Art. 4.
936. *Ibid.*, Art. 5.
937. CCP, Art. 277.

court shall, taking all circumstances into consideration, determine whether an admission has been made. Except as otherwise provided, no admission may be withdrawn unless the party making such admission either proves that such admission is contrary to the truth or the opposing party agrees to such withdrawal.[938] A fact presumed de jure need not be proved absent proof to the contrary.[939] The court may presume the truth of a disputed fact by drawing inferences from the facts already established.[940] Where a party intentionally destroys or hides a piece of evidence, or makes it difficult to use, for the purpose of obstructing the use of such evidence by the opposing party, the court may, in its discretion, take as the truth the opposing party's allegation with regard to such evidence or the disputed fact to be proved by such evidence.[941]

602. The court shall accept evidence introduced by the parties, except for evidence which is considered by the court to be unnecessary.[942] In the case of any obstacle that makes it impossible to designate the time in advance for taking evidence, the court may, on motion, designate a period of time within which the evidence shall be taken. Notwithstanding, the evidence shall still be taken after such period expires insofar as the litigation will not be delayed as a result.[943] When the court cannot obtain conviction from the evidence introduced by the parties, the court may take evidence on its own initiative if such is necessary for finding the truth.[944] Either the court in which the action is pending, the commissioned judge, or the assigned judge may, if necessary, take evidence outside the jurisdictional boundaries of the court.[945]

II. Foreign Laws and Foreign Evidences

603. The legal treatment of foreign law in the CCP differs significantly from domestic law and from factual evidence. Article 283 provides: 'A party has the burden of proof with regard to customs, local ordinances, and foreign laws which are unknown to the court. Notwithstanding, the court may investigate on its own initiative.' One of the parties has to take the initiative and show a certain level of diligence in order to establish foreign law. Since foreign laws are treated in an international civil procedure as laws that are the legal foundations to decide the disputes between the parties[946], according to the Latin maxim '*Iura novit curia*' which means 'the court knows the law', they are subject to the investigation on the court's own initiative.

938. CCP, Art. 279.
939. CCP, Art. 281.
940. CCP, Art. 282.
941. CCP, Art. 282-1.
942. CCP, Art. 286.
943. CCP, Art. 287.
944. CCP, Art. 288.
945. CCP, Art. 293.
946. Liu & Chen, *supra* n. 12, at 193.

604. To make a preliminary showing of a factual allegation, all kinds of evidence may be used to establish the truth of such allegation to the belief of the court, except for the kind of evidence which cannot be submitted immediately.[947] Witnesses, expert's testimony, documentary evidence and other objects are all permitted in the CCP. The court may request an agency, a school, a chamber of commerce, an exchange or any other organization to conduct a necessary investigation; the requested organization is under a duty to conduct such investigation. Where the court considers it appropriate, it may also request a foreign agency or organization to conduct a necessary investigation.[948]

605. Where the evidence is to be taken in a foreign country, the evidence-taking shall be entrusted to be conducted by the competent jurisdictional authorities of such country or the relevant ROC ambassador/minister envoy/consul or other institution or organization in that country authorized to do so. The evidence-taking conducted by a foreign authority shall take effect insofar as it is not contrary to the laws of the ROC irrespective of the contravention, if any, with the laws of the country of such foreign authority.[949] Where the evidence is taken outside the court in which the action is pending, the parties shall state the outcome of such evidence-taking in the oral-argument sessions. Notwithstanding, the presiding judge may order the court clerk to read aloud the evidence-taking transcript or other documents instead.[950]

606. The principal sources of evidence for foreign law are documents (particularly public documents) and expert opinions. The court, in its discretion, can determine the authenticity of a foreign public document. Notwithstanding, where the document has been certified by the ROC ambassador/minister envoy/consul or other authorized institution in that country, it shall be presumed to be authentic.[951] Where the court considers it necessary, the court may request any agency, organization, or a foreign agency or organization to give expert testimony or to review the expert testimony given. Where an explanation is needed, such explanation shall be provided by the person appointed by such agency or organization.[952]

607. In family matters, the evidences are sometimes focused on the parties' real intention and interest of the minors. The Procedural Rules for Courts in Handling Family Matters[953] therefore stipulates clearly. 'Where a matter of adoption relates to one or more foreigners, the adopter shall be called to the court for oral statement

947. CCP, Art. 284.
948. CCP, Art. 289.
949. CCP, Art. 295.
950. CCP, Art. 297 para. 2.
951. CCP, Art. 356.
952. CCP, Art. 340 para. 1.
953. Procedural Rules for Courts in Handling Family Matters (Jia-Shi-Shi-Jian-Shen-Li-Xi-Ze, 家事事件審理細則) was adopted in 2012 and last revised in 2020.

to confirm their real intention to adopt the adoptee. The court may also, if necessary, entrust the relevant ROC ambassador/minister envoy/consul or other institution or organization in foreign country to investigate into it.'[954]

§6. TEMPORARY RELIEF

I. General Principles

608. The courts are sometimes asked for a decree of 'temporary relief' after a case is filed, but before it is resolved. Taiwanese courts have the power to award 'temporary relief' or 'provisional measures' under the circumstances prescribed by the CCP. Provisional attachment and provisional injunction are deployed as the two measures as temporary relief. The former is awarded to ensure the satisfaction of potential judgment when the parties have a dispute about payment of ongoing bills, support, or issues involving money. The latter is awarded to impose an order keeping the 'status quo' and allow an 'interim' (temporary) exclusive use and possession of immovable or movable property, management of corporation or custody of a child until further order of the court or until the case has concluded. The relevant provisions apply to the non-contentious, family and labour matters *mutatis mutandis* as well.

609. In order to protect his/her rights, a person who restrains, seizes, or destroys the liberty or the property of another, according to the CC, is not liable to compensate for any injury arising therefrom, provided the assistance of the court or other relevant authorities could not be obtained in due time and there was a fact that if the person did not act immediately, the exercise of his rights would be rendered impossible or manifestly arduous.[955] To cope with this provision, the CCP stipulates that where the creditor has seized property or restrained the liberty of the debtor accordingly, the creditor must immediately apply to the court for a ruling for provisional attachment or provisional injunction. The court for the place where the property of the debtor is seized or where the liberty of the debtor is restrained has exclusive jurisdiction over such application.[956]

II. Provisional Attachment

610. According to the CCP, a court can order to impose a temporary relief in a national or international civil procedure. A creditor may apply for provisional attachment with regard to monetary claims or claims exchangeable for monetary claims for purposes of securing the satisfaction of a compulsory execution. Such application may be made with regard to claims subject to a condition or time.[957] No

954. *Ibid.*, Art. 110.
955. CC, Art. 151.
956. CCP, Art. 537-1.
957. CCP, Art. 522.

provisional attachment is to be granted unless there is a showing of the impossibility or extreme difficulty to satisfy the claim by compulsory execution in the future. In cases where the compulsory execution must be performed in a foreign country, extreme difficulty shall be deemed to be shown.[958]

611. The court having jurisdiction over the principal case, or the court at the place where the object of the provisional attachment is located, has jurisdiction over the application for provisional attachment. The court having jurisdiction over the principal case shall be the court of first instance in which the action is pending or to be pending. Notwithstanding, where the action is pending in a court of second instance, that court of second instance is deemed to be the court having jurisdiction over the principal case. Where the object of the provisional attachment is a creditor's right, or a proprietary right which must be registered, the place where the object of the provisional attachment is located shall be the place where the debtor domiciles or the object of security therefor is located or registered.[959]

612. A preliminary showing of the claim and the ground for the provisional attachment must be made. In cases of insufficiency in the preliminary showing, where the creditor has represented willingness to provide a security or where it is deemed appropriate by the court, the court may assess an amount for the security and issue a ruling for a provisional attachment upon the creditor's provision of such security. The court may still order the creditor to provide a security for the provisional attachment sought despite the fact that the preliminary showing of the claim and the ground for the provisional attachment has been made by the creditor. Where a husband or a wife petitions for a provisional attachment, based on the right to claim for distribution of the remainder of a husband and wife's property, the dollar amount ordered by the court for security shall not be more than one tenth of the petitioned amount.[960]

III. Provisional Injunction

613. A creditor may apply for a provisional injunction with regard to non-monetary claims for purposes of securing the satisfaction of compulsory execution. A provisional injunction shall not be granted unless there is a showing of impossibility or extreme difficulty to satisfy the claim by compulsory execution in the future should there arise a change in the status quo of the claimed object.[961] Where necessary for purposes of preventing material harm or imminent danger or other similar circumstances, an application may be made for an injunction maintaining a temporary status quo with regard to the legal relation in dispute. Such a ruling may be issued only where the legal relation in dispute may be ascertained in an action on the merits. The injunction may order certain prestation to be performed in

958. CCP, Art. 523.
959. CCP, Art. 524.
960. CCP, Art. 526.
961. CCP, Art. 532.

advance. The court shall accord the parties an opportunity to be heard before issuing the rulings except where the court considers it inappropriate to do so.[962]

614. The necessary means of effectuating a provisional injunction shall be determined in the court's discretion by a ruling to such effect. The court may, by such ruling, appoint a manager and order the debtor to conduct or prohibit the debtor from conducting specific acts.[963] The court may provide in the ruling of provisional injunction that the debtor may be exempt from, or move for revocation of, the ruling for provisional injunction by the debtor providing the court-assessed counter-security only in cases where the claim secured by a provisional injunction may be satisfied by money payments or where the provisional injunction will result in irreparable material harm to the debtor or where there exist other special circumstances.[964]

§7. Immunities from Jurisdiction

I. Legislative Provisions

615. Taiwanese courts' jurisdiction over a civil matter involving foreign elements is based on express languages of legislation or, in their absence, the underlying legislative spirit of the provisions for allocating domestic jurisdiction to courts. It is noteworthy that some entities enjoy immunity under international law. The CCP recognizes such reality and stipulates a supplement to the principle '*actor sequitur forum rei*'. Where a Taiwanese citizen is located in a foreign nation and enjoys immunity from the jurisdiction of such foreign nation, he/she cannot be sued in the courts of such nation. To ensure that justice prevails, the CCP stipulates that if no Taiwanese court can exercise jurisdiction on the basis of his/her domicile or residence, then the place where the central government is located shall be deemed to be the place of domicile of such citizen.[965]

616. Under the principle '*par in parem non habet imperium*', a country that exercises jurisdiction to adjudicate on the conduct of a foreign country would violate the basic principle of sovereign equality under international law as well as the principle of comity. Such principles lie at the very heart of international practice, and it is widely accepted that each country's sovereignty and dignity should be equally respected. Immunity is based on the classical concept of sovereignty in the sense that all sovereign states are equal and shall not be subject to the jurisdiction of another sovereign state without its consent. The courts would therefore not have jurisdiction to hear a plea against another sovereign.[966]

---

962. CCP, Art. 538.
963. CCP, Art. 535.
964. CCP, Art. 536 para. 1.
965. CCP, Art. 1 para. 3.
966. Taiwan High Court Civil Decision Shang 1224 of 1998.

617. There is no such comprehensive legislation on sovereign immunity in Taiwan similar to the US Foreign Sovereign Immunity Act 1976.[967] The immunity of foreign heads of states and foreign states are to be decided by the relevant principles under international law.[968] Just two years after the United Nations was founded, the ROC promulgated its Regulations Governing the Privileges and Immunities of the United Nations Missions and Their Personnel in the ROC[969] to grant the UN employees performing official functions in the ROC privileges and immunities. They are immune from all litigations arising out of their exercise of official functions. The scope limitation of 'their exercise of official functions' implies that the restrictive immunity approach was adopted.[970] These provisions can hardly apply since the ROC was ousted from the UN in 1971.

618. Taiwan promulgated its Statute Governing the Privileges and Immunities of Foreign Offices and their Personnel in the Republic of China[971] in 1982 to deal with the problems of diplomatic immunity. It stipulates that a foreign office itself and its personnel shall be immune from civil, criminal and administrative jurisdictions to the extent that the acts concerned are within the scope of their authorized functions.[972] An Article was added for the purpose of granting the office and personnel of the World Trade Organization (WTO) with the same privileges and immunities. It stipulates that the provisions on privileges and immunities of foreign offices and their personnel may apply, *mutatis mutandis*, to its offices stationed in the ROC and its personnel, and to the officials and representatives of its members for their exercise of official functions as well. [973]

619. Many countries are moving away from the doctrine of absolute immunity, which grants foreign sovereign absolute immunity from the jurisdiction of local courts for all transactions in which the foreign sovereign is involved. The move toward the restrictive immunity approach grants a foreign sovereign immunity for

967. The Foreign Sovereign Immunities Act (FSIA) of 1976 is codified at Title 28, §§ 1330, 1332, 1391(f), 1441(d), and 1602–1611 of the United States Code.

968. The United Nations Convention on Jurisdictional Immunities of States and Their Property was adopted by the General Assembly on 2 December 2004 and was open for signature by all States until 17 Jan. 2007 and may enter into force on the thirtieth day following the date of deposit of the thirtieth instrument of ratification, acceptance, approval or accession. As of 12 Oct. 2020, there are twenty-eight signatories to the Convention and twenty-two instruments of ratification have been deposited. *See* https://treaties.un.org/Pages/ViewDetails.aspx?src=IND&mtdsg_no=III-13&chapter=3&clang=_en (accessed 12 Oct. 2020).

969. Regulations Governing the Privileges and Immunities of the United Nations Missions and Their Personnel in the Republic of China (Lian-He-Guo Ge Zu-Zhi Ji Ren-Yuan Zai-Hua Ying-Xiang-Shou Zhi Te-Quan Ji Huo-Mian Ban-Fa, 聯合國各組織及人員在華應享受之特權及豁免辦法) was adopted in 1947.

970. *Ibid.*, Art. 2.

971. Statute Governing the Privileges and Immunities of Foreign Offices and their Personnel in the Republic of China (Zhu-Hua Wai-Guo Ji-Gou Ji Qi Ren-Yuan Te-Quan Ji Huo-Mian Tiao-Li駐華外國機構及其人員特權暨豁免條例) was adopted in 1982 and last revised in 1997.

972. *Ibid.*, Art. 5 and Art. 6 para. 1.

973. *Ibid.*, Art. 7-1 (effective on 1.1.2002).

its official act or act *jure imperii* only. A foreign sovereign is not immune to the jurisdiction of local courts if the action is resulted from a private act or act *jure gestionis*.

620. The restrictive immunity approach is adopted in the Statute Governing the Privileges and Immunities of Foreign Offices and their Personnel in the Republic of China. The following four exceptions are explicitly stated in it: 1. waiver of immunity by the foreign office; 2. a counterclaim with respect to any action brought by the foreign office; 3. an action arising from a commercial activity carried on by the foreign office; and 4. an action arising from disputed immovable property situated in the ROC.[974] Item 3 enunciates the policy of restrictive immunity.

II. Judicial Practice

621. The Supreme Court ruled on the permissibility of a suit brought against the Japanese Prime Minister and the Coast Guard of Japan in a recent case. It said: 'In accordance with the principle of sovereignty equality, with the exception that a sovereign voluntarily involves itself in a civil litigation, or where the subject matter involves private legal relations such as real property, commercial transactions or other non-governmental business activities within the territory of ROC, the courts of ROC will not be the competent court for adjudicating matters where foreign governments and its representative bodies are parties to a claim. The Japanese government's act to expel Taiwanese fishing vessels was not an act conducted in its private capacity (*acta iure gestionis*). Japan did declare its refusal to be subjected to the Taiwanese courts' competence to adjudicate on such matter. The action brought before this court is impermissible and shall be duly dismissed.'[975]

622. When the United States of America, the United States International Trade Commission and the United States Department of Commerce were sued for the asserted wrongful acts in the United States, the Taiwan High Court ruled in 1998 that such case is beyond the reach of Taiwanese Courts' competence and jurisdiction and shall be dismissed.[976] It quoted the Latin maxim '*Par in parem non habet imperium*' and stated that under international law, the right of equality is one of the fundamental powers of each State. The fundamental right under international law of a state will be infringed if it is subject to adjudication by the courts of another state. The exercise of adjudicatory jurisdiction is one of the supreme functions of a state's sovereignty. So, a sovereign state shall no way be subject to the courts' jurisdiction of another state unless it consented to. It is so required by the principle of comity in international law. Such principle is necessary for international relations and receives worldwide acceptance among scholars and courts around the world. Hence, all states shall respect the independence and equality of each state's sovereignty and

---

974. *Ibid.*, Art. 5 Item 4.
975. Supreme Court, Civil Judgment, Tai-Shang 46 of 2017.
976. Taiwan High Court, Civil Decision, Shang 12 of 1998.

its dignity. When a state asserts for its official act or act *jure imperii* immunity from courts' adjudication of other states, such courts shall dismiss the case as they will have no jurisdiction over the case.[977]

623. In its Civil Decision Kang-850 of 2012, Taiwan High Court ruled that the United States and other foreign governmental bodies can assert their immunity from suit initiated in the Taiwanese court. It mentioned that pursuant to international customary law, unless there is voluntary submission to the case or a treaty to the same effect is present, immunity is not waived. As a result, it ruled that the Taiwanese courts have no competence over the criminal case against them.[978] The civil case before this court as supplementary action to the criminal trial is therefore not permissible. It also ruled as *obiter dicta* that the Taiwanese courts will have no international jurisdiction due to the fact that both the act and its consequence took place in the United States. The Taiwanese courts are thus entitled to reject exercising jurisdiction over this civil case on the basis of forum *non conveniens* and *actor sequitur forum rei*.[979]

624. The Taiwan High Court's Civil Judgment Shang-Yi 875 of 2003 illustrates the judicial practice on distinguishing the acts of a foreign sovereign nature (act *jure imperii*) and acts of a commercial nature (acts *jure gestionis*). In this case, the Taiwanese plaintiff sued the Panama's Embassy for unjust enrichment resulting from receiving proceeds of the selling a luxurious limousine that belongs to the plaintiff but is registered under the defendant's name. [980]

625. Taiwan High Court ruled that the Panama's Embassy is not immune from jurisdiction of Taiwanese courts. Several reasons were included in the ruling. 1. The Panama's Embassy carries out sovereign functions of the Republic of Panama, and the ambassador is its diplomatic agent to Taiwan. 2. According to Article 31 Sec. 1 Vienna Convention on Diplomatic Relations 1961, the embassy and the ambassador may enjoy immunity from civil jurisdiction of the receiving state. 3. In light of the fact that the defendant is the embassy rather than the ambassador, although the ambassador is the representative of the embassy, the issue is about whether the embassy, not the ambassador, is immune from jurisdiction of Taiwanese courts. 4. The principle of absolute sovereign immunity used to prevail in the early age, yet the contemporary international practice and customary international law seem to prefer the restrictive sovereign immunity approach. 5. Along with the US Foreign Sovereign Immunities Act 1976 and the UK State Immunity Act 1978, the foreign sovereign acts are to be distinguished between non-commercial acts (acts *jure imperii*) and commercial acts (acts *jure gestionis*). 6. The nature of a foreign sovereign act shall be decided by the court where the issue is brought up. 7. In this case,

977. *Ibid.*
978. Taiwan High Court, Criminal Judgment, Shang-Su 1591 of 2001.
979. Taiwan High Court, Civil Decision, Kang 850 of 2012. The case was duly dismissed under the CCP, Art. 249 para. 1.
980. For discussions on this case, *see* Rong-Chwan Chen, *Private International Law in Practice: Analytical Study on Civil Cases with Foreign Elements* (國際私法實用-涉外民事案例研析) 1–6 (Wunan Publisher 2015).

the plaintiff alleged that the defendant had no power to dispose of the limousine that had been sold to him, the receiving of proceeds from the second sale conferred interest to the embassy at the cost of his damage and constituted an unjust enrichment. The nature of reselling the limousine to get the proceeds is commercial. It is far from the defendant's exercise of sovereign power. Therefore, the defendant is not immune from the civil jurisdiction of this litigation. The Taiwanese courts have jurisdiction over this litigation.[981]

981. Taiwan High Court, Civil Judgment, Shang-Yi 875 of 2003.

Chapter 5. Recognition and Enforcement of Foreign Judgments

§1. Basic Rules for Foreign Judgments

626. A judgment rendered by the court of a foreign country shall face the problem whether it may be recognized and enforced within the territory of the ROC. The CCP addresses the issues in Article 402. '(1) A final and binding judgment rendered by a foreign court shall be recognized, except in case of any of the following circumstances: 1. where the foreign court lacks jurisdiction pursuant to the ROC laws; 2. where a default judgment is rendered against the losing defendant, except in the case where the notice or summons of the initiation of action had been legally served in a reasonable time in the foreign country or had been served through judicial assistance provided under the ROC laws; 3. where the performance ordered by such judgment or its litigation procedure is contrary to ROC public policy or good morals; and 4. where there exists no mutual recognition between the foreign country and the ROC.'[982] '(2) The provision of the preceding paragraph shall apply *mutatis mutandis* to a final and binding ruling rendered by a foreign court.'[983]

627. Given the facts that the CCP focuses on the procedural problems around civil litigations, the above provisions apply to the foreign court decisions or judgments rendered through litigations. The Act on Non-contentious Matters addresses the issues on recognizing foreign non-contentious decisions. 'A final and binding judgment or decision rendered by a foreign court in a non-contentious shall not be recognized in case of any of the following circumstances: 1. where the foreign court lacks jurisdiction pursuant to the ROC laws; 2. where an interested party who is a ROC citizen asserted that the notice or summons of the initiation of action had not been legally served in time so that his/her rights cannot be duly exercised; 3. where the foreign court judgments or decisions are contrary to ROC public policy or good morals; and 4. where the mutual recognition does not exist, with exception that the foreign court judgment or decision is in favour of citizens of the ROC.'[984]

628. The above provisions in the Act on Non-contentious Matters, by distinguishing from that of the CCP, apply only and directly to the foreign court judgments and decisions rendered in non-contentious procedure. The enforcement of foreign court judgments is dealt with in the Compulsory Enforcement Act.[985] A foreign court judgment is not 'an irrevocable final judgment' which is prescribed as a valid title to compulsory enforcement under Article 4 of it.[986] Article 4-1 Paragraph

982. CCP, Art. 402 para. 1.
983. CCP, Art. 402 para. 2.
984. Act on Non-contentious Matters, Art. 49 para. 1.
985. The Compulsory Enforcement Act (Qiang-Zhi Zhi-Xing Fa,強制執行法) was adopted in 1940 and last revised in 2019.
986. Art. 4 para. 1 of the Compulsory Enforcement Act provides: 'The compulsory enforcement can be carried out on the grounds of the following enforcement titles: 1. An irrevocable final judgment. 2. A decision authorizing the provisional seizure, provisional injunction, or provisional enforcement,

1 of it hence adopts the same standards and states that: 'petitions for the compulsory enforcement on the grounds of an irrevocable foreign court judgment is permissible for compulsory enforcement only when none of the conditions enumerated under Article 402 of the CCP apply and a court of the ROC has approved the enforcement by a judgment.' Those provisions form the basic structural legal ground for recognizing and enforcing the judgments rendered by foreign courts. The following discussions focus on the situations prescribed in Article 402 Paragraph 1 of the CCP that a foreign court judgment may be refused to recognize.[987]

§2. Indirect International Jurisdiction

629. The legislature set the criteria for recognizing a foreign court judgment in the provisions mentioned above. The criteria need to be checked on a case-by-case basis in practice. The Supreme Court has addressed many details in its reported judgments. The first criteria is whether the foreign court rendering the judgment or decision has indirect international jurisdiction. As the condition is stated as 'the foreign court lacks jurisdiction pursuant to the ROC laws', and it is the fundamental that the foreign courts' direct jurisdiction does not fall into the realm of the ROC legislations, the jurisdiction here denotes indirect jurisdiction and is developed basically gradually by judicial practice.

630. In its Civil Judgment Tai-Shang 1943 of 2004, the Supreme Court discussed the requirement of the rendering court having indirect international jurisdiction in affirming the lower court's decision recognizing a divorce decree rendered by a Hong Kong court. It advanced the following opinions:

> 'There is no provision on international jurisdiction over divorce matters with foreign elements in the Choice-of-law Act 1953. Article 568 Paragraph 1 of the CCP shall be applied by analogy to it. It is this court's opinion that not only the courts of the country of which the husband and the wife are citizens, but also the courts of the country where the husband and the wife have their domicile and the courts of the country where the facts, upon which the action was based, occurred have jurisdiction over such case. According to Article 20 Paragraph 2 of the Civil Code, every person has, at any given time, one domicile, and no person has more than one domicile at a time. This provision is limited to regulating the household registration in Taiwan; the domiciles in foreign countries are not covered by its prohibition. The lower court held that the Hong

---

or any decision that authorizes the compulsory enforcement pursuant to the Code of Civil Procedure. 3. A settlement or mediation pursuant to the Code of Civil Procedure. 4. A notarized document authorizing the compulsory enforcement pursuant to the Notary Act. 5. A ruling of the court authorizing the compulsory enforcement that grants a mortgagee's or pledgee's petition to auction the mortgaged or pledged property. 6. Others that can serve as enforcement titles pursuant to other laws.'

987. For relevant discussions, *see* Fuldien Li & Yen-Te Wu, *Taiwan*, in *Recognition and Enforcement of Judgments in Civil and Commercial Matters* 87–91 (Anselmo Reyes ed., Hart Publishing 2019); Rong-Chwan Chen, *supra* n. 832, at 34–37.

> Kong courts have jurisdiction over the matter of the parties' divorce and the guardianship over their minor children on the grounds that the parties established their domicile in Hong Kong and the facts, upon which the action was based, occurred there. This holding is not contradictory to the law.'[988]

§3. Natural Justice

631. The second test is whether the foreign court judgment or decision is contradictory to the principle of natural justice or whether the parties' were neglected in the procedure. In a case of 2007, the Supreme Court discussed the requirement that the rendering court's proceedings be properly notified to the defendant in deciding upon the recognition of a divorce decree rendered by a New Zealand court. It stated:

> The purpose of Article 402 Paragraph 1 Item 2 of the CCP is to protect the interests of ROC citizens in litigation. 'Default' in the provision means that the defendant's essential right of defense was not sufficiently protected. The judgment at issue was rendered on 2 August 2002. The lower court did not investigate into the nature of the notice of litigation served by the Oakland District Court on 6 September 2001. The question whether it was legally served, and the question whether the appellant's essential right of defense was sufficiently protected remain to be answered. It was held that the requirements of Article 402 Paragraph 1 Item 2 proviso of the CCP were met on the grounds that the appellant was served by the Oakland District Court on 6 September 2001 and the appellant had contested twice the court's jurisdiction. This holding is not sufficiently conscientious and careful.[989]

§4. *Ordre Public*

632. The third test is whether the foreign court judgment or decision is contradictory to the public order or good morals in the ROC. In its Civil Judgment Tai-Shang 582 of 2007, refusing to recognize a foreign court judgment to distribute matrimonial properties between separated spouses, the Supreme Court discussed the role of public order and good morals (public policy) in respect of Taiwan. It stated:

> It is provided in Article 1030-1 Paragraph 1 of Taiwan's Civil Code that upon dissolution of the statutory marital property regime, the remainder of the property acquired by the husband or wife in marriage, after deducting the debts incurred during the continuance of the marriage relationship, if any, shall be equally distributed between the husband and the wife. The phrase 'dissolution of the statutory marital property regime' is interpreted as including the death

988. Supreme Court's Civil Judgment, Tai-Shang 1943 of 2004.
989. Supreme Court's Civil Judgment, Tai-Shang 582 of 2007.

of the husband or wife, divorce, annulment of marriage, invalidation of marriage, or a shift to other matrimonial property regimes. Article 1001 of the Civil Code allows a party to contend that the husband and the wife cannot cohabit, yet he/she is not allowed to apply for a judicial separation under the same circumstances. The separation of the husband and wife is therefore not a ground for dissolution of the statutory marital property regime. Neither the husband nor the wife can claim distribution of the remainder of the property upon their separation. The spouses were just separated. Their marriage still existed when the final judgment in question was rendered on 2 August 2002. The parties had neither shifted to another marital property regime nor dissolved their existing statutory marital property regime. It is thus not without any merit for the appellant to contend that the final judgment in question is contradictory to public order and good morals.[990]

633. Taiwan is among the countries which has encountered the problem of recognizing and enforcing foreign court judgments ordering punitive damages as rendered by the courts of common law countries.[991] In the Supreme Court's Civil Judgment Tai-Zai 46 of 2009, a UK court judgment was examined for recognition. A prominent German company had initiated in a court in UK an action claiming damages for the infringement of a trademark right, asserting that a Taiwanese company unlawfully registered and used a mark similar to its protected trademark in similar products. The UK High Court decided for the German company in a final court judgment. When the German company court brought an action seeking recognition and enforcement of the UK court final judgment, the Taiwanese company interposed many objections, yet the Supreme Court upheld the trial court's judgment approving enforcement.

634. The following findings and reasons were all upheld by the Supreme Court in that judgment: 1. the final judgment has been proved as authentic; 2. enforcement shall not be denied based on the fact that it is labelled differently than as provided in Taiwan's law; 3. the tortious act was committed in UK, so the UK courts have jurisdiction over this case of infringement; 4. the Taiwanese company was not deprived of its procedural rights; and 5. a Taiwanese court is not allowed to review the merits of a foreign court judgment. Its effects are not recognized in Taiwan if its results are especially incompatible with the basic rules or concepts of Taiwan's legal or ethical order. No evidence indicates that the same case has been decided in Taiwan. Even though the attorney's fee granted in such foreign judgment is not allowed to be included in a Taiwanese judgment, under the principle of international mutual respects, the UK court's final decision is not incompatible with Taiwan's public

990. Supreme Court's Civil Judgment, Tai-Shang 582 of 2007.

991. For further discussions, *see* Rong-Chwan Chen, *The Recent Development of Private International Law in Taiwan*, in Wen-Yeu Wang (ed.), *supra* n. 26, at 245–247.

order or good morals. 6. The UK High Court has recognized the effects of judgments of the Kaohsiung District Court and the Supreme Court in a decision of 1996, so mutual recognition of each other's final judgments exists between Taiwan and the UK.[992]

635. It has been this author's opinion that punitive damages are to some extent recognized in Taiwan's legislation.[993] Article 51 of the Consumer Protection Act[994] allows the consumer to claim for punitive damages up to three times the amount of actual damage as a result of injuries caused by a wilful misconduct of business operators. Article 32 Paragraph 1 of the Fair Trade Act[995] empowers a court, taking into consideration the nature of the infringement, to award damages up to three times the amount of the actual damage that is proven. Under such conditions, foreign court judgments of punitive damages shall, at least in some limited extent, be recognized and enforced in Taiwan to protect the party's interests. It is also suggested that the extent of recognition expand to cope with the development of the relevant domestic legal system. This opinion has been adopted by the Supreme Court in 2008.[996]

§5. Reciprocity

636. The fourth test is whether international reciprocity exists between the foreign country and Taiwan. Reciprocity means the facts that the courts of the rendering foreign country had recognized or is likely to recognize the ROC judgments in the future. So, neither international official relationship nor mutual diplomatic recognition of state or government is required. Reciprocity can exist between courts of two countries that had no official or diplomatic relation under international law. Recognizing the court judgments of an unrecognized state that does not recognize the ROC or Taiwan as a sovereign state in judicial practice is an expression of the judiciary independence from the political branches.

637. For example, the courts in the British Virgin Islands have not expressed their willingness to recognize judgments rendered by Taiwanese courts, this author urged the Taiwanese courts the recognize the BVI court judgments.[997] The Supreme Court adopted this opinion and ruled in a case of 2019 that the BVI judgments are recognized accordingly.[998] It seems that reciprocity lacks only in the situation that the rendering state had declared that the ROC court judgments will not be recognized in that country.

---

992. Supreme Court's Civil Judgment, Tai-Zai 46 of 2009.
993. Liu & Chen, *supra* n. 12, at 665.
994. The Consumer Protection Act (Xiao-Fei-Zhe Bao-Hu Fa, 消費者保護法) was adopted in 1994 and last revised in 2015.
995. The Fair Trade Act (Gong-Ping Jiao-Yi Fa, 公平交易法) was adopted in 1991 and last revised in 2017.
996. Supreme Court's Civil Judgment, Tai-Shang 835 of 2008.
997. Rong-Chwan Chen, *supra* n. 132, at 16–18.
998. Supreme Court's Civil Judgment, Tai-Shang 517 of 2019.

§6. Enforcement of Foreign Judgments

638. There is a difference between recognition and enforcement of foreign court judgments. Recognition concerns the acknowledgement of the effects of the recognized judgment. The criteria is whether the judgment meets the requirements that are set in the relevant provisions. It's unnecessary to file for a domestic court's ruling to validate the foreign judgment. The officials in household registry can decide to recognize or not.[999] An action is only initiated to declare the validity of the foreign judgment and to resolve the dispute between the parties.

639. Enforcement of a foreign judgment is based on the facts that the judgment is recognized and the judicial power to enforce it is ignited by the enforcing court. Article 4-1 of the Compulsory Enforcement Act thus provides that an application for compulsory enforcement of a foreign court final judgment may be permitted provided that such judgment did not meet any situation provided in Article 402 Paragraph 1 of the CCP and has been declared approved for enforcement by a ROC court judgment. The action applying for the permission of enforcement is subject to the jurisdiction of the court for the place of the debtor's domicile. Where the debtor has no domicile in the ROC, the action is subject to jurisdiction of the court where the object of the enforcement is located or where the enforcement action shall be performed.

§7. Court Judgments of the Mainland China, Hong Kong and Macau

640. It is worth noting that judgments rendered by courts in Mainland China are not characterized as 'foreign' court judgments in the constitutional and legal sense. Their recognition and enforcement are stipulated in Article 74 of the Act on the Taiwan Area and the Mainland Area. '(1) To the extent that an irrevocable civil ruling or judgment, or arbitral award, rendered in the Mainland Area is not contrary to the public order or good morals of the Taiwan Area, an application may be filed with a court for a ruling to recognize it.' '(2) Where any ruling or judgment, or award recognized by a court's ruling, as referred to in the preceding paragraph, requires performance, it may serve as a writ of execution.' '(3) The preceding two paragraphs shall not apply until the time when, for any irrevocable civil ruling or judgment, or arbitral award rendered in the Taiwan Area, an application may be filed with a court of the Mainland Area for a ruling to recognize it, or it may serve as a writ of execution in the Mainland Area.'

641. A Chinese Mainland court's divorce decree that has been recognized by a Taiwanese court has the same effect as a Taiwanese decree. The legal relations resulting from the status of a spouse or an effective marriage have thereby been adjusted.[1000] In the judicial practice, 'divorce conciliation documents' issued by the Chinese Mainland courts attract considerable attention and interest. The phrase

999. Liu & Chen, *supra* n. 12, at 651.
1000. Ministry of Justice's Interpreting Letter, Fa-84-Lu-Jue 9393 (27 April 1995).

'civil ruling or judgment' found in the above Article is interpreted very narrowly, so that other documents which are not deemed a 'ruling or judgment' are excluded from recognition, even if they are as effective as a 'ruling or judgment' in Mainland China. Divorce conciliation documents issued by Chinese Mainland courts are therefore not recognized, and such a divorce is not effective in Taiwan.[1001]

642. As a result, if the parties reached divorce conciliation in a court of the Mainland China and a divorce conciliation document was accordingly issued, the document has the same effect as a divorce decree in Mainland China. However, the conciliation document is not recognized in Taiwan so as to make the divorce effective. The same marriage which was dissolved in Mainland China by these divorce proceedings will continue to exist in Taiwan. The limping marriage and limping divorce are the products of an unreasonable interpretation.[1002] The following provision was added in 2009 to pave the way to recognizing divorce conciliation documents issued by a court outside Taiwan: 'when a divorce through court mediation or court settlement is sustained, the marriage relationship is dissolved; and the court is required to notify the couple's household registration office.'[1003] But its influence on the judicial interpretation of the practice of the above Article remains to be seen.

643. The Supreme Court ruled in its Judgment Tai-Shang 2376 of 2008 that a judgment of Chinese Mainland approved for compulsory enforcement under the above Article is granted the effect to be enforced, but unlike a foreign court judgment, its effect of *res judicata* is not included in the scope of the recognizing ruling. The dispute can therefore be the subject matter in an action initiated in the ROC court.

644. Given the fact that Hong Kong and Macau belonged to foreign countries before their handover to China in 1997 and 1999, their court judgments deserve special treatment in ROC law. Article 42 Paragraph 1 of the Act Governing Relations with Hong Kong and Macau 1997 thus provides that 'in determining the conditions for the validity, jurisdiction, and enforceability of civil judgments made in Hong Kong or Macau, Article 402 of the Code of Civil Procedure and Article 4 Paragraph 1 of the Compulsory Enforcement Act shall apply *mutatis mutandis*.' The standards for recognizing court judgments of Hong Kong and Macau are therefore almost the same as required for recognizing foreign court judgments.

645. In its Civil Judgment Tai-Shang 1943 of 2004, affirming that mutual reciprocity exists between Hong Kong and Taiwan in recognizing each other's judgments, the Supreme Court explained the spirit of reciprocity. It stated: 'Furthermore, the mutual recognition provided in Article 402 Paragraph 1 Item 4 of the Code of Civil Procedure is interpreted to mean the mutual recognition between judicial authorities; it is different from the recognition in international law or political recognition. The mutual recognition between judicial authorities exists as soon as the

1001. Ministry of Justice's Interpreting Letter, Fa-85-Lu-Jue 9503 (23 April 1996).
1002. Ministry of Justice's Interpreting Letter, Fa-83-Lu-Jue 27860 (22 December 1994).
1003. CC, Art. 1052-1.

foreign court had concretely recognized Taiwan's court judgments, or if it can be objectively expected that it will recognize Taiwan's court judgments in the future.'[1004]

646. It was quite pleasing that the Taiwanese courts reversed their previous position and recognized the judgments rendered by Hong Kong courts in reliance on the author's advocacy and finding that one Hong Kong court had begun to recognize Taiwan's court judgments no later than 27 January 2000.[1005] It is noted in the court ruling that the court judgments of Hong Kong are reciprocally recognized by the ROC courts.

1004. Hong Kong is no longer a foreign territory to the ROC after its handover by the United Kingdom to China in 1997.

1005. *Chen Li Hung & Anor v Ting Lei Miao & Ors*, 2000-1 HKC 461. Before Hong Kong was handed over to the People's Republic of China and before this decision, Taiwan's court judgments were not recognized by Hong Kong courts for political reasons. Following this decision, the author advocated for mutual recognition on the basis of reciprocity and the courts followed with no delay. *See* Rong-Chwan Chen, *The Recognition of Hong Kong Court's Judgments*, 81 Taiwan Law Review (月旦法學雜誌) 32–33 (2001).

Chapter 6. International Insolvency Law

§1. CORPORATION INSOLVENCY

647. Corporations are legal entities with personality that were established under corporation law. There are two categories of jurisdictional problems around them. First, which court has jurisdiction over a litigation of which the defendant is a corporation? Second, which court has jurisdiction over a non-contentious matter of which the court is required by the Company Act to make a decision for the corporation?

648. The first category runs into litigations that is addressed in the CCP. A private juridical person or unincorporated association that has the capacity to be a party to an action may be sued in the court for the location of its principal office or principal place of business.[1006] No matter what nationality the defendant corporation has, the Taiwanese courts can exercise international jurisdiction over it if its principal office or principal place of business is located in Taiwan. A foreign juridical person or unincorporated association may be sued in the court for the location of its principal office or principal place of business in Taiwan.[1007] In other words, a foreign corporation with offices or businesses in Taiwan is subject to the court jurisdiction for the location of its Taiwanese principal office or principal place of business, despite that its principal office and principal place of business are located abroad. As mentioned earlier, actions against the foreign corporations that have not sought the ROC government's recognition or set branches within its territory face the problems of service of process in their own nation.

649. Corporation insolvency and its reorganization is specifically addressed in Company Act. 'Where a company which publicly issues shares or corporate bonds suspends its business due to financial difficulty or there is an apprehension of suspension of business thereof, but there is a possibility for the company to be constructed or rehabilitated, the company or any of the following interested parties may apply to the court for reorganization: 1. shareholders who have been continuously holding shares representing ten per cent or more of the total number of issued shares for a period of six months or longer; 2. creditors of the company who have claims equivalent to ten per cent or more of the capital from the total number of issued shares; 3. labour unions; or 4. two-third or more of the Employees of a company.'[1008] 'For filing the reorganization application by a company under the preceding Paragraph, the Board of Directors of the company shall adopt a resolution by a majority vote of the directors present at a meeting of the Board of Directors attended by over two-thirds of all directors.'[1009]

1006. CCP, Art. 2 para. 2.
1007. CCP, Art. 2 para. 3.
1008. Company Act, Art. 282 para. 1.
1009. Company Act, Art. 282 para. 2.

650. The filing for a company's reorganization falls into the second category which is dealt with by the Act on Non-contentious Matters. The matter concerning registration of a legal person is subject to the jurisdiction for the place where the office is located.[1010] The company matter with which the court is required by Company Act to deal is subject to the jurisdiction for the place where the company is present.[1011] Logically, the Taiwanese courts hear and decide the non-contentious matters as required by the Taiwanese law, therefore, they can exercise such subject matter jurisdiction over corporations which are governed by the Taiwanese law.

651. According to the Choice-of-law Act 2010, the Taiwanese law is applicable to the internal affairs of the domestic corporations which were established under Taiwanese law.[1012] The specific court for the place where the principal office of the corporation is located can exercise its domestic jurisdiction over the relevant matters. It is understandable that the substantive requirements are governed by the national law of the corporation and the procedural problems by the *lex fori.*

§2. Bankruptcy Law

652. Bankruptcy is a legal process that applies to a debtor who cannot repay debts to creditors. It can only be imposed by a court order. The standard and procedure are provided for in Bankruptcy Act.[1013] The bankruptcy matter is exclusively subject to the jurisdiction of district court for the place where the debtor or the bankrupt is domiciled; if the debtor or the bankrupt has a place of business, to the jurisdiction of district court for the place of business. If the principal place of business of the debtor or the bankrupt locates in a foreign country, the bankruptcy matter is exclusively subject to the jurisdiction of district court for their Taiwanese principal place of business. If the court of jurisdiction cannot be decided by the above rules, the district court for the place where the principal property of the debtor or the bankrupt is located can exercise its jurisdiction.[1014]

653. In simple terms, the Taiwanese courts have jurisdiction over a bankruptcy matter if the debtor or the bankrupt has a domicile or an office of business within Taiwan, or the principal property of the debtor or the bankrupt is located within Taiwan. The law applicable to the substantive problems in a bankruptcy matter is decided in accordance with the Choice-of-law Act. The procedure is subject to the *lex fori*. It seems the substantive problems included in the procedural rules are characterized as procedural in nature. The Supreme Court ruled in a case of 2005 that whether the debtor is capable of repaying the debts or shall be declared bankrupt is within the exclusive jurisdiction of the aforementioned court.[1015]

1010. Act on Non-contentious Matters, Art. 82.
1011. Act on Non-contentious Matters, Art. 171.
1012. Choice-of-law Act 2010, Arts 13 & 14.
1013. The Bankruptcy Act (Po-Chan-Fa, 破產法) was adopted in 1935 and last revised in 2018.
1014. Bankruptcy Act, Art. 2.
1015. Supreme Court's Civil Decision, Po-Kang 1195 of 2005.

654. With regard to the international effects of bankruptcy settlements or court orders, it is stipulated that a bankruptcy settlement concluded in abroad or a bankruptcy order rendered by a foreign court has no binding force over the properties of the debtor or the bankrupt which locate within Taiwan.[1016] This protective policy may raise the problem of recognition of foreign court judgments and the disharmony of rules of property around the world. The question whether a bankruptcy order rendered by a Taiwanese court has binding force or legal effects in a foreign country is governed by the law of such foreign country.

655. As the Bankruptcy Act was not adequate to solve the problems arising in the tide of consumer debtors, the Act on Liquidation of Consumers' Debts[1017] was adopted in 2007 to provide an easier procedure for the consumer debtors to seek settlements imposed by the court and to get an opportunity to freshly restart the adjusted legal relations with the creditors and other interested parties. The matters of regeneration or liquidation are subject to exclusive jurisdiction of the court for the place of the debtor's domicile or residence; if the court of jurisdiction cannot be decided by the above rules, the district court for the place where the principal property of the debtor is located can exercise its jurisdiction.[1018] The international elements are not addressed in this Act, it is likely that the practice in the Bankruptcy Act will be followed in a dynamic way to protect the consumer debtors.

1016. Bankruptcy Act, Art. 4.
1017. The Act on Liquidation of Consumers' Debts (Xiao-Fei-Zhe Zhai-Wu Qing-Li Tiao-Li, 消費者債務清理條例) was adopted in 2007 and last revised 2018.
1018. Act on Liquidation of Consumers' Debts, Art. 5.

Chapter 7. International Arbitration

§1. Basic Background and Legal Sources

656. As the ROC on Taiwan lost its UN membership in 1970, it is not allowed either to sign or to accede to the New York Convention.[1019] It is worth noting that three years after the New York Convention was passed, Taiwan promulgated its Commercial Arbitration Act in1961 to promote arbitration as an alternative dispute resolution mechanism as well as to govern the proceedings of arbitration and enforceability of arbitral awards.[1020] The current Taiwanese arbitration legislation is the Arbitration Act of 1998. It adopted the spirit of the New York Convention and the UNCITRAL Arbitration Model Law[1021]. However, it differs in some respects with the New York Convention to reflect the reality that Taiwan cannot participate as a member and has to recognize and enforce foreign arbitral awards under the its own domestic criteria which can only relate tangentially to the international standards set forth in the Convention.

657. In spite of the fact that some major Articles of the New York Convention have been incorporated into Taiwan's Arbitration Act, differences still exist between the two legal regimes. The courts of Taiwan do not apply the New York Convention directly. Since it lacks the direct connection to the New York Convention, Taiwan was forced to codify the respective rules for recognizing arbitral awards of foreign countries of Mainland China, Hong Kong and Macau. The inevitable overlapping and conflict of the relevant laws brought about new problems within the Taiwanese legal system.[1022]

§2. Domestic Arbitration

658. A Taiwanese or domestic arbitral award is an arbitral award rendered in Taiwan according to Taiwan's arbitration procedure formulated by the Arbitration Act 1998. The basic legal components of a domestic arbitration and norms for deciding whether a domestic arbitral award is duly rendered and enforceable. With the detailed criteria for recognizing foreign arbitral awards, it is apparent that international arbitration (in Taiwan) is not distinguished out and stipulated in it.

1019. New York Convention of 10 June 1958 on the recognition and enforcement of foreign arbitral awards, 330 UNTS 3 (1959).

1020. Commercial Arbitration Act, Art. 1: 'With regard to a dispute arising from commercial activities at present or in the future, the parties may enter into an arbitration agreement in accordance with the present Act, designating a single arbitrator or an odd number of arbitrators to arbitrate such dispute. The arbitration agreement shall be in writing. '

1021. United Nations Commission on International Trade Law, UNICITRAL Model Law on International Commercial Arbitration as adopted on 21 June 1985, and as amended on 7 July 2006, UN doc A/40/17 and A/61/17.

1022. Rong-Chwan Chen, *Interpretation and Application of the New York Convention in Taiwan*, in *Recognition and Enforcement of Foreign Arbitral Awards – The Interpretation and Application of the New York Convention by National Courts* 945, 949–950 (George A. Bermann ed., Springer 2017).

I. Arbitration Agreements

659. Arbitration Act specifies arbitration agreements as the core basis of arbitration. It provides that parties to a dispute arising at present or in the future may enter into an arbitration agreement designating a single arbitrator or an odd number of arbitrators to constitute an arbitral tribunal to determine the dispute.[1023] The dispute is limited to those which may be settled in accordance with the law.[1024]

660. Arbitration is an alternative to litigation, but the court would be willing and is actually required by the ROC Constitution and laws to entertain the action if there is no valid arbitration agreement. In case the parties dispute the validity of the arbitration agreement in front of the arbitral tribunal and the tribunal decides to arbitrate, the court will allow it to decide in the first instance. The threshold issues of arbitration are dealt with by the arbitral tribunal before addressing the merits the case. If such issues are raised in litigation as a principal or preliminary question, the court undoubtedly has the authority to decide issues or to review the decisions made by the arbitral tribunal.

661. The Arbitration Act thus states the relationship between an arbitration and a court proceedings.[1025] In the event that one of the parties to an arbitration agreement commences a legal action contrary to the arbitration agreement, the court may, upon application by the adverse party, suspend the legal action and order the plaintiff to submit to arbitration within a specified time, unless the defendant proceeds to respond to the legal action. If a plaintiff fails to submit to arbitration within the specified time period, the court shall dismiss the legal action. After the suspension mentioned above, the legal action shall be deemed to have been withdrawn at the time an arbitral award is made.

662. According to the Arbitration Act, the arbitration agreements shall be in writing. Written documents, documentary instruments, correspondence, facsimiles, telegrams or any other similar types of communications between the parties evincing *prima facie* arbitration agreement shall be deemed to establish an arbitration agreement.[1026] No arbitration agreement shall be valid unless it was entered in respect of a legal relationship or a dispute thereto.[1027] Under the principle of severability and independence of arbitration clauses, the validity of an arbitration clause which forms part of a principal contract between the parties may be determined separately from the rest of the principal contract. A decision that the contract is nullified, invalid, revoked, rescinded or terminated shall not affect the validity of the arbitration clause.[1028]

1023. Arbitration Act, Art. 1 para. 1.
1024. Arbitration Act, Art. 1 para. 2.
1025. Arbitration Act, Art. 4.
1026. Arbitration Act, Art. 1 paras 3 & 4.
1027. Arbitration Act, Art. 2.
1028. Arbitration Act, Art. 3.

II. Arbitration Proceedings

663. The provisions about the constitution of an arbitral tribunal and the arbitration proceedings are the foundation of a domestic arbitration. An arbitral award duly awarded is enforceable in Taiwan. The arbitral award shall be binding on the parties and have the same force as a final judgment of a court. An award may not be enforceable unless a competent court has, on application of a concerned party, granted an enforcement order.[1029] However, the arbitral award may be enforced without having an enforcement order granted by a competent court if the contending parties so agree in writing and the arbitral award concerns any of the following subject matters: 1. payment of a specified sum of money or certain amount of fungible things or valuable securities; or 2. delivery of a specified movable property.[1030]

664. Furthermore, the court shall reject an application for enforcement in any of the following circumstances: 1. the arbitral award concerns a dispute not contemplated by the terms of the arbitration agreement, or exceeds the scope of the arbitration agreement, unless the offending portion of the award may be severed and the severance will not affect the remainder of the award; 2. the reasons for the arbitral award were not stated, as required, unless the omission was corrected by the arbitral tribunal; and 3. the arbitral award directs a party to act in contradiction to the law.[1031]

III. Arbitral Awards

665. Once an arbitral award is awarded, a party may only resist the other party's enforcement by applying to a court to set aside it. The Arbitration Act specifies the following circumstances that an arbitral award can be set aside:[1032] 1. the existence of any one of the three circumstance stated in prior paragraph;[1033] 2. the arbitration agreement is nullified, invalid or has yet to come into effect or has become invalid prior to the conclusion of the arbitral proceedings; 3. the arbitral tribunal fails to give any party an opportunity to present its case prior to the conclusion of the arbitral proceedings, or if any party is not lawfully represented in the arbitral proceedings; 4. the composition of the arbitral tribunal or the arbitral proceedings is contrary to the arbitration agreement or the law; 5. an arbitrator fails to fulfil the duty of disclosure as prescribed[1034] herein and appears to be partial or has been requested to withdraw but continues to participate, provided that the request for withdrawal has not been dismissed by the court; 6. an arbitrator violates any duty in the entrusted arbitration and such violation carries criminal liability; 7. a party or any representative has committed a criminal offence in relation to the arbitration; 8.

1029. Arbitration Act, Art. 37 paras 1 & 2.
1030. Arbitration Act, Art. 37 para. 3.
1031. Arbitration Act, Art. 38.
1032. Arbitration Act, Art. 40.
1033. Arbitration Act, Art. 38.
1034. Arbitration Act, Art. 15 para. 2.

if any evidence or content of any translation upon which the arbitration award relies, has been forged or fraudulently altered or contains any other misrepresentations; and 9. if a judgment of a criminal or civil matter, or an administrative ruling upon which the arbitration award relies, has been reversed or materially altered by a subsequent judgment or administrative ruling.

IV. Settlement and Mediation

666. Settlement and mediation are alternative resolutions to arbitration under the Arbitration Act. Parties to an arbitration may explore settlement options to their dispute prior to the issuance of an arbitral award. If the parties reach a settlement prior to the conclusion of the arbitration, the arbitrator shall record the terms of settlement in a settlement agreement. Such a settlement agreement has the same force and effect as that of an arbitral award. However, the terms of the settlement agreement may be enforced only after the court has granted an application by a party for enforcement and issued an enforcement order.[1035] Unless otherwise agreed in the arbitration agreement, the parties may choose to submit their dispute to mediation and jointly appoint an arbitrator to conduct the mediation. Upon the successful conclusion of the mediation between the parties, the arbitrator shall record the results of the mediation in a mediated agreement. Such a mediated agreement has the same force and effect as that of an arbitral settlement agreement. However, the terms of the mediated agreement may be enforced only after the court has granted an application for enforcement by a party and issued an enforcement order.[1036]

§3. Recognition and Enforcement of Foreign Arbitral Awards

I. Distinction of Domestic and Foreign Arbitral Awards

667. Eight chapters are included in the Arbitration Act, namely, Arbitration Agreements, Constitution of Arbitral Tribunals, Arbitral Proceedings, Enforcement of Arbitral Awards, Revocation of the Arbitral Awards, Settlement and Mediation, Foreign Arbitral Awards, and Additional Provisions. It is evident that Chapter 7 applies to 'foreign arbitral awards', while the other chapters apply to 'domestic arbitral awards'. In deciding which provisions are applicable to the arbitral award in question, the court is required to characterize the nature of it. The focus is on the definition and scope of 'foreign', as the domestic awards are those awards that are not 'foreign'.

668. The New York Convention defines the scope of foreign arbitral awards as 'arbitral awards made in the territory of a state other than the state where the recognition and enforcement of such awards are sought, and arising out of differences between persons, whether physical or legal' and the 'arbitral awards not considered

1035. Arbitration Act, Art. 44.
1036. Arbitration Act, Art. 45.

as domestic awards in the state where their recognition and enforcement are sought'.[1037] This definition cannot be applied directly as Taiwan's law.[1038]

669. In 1982, five Articles on recognizing the foreign arbitral awards were added to the Commercial Arbitration Act to reflect the international trend and legal needs.[1039] The added Article 30 provides: 'A foreign arbitral award is an arbitral award rendered outside the territory of the ROC. A foreign arbitral award, after an application for recognition has been granted by the court, shall be enforceable.'[1040] Article I (1) of the New York Convention was referred to in the legislative Bill when defining a foreign arbitral ward.[1041]

670. The Arbitration Act expands the scope of foreign arbitral awards to include arbitral awards rendered under a foreign law.[1042] It redefines foreign arbitral award as an 'arbitral award which is issued outside the territory of the ROC or issued pursuant to foreign laws within the territory of the ROC.'[1043] This definition deviates from the standard set in Article I (1) of the New York Convention.[1044] Under this provision, both an arbitral award issued outside the territory of Taiwan and an arbitral award issued pursuant to foreign laws within the territory of Taiwan are characterized and considered as 'foreign.'

671. The elements of 'territory' and 'applicable law' are adopted as alternative connectors to expand the scope of the foreign arbitral awards. The explanatory comments show that the term 'foreign laws' refers to all rules other than the laws of Taiwan, so that foreign arbitral awards include the awards made in accordance with the following three legal norms: 1. arbitration laws or rules of a foreign country; 2. rules of a foreign arbitration institution (such as LICA or ICC); and 3. arbitration rules of an international organization (such as the UNCITRAL Model Law).[1045]

1037. New York Convention, Art. I (1).
1038. *See* General Comment in the Bill for Revising the Commercial Arbitration Act, 71 Legislative Yuan Gazette (Li-fa-yuan Gong-bao) (no. 41) 39 (1982).
1039. Commercial Arbitration Act, Arts 30 to 34.
1040. Commercial Arbitration Act (Amendment) of 1982, Art. 30.
1041. *See* Explanation no. 9, 71 Legislative Yuan Gazette (Li-fa-yuan Gong-bao) (no. 41) 41 (1982).
1042. Explanation to Art. 47 of Arbitration Act 1998, 87 Legislative Yuan Gazette (Li-fa-yuan Gong-bao) (no. 31) 266 (1998).
1043. Arbitration Act, Art. 47 para. 1.
1044. Art. I(1) of the New York Convention states: 'This Convention shall apply to the recognition and enforcement of arbitral awards made in the territory of a State other than the State where the recognition and enforcement of such awards are sought, and arising out of differences between persons, whether physical or legal. It shall also apply to arbitral awards not considered as domestic awards in the State where their recognition and enforcement are sought.' The first sentence signifies that a 'foreign arbitral award' is an arbitral award made in a foreign country. If a non-foreign arbitral award is not considered domestic under national law, it can be treated in the same way as a foreign one. If Taiwan can accede to the Convention, it is possible to apply its provisions to arbitral awards made in the Mainland China, Hong Kong and Macau even though they are not considered as domestic or Taiwanese arbitral awards.
1045. Explanation to Art. 47 of the Arbitration Act and its original Bill submitted by the Executive Yuan, 87 Legislative Yuan Gazette (Li-Fa-Yuan Gong-Bao) (no. 31) 309 (1998).

672. Given the fact that Taiwan is not a member to the Convention, the Convention can automatically apply neither to a foreign arbitral award nor any other non-domestic arbitral award. The above provisions opened the possibility of allowing the latter to be dealt with as a foreign arbitral award. The provisions on foreign arbitral awards were thus ruled to apply to an arbitral award made under the UNCITRAL Arbitration Rules by the parties' agreement.[1046]

II. Compulsory Grounds for Denying Recognition

673. As mentioned above, a foreign arbitral award is an arbitral award which is issued outside the territory of the ROC or issued pursuant to foreign laws within the territory of the ROC. A foreign arbitral award, after an application for recognition has been granted by the court, shall have the same force between the parties as a final judgment rendered by court and may be a ground of execution. Similar to the policy adopted in the New York Convention that the grounds for refusing to recognize a foreign arbitral award should be exceptional.[1047] The underlying policy is to promote the recognition and enforcement of foreign judgments and arbitral awards. Taiwan courts can only recognize and enforce them if there is a lack of the negative factors.

674. The basic policy of the Arbitration Act is to favour recognition and enforcement of foreign arbitral awards. A Taiwanese court that is asked to deny recognition or enforcement of a foreign arbitral award can only review and consider the law and the circumstances alleged by the parties. Other situations are not good causes for the court to deny recognition.[1048] The following are the good causes for which the courts 'shall' refuse recognizing.[1049] When the courts are required by law to refuse recognition, their recognition will be in contradiction to the law even if no party ever argues so.

1046. Taiwan High Court's Civil Decision, Fei-Kang 61 of 2008.
1047. New York Convention, Art. V.
1048. Arbitration Act, Art. 48: 'To obtain recognition of a foreign arbitral award, an application shall be submitted to the court and accompanied by the following documents: 1. the original arbitral award or an authenticated copy; 2. the original arbitration agreement or an authenticated copy; 3. the full text of the foreign arbitration law and regulation, the rules of the foreign arbitration institution or the rules of the international arbitration institution which applied to the foreign arbitral award.' 'If the documents in the preceding paragraph are made in a foreign language, a copy of the Chinese translation of the same shall be submitted.' 'The word 'authenticated' mentioned in Items 1 and 2 of paragraph 1 herein means the authentication made by the embassies, consulates, representative offices, liaison offices or any other organizations authorized by the government of the ROC.' 'Copies of the application mentioned in paragraph 1 herein shall be made corresponding to the number of respondents and submitted to the court which shall deliver those copies to the respondents.'
1049. Arbitration Act, Art. 49 para. 1.

A. Ordre Public

675. The Arbitration Act states that a foreign arbitral award shall be refused recognizing if 'its recognition or enforcement is contrary to the public order or good morals of the ROC.'[1050] This provision's reference to 'public order or good morals' emphasizes that the recognition or enforcement results in such a contradiction to it.[1051] It does not mean that Taiwanese courts can review the merits of the award to confirm whether it contradicts the public order or good morals of the ROC.[1052]

676. Taiwanese law does not rely on the distinction between 'international public policy' *(ordre public international)* and 'domestic public policy' *(ordre public interne)* to guarantee the exceptional application of this clause. The *ordre public* clause can only be asserted if the foreign judgment or arbitral award has consequences that are markedly incompatible with the basic rules or concepts of Taiwan's legal or ethical order.[1053] In a case of 1984, the Supreme Court upheld the decision to recognize an arbitral award rendered by an American Arbitration Association tribunal in New York City, USA and ruled that neither a foreign arbitral award in which the reasoning is not attached nor a foreign arbitral award in which the amount of rendered compensation is very high is contradictory to the public order or good morals of the ROC.[1054]

B. Arbitrability of the Dispute

677. The foreign arbitral award shall also be refused recognizing if 'the dispute is not arbitrable under the laws of the ROC.'[1055] The arbitrable disputes are limited to 'those which may be settled in accordance with the law.'[1056] In other words, any dispute on a subject matter that cannot be disposed of by the parties will not be arbitrable. It is the opinion of this author that a dispute in the nature of public law is not arbitrable under the currently effective rules.[1057] Accordingly, the Supreme Administrative Court ruled in 2004 that since competent governmental authority must exercise its public function in adding to public listings of securities, the dispute relating to this issue is not arbitrable.[1058]

1050. Arbitration Act, Art. 49 para. 1 Item 1.
1051. Liu & Chen, *supra* n. 12, at 689.
1052. Chong-Shen Yang et al., *New Theories of the Arbitration Law* (Zhong-Cai Fa Xin-Lun, 仲裁法新論) 364 (Chinese Arbitration Association 2008).
1053. Supreme Court's Civil Judgment, Tai-Zai 46 of 2009.
1054. Supreme Court's Civil Decision, Tai-Kang 234 of 1984. *See* Chen-Huan Wu, R*ecognition and Enforcement of Foreign Arbitration Awards in the Republic of China*, 51 (Chinese Arbitration Association 2005).
1055. Arbitration Act, Art. 49 para. 1 Item 2.
1056. Arbitration Act, Art. 1 para. 2.
1057. Liu & Chen, *supra* n. 12, at 690.
1058. Supreme Administrative Court's Judgment, Pan 510 of 2004.

III. Reciprocity as a Discretionary Ground

678. Given the fact that Taiwan is not a member to the New York Convention, foreign arbitral awards cannot enjoy the benefits of mutual multilateral recognition under the Convention umbrella in Taiwan. The standards for recognizing rely on the provision of Taiwan's domestic legislation and the bilateral arrangements signed with foreign States. The Arbitration Act states that 'the court may issue a dismissal order with respect to an application for recognition of a foreign arbitral award if the country where the arbitral award is made or whose laws govern the arbitral award does not recognize the arbitral awards of the ROC.'[1059] Bilateral reciprocity is thus required to recognize a foreign arbitral award.[1060]

679. In judicial practice, the above provision is interpreted in a relatively liberal and flexible manner to favour recognizing foreign arbitral awards. It is established that the reciprocity requirement is satisfied if the foreign court has recognized or is expectedly to recognize Taiwan's court judgments or arbitral awards.[1061] Furthermore, the reciprocity requirement does not mean that the applicant has to prove that Taiwanese arbitral awards have been recognized by the foreign country in question, objective possibility of recognition in the future is sufficient for Taiwan to step forward toward mutual recognition.[1062]

680. When an arbitral award made by a tribunal in the United Kingdom of Britain was recognized, the Supreme Court emphasized that given the fact that there is no diplomatic relationship between Taiwan and the UK, and that Taiwanese court judgments and arbitral awards were not recognized in the UK, the competent Taiwanese court was still not bound to refuse recognition. It ruled that in order to implement the spirit of comity and to facilitate the international judicial co-operating, the court has discretion to decide whether to refuse recognition or not.[1063]

IV. Waivable Grounds for Denying Recognition

681. Upon the application for recognizing a foreign arbitral award, the Taiwanese courts are asked to review its conditions as required by the above provisions.

1059. Arbitration Act, Art. 49 para. 2.

1060. In Taipei District Court's Decision, Zhong-Sheng 17 of 1993, an arbitral award rendered in Malaysia was refused recognizing due to the position that Malaysian courts did not recognize and enforce Taiwanese arbitral awards. 2 *Selected Court Decisions and Judgments on Arbitration* (Zhong-Cai Shi-Jian Fa-Yuan Cai-Pan Xuan-Ji, 仲裁事件法院裁判選輯) 595–597 (Chinese Arbitration Association ed., Chinese Arbitration Association 1997).

1061. Supreme Court's Civil Judgment, Tai-Shang 1943 of 2004.

1062. Supreme Court's Civil Judgment, Tai-Shang 1943 of 2004. Such attitude toward recognizing foreign court judgments is also adoptable to foreign arbitral awards. Taiwanese courts are expected to recognize arbitral awards of a foreign country in order to pave the way for reciprocity and so the foreign country in future occasions will recognize Taiwanese arbitral awards. Liu & Chen, *supra* n. 12, at 691.

1063. Supreme Court's Civil Decision, Tai-Kang 335 of 1986.

They can only refuse recognition when they shall or may do so. Foreign arbitral awards shall be recognized except when certain conditions exist. The courts 'may' refuse recognizing a foreign arbitral award by due request if any one of the stipulated situations exists. The Arbitration Act provides six Items to describe the situations in which the award may also be dismissed within twenty days at the request of the respondent.[1064]

682. The courts cannot refuse recognition due to the existence of the stipulated situation without the party's due request. So, the parties can waive its rights to deny recognition. It would constitute a waiver if the respondent did not request the court to deny recognition within twenty days upon receipt of the notice of the application. No affirmative intent to waive is required in this situation. However, a pre-dispute waiver of grounds for denying the arbitral award may only be raised as a defence in the court proceedings. Such a waiver will not necessarily preclude the court from reviewing the arbitral award for recognition. Although it may be considered as a disposal of rights by the party, its effects may not affect the court's decision where public interests prevail over party autonomy.

683. The six specified waivable grounds for denying recognition are as follows. (1) The arbitration agreement is invalid as a result of the incapacity of a party according to the law applicable to such party. (2) The arbitration agreement is null and void according to the law chosen to govern the agreement or, in the absence of choice of law, the law of the country where the arbitral award was made. (3) A party is not given proper notice of the appointment of an arbitrator or of any other matter required in the arbitral proceedings, or any other situations which give rise to lack of due process. (4) The arbitral award is not relevant to the subject matter of the dispute covered by the arbitral agreement or exceeds the scope of the arbitration agreement, unless the offending portion can be severed from and will not affect the remainder of the arbitral award. (5) The composition of the arbitral tribunal or the arbitration procedure contravenes the arbitration agreement or, in the absence of an arbitration agreement, the law of the place of the arbitration. (6) The arbitral award is not yet binding upon the parties or has been suspended or revoked by a competent court.

A. *Incapacity of Parties*

684. The first specified situation is that 'the arbitration agreement is invalid as a result of the incapacity of a party according to the law applicable to such party'. It is understood to be the law applicable to the party's capacity to act, and shall be determined in accordance with the relevant conflicts rule in domestic law,[1065] namely Article 10 of the Choice-of-law Act 2010. It literally adheres to the traditional principle of *lex patriae* to decide the party's personal law which governs his/her capacity to act. It is provided that the capacity of a person to act is not lost or

1064. Arbitration Act, Art. 50.

1065. Chong-Shen Yang et al., *supra* n. 1053, at 378.

limited because of a change of nationality by him/her; where an alien of no or limited capacity to act under his/her national law is of full capacity to act under the law of the ROC, he/she is deemed to be of full capacity to act with respect to his/her juridical acts undertaken within the ROC.[1066] It is noteworthy that by applying the principle of *renvoi*[1067], the law finally designated is therefore usually the law of the foreign party's habitual residence.

B. Arbitration Agreements

685. The second specified situation is that 'the arbitration agreement is null and void according to the law chosen to govern the agreement or, in the absence of choice of law, the law of the country where the arbitral award was made.' This provision specifies that the law applicable to the substantive validity of an arbitration agreement is the law agreed by the parties or in the absence of such agreement, the law of the place where the arbitral award was made.

686. A valid arbitration agreement grants the courts power to suspend litigation proceedings. An arbitration agreement is a separate and independent legal relationship from the principal contract.[1068] Thus, it is apparent that the validity of an arbitration agreement shall be governed by the law applicable to the agreement itself, which could possibly be different from the law applicable to the principal contract.

687. The governing law of substantive validity of an arbitration agreement is not stipulated in the Choice-of-law Act 2010. The choice of law rule for obligatory agreements embodied in Article 20 of it is not applicable to arbitration agreements. But it is this author's opinion that it can be apply by way of analogy. In case the governing law was not agreed on, and the law of arbitral procedure differs from the law of the arbitral seat, the law of the closest connection is the law of arbitral procedure.[1069]

688. Whenever the first or second specified situation is argued by a party, the court shall follow the sequence of conflicts rules mentioned above to decide the applicable law before stating whether the arbitration agreement is valid or not. Generally speaking, provisions of the Civil Code and other legislations of private law are mainly applicable to the 'domestic' civil matters.[1070] It has been established that private international law is mandatory and the courts are required to determine which law should govern in civil matters involving foreign parties before applying any law to the legal relationship in question.[1071] Thus, if a court jumped to apply

1066. Choice-of-law Act 2010, Art. 10.
1067. Choice-of-law Act 2010, Art. 6.
1068. Arbitration Act, Art. 3.
1069. Rong-Chwan Chen, *The Governing Law of an Arbitration Agreement Involving Foreign Elements*, in *Essays in Honour of Grand Justice Tieh-Cheng Liu's 80th Birthday* 865 (Taipei, 2018).
1070. CC, Art. 1.
1071. Liu & Chen, *supra* n. 12, at 197–198. A recent case reiterates the established rule. *See* Supreme Court's Civil Judgment, Tai-Shang 781 of 2020.

Taiwanese law to a civil matter involving a foreign party without considering the provisions of private international law, its judgment would be remanded by the superior court on the ground that it is in contravention to the laws and regulations.[1072]

689. In judicial practice, a court can only enforce the arbitration agreement at the request of one of its parties; no court is empowered to suspend the litigation proceedings *ex officio.*[1073] An optional agreement which subjects the dispute to litigation or arbitration empowers the parties with the authority to choose the procedure. Once a party duly chooses the procedure, the other party shall be bound by this choice.[1074] If a party chose arbitration as the way to resolve the dispute, and one of the parties commences a legal action contrary to their optional agreement, the court may, upon application by the adverse party, suspend the legal action and order the plaintiff to submit to arbitration within a specified time, unless the defendant proceeds to respond to the legal action.[1075]

C. *Notice of Proceedings*

690. The third specified situation is that 'a party is not given proper notice of the appointment of an arbitrator or of any other matter required in the arbitral proceedings, or any other situations which give rise to lack of due process.' If a party requests the court to review an alleged lack of due process, the court will review the situation and proceedings which led to the issuance of the foreign arbitral award. The criteria are not necessarily the same as required in domestic litigations.

691. In judicial practice, the party against whom the foreign arbitral award was rendered usually requests the court to refuse recognition in the name of due process. However, it is established that when a party unilaterally ignores the notice made pursuant to the relevant arbitration rules and failed to participate in the arbitration proceedings that this does not constitute a lack of due process.[1076] It is noteworthy that the due process requirements of a foreign arbitral award shall look to such foreign laws instead of the Taiwanese laws.[1077] However, the standard stipulated in Taiwanese law for due process has been stated to be a basic requirement to recognize a foreign arbitral award. A foreign arbitral award made under the UNCITRAL Arbitration Rules by the parties' agreement shall be refused recognizing if the respondent was not given proper notice in the arbitral proceedings as required by Taiwanese law.[1078]

1072. CCP, Art. 468.
1073. Supreme Court's Civil Decision, Tai-Kang 476 of 2001.
1074. Supreme Court's Civil Decision, Tai-Kang 390 of 2006.
1075. Arbitration Act, Art. 4.
1076. Chong-Shen Yang et al., *supra* n. 1053, at 378.
1077. The due process requirements of a Hong Kong arbitral award shall look to the Hong Kong laws instead of the Taiwanese laws. Supreme Court's Civil Decisions, Tai-Kang 88 of 1994 & Tai-Kang 82 of 2000.
1078. Taiwan High Court's Civil Decision, Fei-Kang 61 of 2008.

D. Scope of the Arbitration Agreement

692. The fourth specified situation is that 'the arbitral award is not relevant to the subject matter of the dispute covered by the arbitral agreement or exceeds the scope of the arbitration agreement, unless the offending portion can be severed from and will not affect the remainder of the arbitral award.' This provision deals with the difference between the dispute resolved in the award and the specific terms of arbitration agreement.

693. Under the above provision, the respondent can request the court to deny recognition of an award that is beyond the scope of the agreement to arbitrate. An award granting a remedy that is beyond the scope of the applicant's request concerns the discretion the arbitrators enjoy in making the award and whether the rules of arbitration were strictly followed. An award resolving a dispute that is not covered by the terms of the arbitration agreement has the similar concerns. They both fall into the fourth specified situation mentioned above.'

694. An award granting a remedy specifically excluded by the main contract concerns the discretion the arbitrators enjoy and the criteria they followed in making the award. It basically relates to the award's merit and unless characterized as harmful to the public order or good morals, the court might not be permitted to deny recognition.

E. Composition of Arbitral Tribunal and Compliance of Arbitral Procedure

695. The fifth specified situation is that 'the composition of the arbitral tribunal or the arbitral procedure contravenes the parties' agreement or, in the absence of such an agreement, the law of the place of the arbitration.' According to this provision, the arbitration agreement or the law chosen thereby are the basic rules that the parties cannot violate. In case no agreement was reached, the law of the place where the arbitration was made shall govern. If the rules chosen are not in accordance with the mandatory rules of the place of arbitration, the rules chosen shall prevail. It would hence contravene the agreement if the arbitrator was not chosen as agreed or stipulated by the applicable law or the law chosen to govern was arbitrarily ignored.[1079]

696. It is notable that the above provision applies only to the procedural problems. It is beyond the scope of the court's power to review the material results of the tribunal's resolution. If the composition of the arbitral tribunal was in violation of the South African Arbitration Law, an arbitral award made by such arbitral tribunal in South Africa should be refused recognition.[1080]

1079. Supreme Court's Civil Judgment, Tai-Shang 1100 of 2002.

1080. Supreme Court's Civil Decision, Tai-Kang 517 of 1992. Chinese Arbitration Association (ed.), *supra* n. 1061, at 587–591.

697. In a case to grant recognition to an arbitral award rendered in Japan, the Supreme Court ruled that a foreign arbitral award duly rendered after the parties' arguments on the merits and arbitrators' judgment in substance is different from an enforcement title that is not provided with the opportunity of substantive arguments.[1081] Since the parties chose to have concluded the arbitration agreement and to take the advantage of arbitration, and the qualified arbitrators are experts with professional experiences and prestige, they are not required by the law to discover the facts seriously under the evidence rules in civil procedure law. The arbitral award was rendered under Japanese arbitration law, and the Japanese court found no ground to set it aside in its decision. It shall therefore be recognized in Taiwan.[1082]

F. Legality and Effectiveness of the Arbitral Award

698. The sixth specified situation is that 'the arbitral award is not yet binding upon the parties or has been suspended or revoked by a competent authority.' The legality and effectiveness of the foreign award shall be reviewed in light of the law applicable to such arbitration rather than the *lex fori.*

699. A recognized foreign arbitral can be enforced as if it were a domestic one. A foreign arbitral award that has been set aside by a competent authority is no more binding on the parties. Its recognition shall be accordingly refused or revoked. However, if one party applies for a judicial revocation of such foreign arbitral award or appeals on its recognition, the enforceability of such award is not necessarily suspended immediately. As the parallel procedure of setting aside, revocation and appellation may cause troubles to its enforcement, 'the court at the request of the respondent may order the applicant to pay a suitable and certain security to suspend the recognition or enforcement proceedings prior to issuing any order for recognition or enforcement of the foreign arbitral award.'[1083] If the foreign arbitral award has been revoked accordingly, the court shall dismiss any application for recognition or upon request, revoke any recognition of the arbitral award.[1084]

700. In a case of 2014, an arbitral award rendered by Hong Kong International Arbitration Centre on 11 April 2011 was recognized by a Taiwanese court and was ordered to be enforced. The respondent appealed on its recognition and requested to suspend the enforcement. The Supreme Court ruled that the appellation on recognition does not have the effect to suspend its enforcement. Unless a suitable security has been decided by the court and paid accordingly, the enforcement shall continue without considering the finality of the recognition decision.[1085]

1081. Supreme Court's Civil Judgment, Tai-Shang 2448 of 2017.
1082. Supreme Court's Civil Judgment, Tai-Shang 2448 of 2017.
1083. Arbitration Act, Art. 51 para. 1.
1084. Chong-Shen Yang et al., *supra* n. 1053, at 386.
1085. Supreme Court's Civil Decision, Tai-Kang 121 of 2014.

V. Jurisdictional Issues

701. Questions of court jurisdiction were not directly addressed in the Arbitration Act. However, it states that 'the court in dealing with procedures of arbitral matters shall apply the provisions of the Act of Non-contentious Matters in addition to this Act, and if in the absence of any relevant provisions therein, apply *mutatis mutandis* the provisions of the Code of Civil Procedure.'[1086] Some principles established in Taiwan's procedural law are hardly without controversy, the principle '*actor sequitur forum rei*' in particular. The Supreme Court ruled that provisions in CCP shall apply in cases concerning recognition of foreign arbitral awards. Based on the principles embodied in Articles 1 & 2 of the CCP, a court in the place of the debtor's domicile, residence, principal office or principal place of business can therefore exercise personal jurisdiction over the debtor to enforce a foreign arbitral award.[1087]

702. In addition, the Taiwanese courts can also exercise jurisdiction over actions to recognize foreign awards if other factors stipulated in the CCP exist. For example, in matters relating to awards granted for proprietary rights, an action may be initiated against a defendant who either does not have a place of domicile in the ROC or whose domicile is unknown; where the defendant's attachable property or the subject matter of a claim is a creditor's right, either the place of the debtor's domicile or the location of the subject matter of a security shall be deemed to be the location of the defendant's attachable property or the subject matter of the claim.[1088] In matters relating to awards of debts or rights *in rem* of any real property provided as a security for such debt, an action may be initiated against the same defendant in the court where the real property is located.[1089] In matters relating to awards on the validity and effects of a contract, an action may be initiated in the court for the place agreed to by the parties as the place of performance of the contract.[1090] In matters relating to awards on negotiable instruments, an action may be initiated in the court for the location where the instruments are to be honoured.[1091]

703. A foreign arbitral award is not enforceable in Taiwan unless it is recognized by a Taiwanese court.[1092] Needless to say, the jurisdiction over the enforcement of a foreign arbitral award and its recognition shall be exercised by the same court. According to the Compulsory Enforcement Act, the issue of enforcement is subject to the jurisdiction of the court at the place where the thing to be enforced is located or the enforced act shall be performed, if such a place cannot be established, then subject to the court of the place of the debtor's domicile, residence, official office, principal office or office of business.[1093]

1086. Arbitration Act, Art. 52.
1087. Supreme Court's Civil Decision, Tai-Shang 511 of 2001.
1088. CCP, Art. 3.
1089. CCP, Art. 11.
1090. CCP, Art. 12.
1091. CCP, Art. 13.
1092. Arbitration Act, Art. 47 para. 2.
1093. Compulsory Enforcement Act, Art. 7.

704. A Taiwanese court cannot generally decline to entertain an action for enforcing a foreign arbitral award. The exception being if the specific remedy granted in the foreign arbitral award cannot be effectively enforced within Taiwan since it is impossible for the court to request official assistance from foreign countries. In such circumstances, the Taiwanese court might exceptionally decline to entertain the action to enforce it.

§4. Arbitral Awards of the Mainland China, Hong Kong and Macau

705. It is noteworthy that under the current ROC Constitution, Taiwan, Mainland China, Hong Kong and Macau are respectively treated as one region or area within it.[1094] So, arbitral awards made in the Mainland China, Hong Kong or Macau or made pursuant to their laws are arbitral award of a 'sister region' rather than of a foreign country to Taiwan. The provisions on foreign arbitral awards cannot apply to them.

706. Before their handover to China, Hong Kong and Macau are foreign territories and the arbitral awards made within them are foreign arbitral awards. After their handover, the provisions on foreign arbitral awards shall no apply 'directly' to arbitral awards made in Hong Kong or Macau. The Act Governing Relations with Hong Kong and Macau thus provides: 'Article 30 through Article 34 of the Commercial Arbitration Act shall apply *mutatis mutandis* to the validity, petition for court recognition, and suspension of execution proceedings in cases involving civil arbitral awards made in Hong Kong or Macau.'[1095] Since the standards of refusing recognition are the same, some cases indicate that the courts ignored the difference between the treatments before and after the handover. For example, an arbitral award rendered by Hong Kong International Arbitration Centre on 11 April 2011 was treated as a foreign arbitral award and enforced in 2014 without mentioning the Act Governing the Relations with Hong Kong and Macau.[1096]

707. It is stated that an arbitral award rendered in the Mainland Area, under the condition that it is not contrary to the public order or good morals of the Taiwan Area, may be filed with a court for a ruling to recognize it.[1097] A recognized arbitral award may serve as a writ of execution. In a case of 2015, the Supreme Court distinguished the provisions in the Act Governing Relations with Hong Kong and Macau and that in the Act on the Taiwan Area and the Mainland Area, and ruled

1094. ROC Constitution, Art. 4 provides: 'The territory of the Republic of China according to its existing national boundaries shall not be altered except by resolution of the National Assembly.' Art. 11 of the Additional Articles of the ROC Constitution of 2005 says: 'Rights and obligations between the people of the Chinese mainland area and those of the free area, and the disposition of other related affairs may be specified by law.' The distinction between a foreign country and a sister region or area is thus demanded in legislative and judicial practice. For a brief discussion, *see* Rong-Chwan Chen, *supra* n. 832, at 19–20.
1095. Act Governing Relations with Hong Kong and Macau, Art. 42 para. 2.
1096. Supreme Court's Civil Decision, Tai-Kang 121 of 2014.
1097. Act on the Taiwan Area and the Mainland Area, Art. 74 para. 1.

that the effects of the arbitral awards recognized under the two acts are different.[1098] It also ruled that although the recognized arbitral award rendered in the Mainland China has the effect to be enforced in Taiwan as an enforcement title, it does not have the same effect of *res judicata* as an irrevocable court judgment. Therefore, under Article 14 Paragraph 2 of the Compulsory Enforcement Act, the debtor may, prior to the conclusion of the compulsory enforcement proceedings, institute an objection suit if the claim does not exist or the events extinguishing or preventing the creditors' claim arise before the enforcement title is created.[1099]

1098. Supreme Court's Civil Judgment, Tai-Shang 33 of 2015.
1099. Supreme Court's Civil Judgment, Tai-Shang 33 of 2015.

Annex: Act Governing the Choice of Law in Civil Matters Involving Foreign Elements

Translated by Rong-Chwan Chen (University Distinguished Professor of Law, National Taipei University) in consultation with Frederick Tse-shyang Chen (Professor of Law Emeritus, Quinnipiac University) and Jamison Wilcox (Associate Professor of Law, Quinnipiac University)

Chapter I: General Principles

Article 1

Civil matters involving foreign elements are governed, in the absence of any provisions in this Act, by the provisions of other statutes; in the absence of applicable provisions in other statutes, by the principles of law.

Article 2

Where the applicable law in accordance with this Act is the national law of a party, but such party has multiple nationalities, the national law is the law of the nationality most closely connected with the party.

Article 3

Where the applicable law in accordance with this Act is the national law of a party, but the party is stateless, the law of the place in which the party is domiciled is applied.

Article 4

Where the applicable law in accordance with this Act is the law of the place in which a party is domiciled, but the party has multiple domiciles, the law of the domicile most closely connected with the party is applied.

If no domicile of a party can be established, the law of the place in which the party resides is applied.

Where a party has multiple residences, the law of the residence most closely connected with the party is applied. If no residence of a party can be established, the law of the place in which the party is present is applied.

Article 5

Where reference is made by this Act to the national law of a party, but the national law of the party differs by reference to sub-national region or another factor, the applicable law is the law as indicated by the rules on choice of law of that national law; if the rules on choice of law of that national law are unclear, the law with which the party is most closely connected, whether by region or by the other factor, is applied.

Article 6

Where this Act provides that the national law of a party is applicable, but the national law of the party indicates that another law should govern the legal relation in question, such other law is applied. However, if the national law of the party or the other law indicates, in turn, the law of the Republic of China as applicable, the internal law of the Republic of China is applied.

Article 7

Where a party to a civil matter involving foreign elements evades a compulsory provision or a prohibition of the law of the Republic of China, that compulsory provision or prohibition is nevertheless applied.

Article 8

Where this Act provides that the law of a foreign State is applicable, if the result of such application leads to a violation of the public order or *boni mores* of the Republic of China, that law of the foreign State is not applied.

Chapter II: The Subject of Rights

Article 9

The legal capacity of a person is governed by his/her national law.

Article 10

(1) The capacity of a person to act is governed by his/her national law.
(2) The capacity of a person to act is not lost or limited because of a change of nationality by him/her.
(3) Where an alien of no or limited capacity to act under his/her national law is of full capacity to act under the law of the Republic of China, he/she is deemed to be of full capacity to act with respect to his juridical acts undertaken within the Republic of China.
(4) The preceding paragraph does not apply to a juridical act governed by family law or law of succession or to a juridical act regarding immovable property located in a foreign State.

Article 11

(1) Where an alien having a domicile or residence within the Republic of China has disappeared, a declaration of death of that alien may be decreed with respect to his property located within the Republic of China or with respect to those legal relations affecting him that are required to be determined by reference to the law of the Republic of China.
(2) A declaration of death of an alien may be decreed in accordance with the law of the Republic of China and without regard to the limitations mentioned in the preceding paragraph, upon the application of the spouse or a lineal relative by blood of the disappeared alien if the spouse or lineal relative is a national of the Republic of China and has a domicile or residence within the Republic of China.
(3) The effect of a declaration of death decreed under either of the preceding two paragraphs is governed by the law of the Republic of China.

Article 12

(1) Where there is a valid ground to declare guardianship or curatorship in respect of an alien under both his/her national law and the law of the Republic of China, a declaration of guardianship or curatorship may be decreed if he/she has a domicile or residence within the Republic of China.
(2) The effect of a declaration of guardianship or curatorship decreed under the preceding paragraph is governed by the law of the Republic of China.

Article 13

The national law of a legal person is the law under which it was incorporated.

Article 14

The following internal affairs of an alien legal person are governed by its national law:

(1) The incorporation, legal nature, legal capacity and capacity to act of the legal person;
(2) The acquisition or withdrawal of membership in the corporation;
(3) The rights and obligations of membership in the corporation;
(4) The organs and organization of the legal person;
(5) The representative of the legal person and the limitation on his/her power of representation;
(6) The internal distribution of liability toward a third person between the legal person and its organs;
(7) The amendment of the bylaws;
(8) The dissolution and liquidation of the legal person; and
(9) Other internal affairs of the legal person.

Article 15

If an alien legal person establishes a branch under the law of the Republic of China, the internal affairs of that branch are governed by the law of the Republic of China.

Chapter III: Formal Requisites of Juridical Acts; Agency

Article 16

The formal requisites of a juridical act; are governed by the law applicable to the act. However, a juridical act that conforms to the formal requisites provided for in the law of the place where the act was undertaken is also effective; where a juridical act is undertaken at different places, it is effective if it conforms to the formal requisites of the law of any one of the places.

Article 17

Where an agent's authority is conferred by a juridical act, the formation of the agency and the relationship between the principal and the agent are governed by the law expressly chosen by them; in the absence of an express choice, by the law of the place with which the agency relationship is most closely connected.

Article 18

Where an agent undertakes a juridical act in the name of the principal with a third person, as between the principal and the third person, the existence, extent, and effect of an exercise of the agent's authority is governed by the law as expressly chosen by the principal and the third person; in the absence of an express choice, by the law of the place with which the act undertaken by the agent is most closely connected.

Article 19

Where an agent undertakes a juridical act in the name of the principal with a third person, as between the third person and the agent, the legal effect of the agent's acting with, in excess of, or without authority is governed by the applicable law as provided in the preceding Article.

Chapter IV: Obligations

Article 20

(1) The applicable law regarding the formation and effect of a juridical act which results in a relationship of obligation is determined by the intention of the parties.
(2) Where there is no express intention of the parties or their express intention is void under the applicable law determined by them, the formation and effect of the juridical act are governed by the law which is most closely connected with the juridical act.
(3) Where among the obligations resulting from a juridical act there is a characteristic one, the law of the domicile of the party obligated under the characteristic obligation at the time he /she undertook the juridical act is presumed to be the most closely connected law. However, where a juridical act concerns immovable property, the law of the place where the immovable property is located is presumed to be the most closely connected law.

Article 21

(1) Where a juridical act results in the creation of rights on a negotiable instrument, the formation and effect of the act are governed by the law determined by the intention of the parties.
(2) However, where there is no express intention of the parties or their express intention is void under the applicable law determined by them, the law of the place where the juridical act was undertaken governs; where the place of the juridical act is unclear, the law of the place of payment governs.
(3) Formal requisites of a juridical act undertaken for the purpose of exercising or preserving a right on a negotiable instrument are governed by the law of the place of the act.

Article 22

Where a juridical act results in an obligation on a security made payable to order or to bearer, and is not governed by Article 21, the formation and effect of the act are governed by the law of the place where the act was performed; where the place of the act is unclear, by the law of the place of payment.

Article 23

An obligation arising from a management of the affairs of another without mandate (‘*negotiorum gestio*’) is governed by the law of the place where the management was undertaken.

Annex, Chapter IV: Obligations

Article 24

An obligation arising from an unjust enrichment is governed by the law of the place where the enrichment was received. However, if the unjust enrichment arises from an intended performance of an obligation, the obligation of the enriched party is governed by the law applicable to the legal relationship which gave rise to the intended performance.

Article 25

An obligation arising from a tort is governed by the law of the place where the tort was committed. However, if another law is the law most closely connected with the tort, it governs.

Article 26

Where an injury has resulted from an ordinary use or consumption of an article of commerce, the legal relationship between the injured person and the manufacturer is governed by the national law of the latter. However, where the manufacturer has agreed in advance or where the manufacturer could have foreseen that the article would be sold in a place whose law is one of the three mentioned below, the law of that place is applied, if the injured person chooses that law as the applicable law:

a. The law of the place of injury;
b. The law of the place where the injured person purchased the article; and
c. The national law of the injured person.

Article 27

Where an obligation has resulted from a disruption of the order of a market by an act of unfair competition or of restriction of competition, the obligation is governed by the law of the place where the market is located. However, where the unfair competition or restriction of competition is produced by a juridical act, and where the law governing the juridical act is more beneficial to the injured person, said law is applied.

Article 28

(1) An obligation arising from a tort which was committed by means of publication, radio, television, internet publication or other medium of communication is governed by the law mentioned below which is the most closely connected with the tort:
   a. The law of the place where the tort was committed; if the place of the tort is unclear, the law of the tortfeasor's domicile;
   b. The law of the place where the injury occurred, if such place could have been foreseen by the tortfeasor; and
   c. The national law of the injured person, if the injury was done to his non-property individual rights.

(2) Where the tortfeasor referred to in the preceding paragraph is in the business of publication, radio, television, internet publication, or other medium of communication, then the law of the place of his/her business governs.

Article 29

The existence of a direct claim of an injured person against the insurer of the person liable for the tort is governed by the law applicable to the insurance contract. However, the injured person also may assert a direct claim if the law applicable to the obligation permits its assertion.

Article 30

An obligation arising from a legal fact other than those referred to in Articles 20–29 is governed by the law of the place where the fact occurred.

Article 31

Where the parties with respect to an obligation which arises otherwise than from a juridical act agree to the application of the law of the Republic of China after a suit has been brought on the obligation in a court of the Republic of China, the law of the Republic of China is applied.

Article 32

(1) Where a claim has been transferred, the effect of the transfer on the debtor is determined by the law governing the formation and effect of the transferred claim.
(2) Where a third person has provided security for a claim, the effect on the third person of a transfer of the claim is determined by the law governing the formation and effect of the security.

Article 33

(1) Where a contract of assumption is concluded between an assuming person and the debtor, the effect of the assumption on the creditor is governed by the law applicable to the formation and effect of the original obligation.
(2) Where a third person has provided security for the performance of an obligation to a creditor, the effect on the third person of an assumption of the obligation is governed by the law applicable to the formation and effect of the security.

Annex, Chapter IV: Obligations

Article 34

Where a third person satisfies an obligation on behalf of a debtor by reason of a particular legal relationship existing between them, the right of reimbursement of the third person against the debtor is governed by the law applicable to the legal relationship.

Article 35

Where an obligation borne by multiple persons has been performed in whole by some of them, the right to reimbursement of those who performed against the others is governed by the law applicable to the legal relationship between all of them.

Article 36

The time limitation of action for a claim is governed by the law applicable to the legal relationship from which the claim arose.

Article 37

The extinction of an obligation is governed by the law applicable to the formation and effect of the obligation.

Chapter V: Rights over Things (‘Rights *in Rem*’)

Article 38

(1) A property right in a thing is governed by the law of the place where the thing is located.
(2) A property right in a right is governed by the law of the place where the right is formed.
(3) Where the location of a thing has changed, the acquisition, loss, or change of a property right in the thing is governed by the law of the location of the thing at the time the decisive fact occurred.
(4) A property right in a ship is governed by the law of the nationality of the ship, and a property right in an aircraft is governed by the law of the State in which the aircraft is registered.

Article 39

The formal requisites of a juridical act concerning a property right are governed by the law applicable to the right.

Article 40

The law of the Republic of China governs the effect of a property right in a movable thing formed in accordance with the law prevailing in the foreign location from which it is brought into the Republic of China.

Article 41

The acquisition, creation, loss, or change of a property right in a movable thing during its transit is governed by the law of its destination.

Article 42

(1) A right in an intellectual property is governed by the law of the place where the protection of that right is sought (‘*lex loci protectionis*’).
(2) Any right in an intellectual property created by an employee in the performance of his/her duties is governed by the law applicable to the contract of employment.

Article 43

(1) The legal relationship arising from an ocean bill of lading is governed by the law specified as applicable on the bill; in the absence of specification, it is governed by the law of the place most closely connected with the bill.

(2) Where goods covered by an ocean bill of lading are claimed by multiple persons on the basis either of the bill or of a property right, the priority of the claims to the goods is governed by the law applicable to claims of property right in the goods.

(3) The provisions of the preceding two paragraphs regarding ocean bills of lading apply *mutatis mutandis* to determine the law applicable to the legal relationship arising from a warehouse receipt or a bill of lading other than an ocean bill of lading.

Article 44

Where a security is held by a centralized depositary, the acquisition, loss, disposition, or change of a right in the security is governed by the law expressly specified as applicable in the contract of centralized deposit; in the absence of express specification, the law of the place most closely connected with the security governs.

Chapter VI: Domestic Relations

Article 45

(1) The formation of an engagement to marry is governed by the respective national law of each party. However, an engagement to marry is also effective if it satisfies the formal requisites of the national law of one of the parties or of the law of the place where the engagement is concluded.
(2) The effect of an engagement to marry is governed by the national law common to the parties; in the absence of a common national law, by the law of the domicile common to them; in the absence of a common law of domicile, by the law most closely connected with them.

Article 46

The formation of a marriage is governed by the national law of each party. However, a marriage is also effective if it satisfies the formal requisites prescribed either by the national law of one of the parties or by the law of the place of ceremony.

Article 47

The effect of a marriage relationship is governed by the national law common to the spouses; in the absence of a common national law, by the law of the domicile common to them; in the absence of a common law of domicile, by the law of the place most closely connected with the marriage relationship.

Article 48

(1) Where the spouses have agreed in writing that either the national law or the law of domicile of one of them shall apply to their matrimonial property regime, the law agreed-upon governs.
(2) Where there is no agreement or where their agreement is void under the applicable law of the preceding paragraph, the matrimonial property regime of the spouses is governed by the national law common to them; in the absence of a common national law, by the law of domicile common to them; in the absence of a common law of domicile, by the law of residence common to them; in the absence of a common law of residence, by the law of the place most closely connected with their marriage relationship.
(3) With respect to the immovable property of the spouses, if the property is subject to special provisions under the law of the place where it is located, the preceding two paragraphs do not apply.

Article 49

Where the applicable law to a matrimonial property regime is a foreign law, but where the spouses have undertaken a juridical act with a third person acting in good faith concerning a property located in the Republic of China, the effect of the matrimonial property regime on the third person is governed by the law of the Republic of China.

Article 50

Divorce and the effect of divorce are governed by the national law common to the spouses; at the time they reach an agreement of divorce or when a suit is brought for the divorce; in the absence of a common national law, by the law of domicile common to them; in the absence of a common law of domicile, by the law of the place most closely connected with the marriage relationship.

Article 51

A child is a legitimate child if he/she was a legitimate child at the time of birth under the national law of the child, of his/her mother, or of the husband of his/her mother. However, where the marriage relationship between the parents has ended before a child was born, the child is a legitimate child if he/she was a legitimate child under his/her national law when born or under the national law of his/her mother or of the husband of his/her mother at the time the marriage relationship ended.

Article 52

Where the natural father and natural mother of a child born out of wedlock become married, the status of the child is governed by the law applicable to the effect of the marriage.

Article 53

(1) An acknowledgement of paternity is effective if, at the time it is made or an action concerning paternity is filed, it is effective under the national law of either the acknowledging person or the acknowledged person.
(2) If, under the preceding paragraph, the acknowledged person is a foetus, the national law of the mother is the national law of the foetus.
(3) The effect of an acknowledgement of paternity is governed by the national law of the acknowledging person.

Article 54

(1) The formation and termination of an adoption of a child are governed for the adoptive parent and for the adopted child by their respective national laws.
(2) The effect of an adoption and its termination is governed by the national law of the adoptive parent.

Article 55

The legal relationship between parents and their children is governed by the national law of the children.

Article 56

(1) A guardianship is governed by the national law of the ward. However, the guardianship of a ward who is an alien, who has a domicile or residence within the Republic of China, and who satisfies one of the following circumstances is governed by the law of the Republic of China:
   a. Where, under the national law of the ward, a guardian should have been appointed for him, but there is no person performing the office of a guardian; and
   b. Where the ward is the subject of a declaration of guardianship in the Republic of China.

(2) The preceding paragraph applies *mutatis mutandis* to a curatorship.

Article 57

A relationship of maintenance, whether or not arising from a matrimonial relationship, is governed by the national law of the person entitled to maintenance.

Chapter VII: Succession

Article 58

A succession upon death is governed by the national law of the decedent. However, if a national of the Republic of China is an heir under the law of the Republic of China, he/she is entitled to inherit that part of the estate which is located within the Republic of China.

Article 59

Where an alien dies leaving property within the Republic of China, if, under the applicable law under the preceding Article, no person is entitled to take the property by descent, such property is dealt with in accordance with the law of the Republic of China.

Article 60

(1) The execution and effect of a last will are governed by the national law of the testator at the time of execution.
(2) The revocation of a will is governed by the national law of the testator at the time of revocation.

Article 61

In addition to the applicable law stated in the preceding Article, a will is also effectively made or revoked by following the formal requisites as provided in any one of the following laws:

a. The law of the place where the will was made;
b. The law of the place in which the testator was domiciled at the time of death; and
c. Where the will concerns immovable property, the law of the place where the immovable property is located.

Chapter VIII: Final Provisions

Article 62

The provisions of this Revised Act do not apply to civil matters which occurred prior to its entering into force. However, where a part of the legal effect of a civil matter does not occur until after this Revised Act has entered into force, the Revised Act applies to such part.

Article 63

This Revised Act enters into force one year after the date of its promulgation.

Selected Bibliography

Books and Articles

Basedow, Jürgen & Pissler, Knut B. eds, *Private International Law in Mainland China, Taiwan and Europe* (Mohr Siebeck 2014).

Basedow, Jürgen et al. eds, *Encyclopedia of Private International Law* (Edward Elgar 2017).

Boele-Woelki, Katharina et al. eds, *Convergence and Divergence in Private International Law – Liber Amicorum Kurt Siehr* (Eleven International Publishing 2010).

Brighnardello, Monica, *Carriage of Goods by Road, Rail and Inland Waters*, in 1 *Encyclopedia of Private International Law* 255 (Jürgen Basedow et al. eds, Edward Elgar 2017).

Chen, Rong-Chwan, *A Boat on A Troubled Strait: The Interregional Private Law of the Republic of China on Taiwan*, 16 Wisconsin International Law Journal 559 (1998).

Chen, Rong-Chwan, *A Comment on The Disputes of Guardianship over the Taiwan-Brazilian Orphan Wu*, 76 Taiwan Law Review (月旦法學雜誌) 147–158 (2001);

Chen, Rong-Chwan, *A Study on the Applicable Law to the Unjust Enrichments,* 8-2 Soochow Law Review 143 (April 1995).

Chen, Rong-Chwan, *Application of Foreign Public Law in Civil Matters with Foreign Elements*, 147 Taiwan Jurist (月旦法學教室) 30–32 (January 2015).

Chen, Rong-Chwan, *Application of the Ordre Public Clause*, 1 Taiwan Law Review (月旦法學雜誌) 70 (May 1995).

Chen, Rong-Chwan, *Cautiousness in Applying the Principle of Forum Non Conveniens,* 142 Taiwan Jurist (月旦法學教室) 36–38 (August 2014).

Chen, Rong-Chwan, *Choice of Law and Statute of Limitation*, 74 Taiwan Law Journal (台灣本土法學雜誌) 111 (September 2005).

Chen, Rong-Chwan, *Conflict of Laws of Divorce: Judicial Practice and Legislative Development of Taiwan*, in *Convergence and Divergence in Private International Law – Liber Amicorum Kurt Siehr* 193 (Katharina Boele-Woelki et al. ed., Eleven International Publishing 2010).

Chen, Rong-Chwan, *Employment Contracts Involving Foreign Elements – Perspectives from Private International Law*, 166 Taiwan Law Review (月旦法學雜誌) 77 (March 2009), 167 Taiwan Law Review (月旦法學雜誌) 82 (April 2009).

Selected Bibliography

Chen, Rong-Chwan, *General Provisions in the Taiwanese Private International Law Enactment 2010*, in *Private International Law in Mainland China, Taiwan and Europe* 65 (Jürgen Basedow & Knut B. Pissler ed., Mohr Siebeck 2014).

Chen, Rong-Chwan, *International Jurisdiction over Disputes of a Foreign Domain Names: An Analytical Study on the Supreme Court's Decision Tai-Kang 1004 of 2015*, 351 Taiwan Law Journal (台灣法學雜誌) 7–33 (14 September 2018).

Chen, Rong-Chwan, *International Trade and Export Control of Cultural Properties,* 13 Chinese Yearbook of International Law and International Affairs 20–75 (August 2002).

Chen, Rong-Chwan, *Interpretation and Application of the New York Convention in Taiwan*, in *Recognition and Enforcement of Foreign Arbitral Awards –The Interpretation and Application of the New York Convention by National Courts* 945 (George A. Bermann ed., Springer 2017).

Chen, Rong-Chwan, *Jurisdiction and Law Applicable to Anti-competition Conducts*, 22-2 Fair Trade Quarterly (公平交易季刊) 93–162 (April 2014).

Chen, Rong-Chwan, *Jurisdiction, Choice of Law and the Recognition of Foreign Judgments in Taiwan*, in *Private International Law in Mainland China, Taiwan and Europe* 26 (Jürgen Basedow & Knut B. Pissler ed., Mohr Siebeck 2014).

Chen, Rong-Chwan, *Legislation and Practice on Choice of Court Agreements in Taiwan*, in *Optional Choice of Court Agreements in Private International Law* 387 (Mary Keyes ed., Springer 2020).

Chen, Rong-Chwan, *New Directions of Private International Law: A Bird View of the Revising Draft for the Act Governing the Choice of Law in Civil Matters Involving Foreign Elements*, 57 Taiwan Law Journal (台灣本土法學雜誌) 207 (2004).

Chen, Rong-Chwan, *Parental Power Shall Not Be Characterized as Effects of a Divorce*, 32 Taiwan Jurist (月旦法學教室) 42–43 (2005).

Chen, Rong-Chwan, *Private International Law in Practice: Analytical Study on Civil Cases with Foreign Elements* (國際私法實用-涉外民事案例研析) (Wu-nan Publisher 2015).

Chen, Rong-Chwan, *Second Comment on the Disputes of Guardianship over the Taiwan-Brazilian Orphan Wu*, 17 Chinese (Taiwan) Yearbook on International Law and International Affairs (中國國際法與國際事務年報) 553–572 (2005).

Chen, Rong-Chwan, *Selected Essays on Private International Law* (國際私法各論集) (Wu-Nan Publisher 1998).

Chen, Rong-Chwan, *Succession to the Property Left by a Deceased Foreigner in Taiwan,* 5 Taiwan Law Review (月旦法學雜誌) 63–64 (September 1995).

Chen, Rong-Chwan, *Taiwan (National Report)*, in 4 *Encyclopedia of Private International Law* 2559 (Jürgen Basedow et al. ed., Edward Elgar 2017).

Chen, Rong-Chwan, *Taiwanese PIL Act 2010 (Translation)*, in *Private International Law in Mainland China, Taiwan and Europe* 453 (Jürgen Basedow & Knut B. Pissler ed., Mohr Siebeck 2014).

Chen, Rong-Chwan, *Territoriality and International Jurisdiction over Copyrights*, 207 Taiwan Jurist (月旦法學教室) 29–31 (January 2020).

Chen, Rong-Chwan, *The Applicable Law of the Assignments and Reassignments of Custodian for Children after Divorce: A Comment on the Supreme Court's Judgment Tai-Shang 1888 of 1993*, in *Selected Essays on Private International Law* (國際私法各論集) ch. 11 (Wu-Nan Publisher 1998).

Chen, Rong-Chwan, *The Applicable Law to the Assigning and Reassigning Custodian for Children after Their Parents' Divorce: A Comment on the Supreme Court Judgment Tai-Shang 1888 of 1993*, (Part One), 24 Taiwan Law Review (月旦法學雜誌) 93 (April 1997); (Part Two), 25 Taiwan Law Review (月旦法學雜誌) 92 (May 1997).

Chen, Rong-Chwan, *The Applicable Law to the Promissory Notes Involving Foreign Elements: Comments on Some Precedents of the Supreme Court*, 55 Taiwan Law Journal (台灣本土法學雜誌) 149–161 (February 2004).

Chen, Rong-Chwan, *The Application of Labour Basic Act in Labour Cases with Foreign Elements: Analytical Comments on the Supreme Court's Decision Tai-Shang 1624 of 2017 and Its Prior Judgments*, 358 Taiwan Law Journal (台灣法學雜誌) 23–44 (28 December 2018).

Chen, Rong-Chwan, *The Application of the Ordre Public Clause*, 1 Taiwan Law Review (月旦法學雜誌) 70–71 (1995).

Chen, Rong-Chwan, *The Bona Fide Acquisition of a Movable Property in Transit*, 11 Taiwan Law Review (月旦法學雜誌) 53 (March 1996).

Chen, Rong-Chwan, *The Characterization and Second Characterization in Private International Law*, 40 Taiwan Law Journal (台灣本土法學雜誌) 129–136 (November 2002).

Chen, Rong-Chwan, *The Characterization in Matters of Parental Power*, 32 Taiwan Jurist (月旦法學教室) 40 (June 2005).

Chen, Rong-Chwan, *The Characterization of and Applicable Law to the Sham Marriages Involving with Foreign Elements*, 75 Taiwan Jurist (月旦法學教室) 24–25 (2009).

Chen, Rong-Chwan, *The Characterization of the Damages Claim for an Air Crash*, 3 Taiwan Jurist (月旦法學教室) 32–33 (2003).

Chen, Rong-Chwan, *The Clauses Involving Foreign Elements in Bills of Lading*, 164 Taiwan Jurist (月旦法學教室) 27–29 (May 2016).

Chen, Rong-Chwan, *The Current Situation and Practice of the Conflict of Laws across the Taiwan Straits* (兩岸法律衝突的現況與實務) (Sharing 2003).

Chen, Rong-Chwan, *The Domestic Effects of an Insolvency Decree of Foreign Court*, 154 Taiwan Jurist (月旦法學教室) 30–32 (August 2015).

Chen, Rong-Chwan, *The Governing Law of an Arbitration Agreement Involving Foreign Elements*, in *Essays in Honour of Grand Justice Tieh-Cheng Liu's 80th Birthday* 865 (Taipei 2018).

Chen, Rong-Chwan, *The Immediate Application of Fair Trade Act to the International Licensing Contracts*, 131 Taiwan Jurist (月旦法學教室) 36–38 (2013).

Chen, Rong-Chwan, *The Inheritance of Stock Shares and Administration of Estate in British Virgin Island: Analytical Comments on the Taiwan High Court's Judgement Shang 493 of 2014*, 366 Taiwan Law Journal (台灣法學雜誌) 1–28 (28 April 2019).

Chen, Rong-Chwan, *The Last Will of an Overseas Taiwanese Notarized Abroad*, 29 Taiwan Jurist (月旦法學教室) 40 (March 2005).

Selected Bibliography

Chen, Rong-Chwan, *The Law Applicable to Compensation for Foreign Workers*, 80 Taiwan Jurist (月旦法學教室) 22–23 (2009).

Chen, Rong-Chwan, *The Law Applicable to Compensation for Foreign Workers*, 80 Taiwan Jurist (月旦法學教室) 22–23 (June 2009).

Chen, Rong-Chwan, *The Law Applicable to Laying Off by a Foreign Corporation*, 197 Taiwan Jurist (月旦法學教室) 15–17 (March 2019).

Chen, Rong-Chwan, *The Law Applicable to the Jurisdictional Agreement with foreign Elements*, 7 Taiwan Law Review (月旦法學雜誌) 39–40 (November 1995).

Chen, Rong-Chwan, *The Law Applicable to the Statute of Limitation*, 74 Taiwan Law Journal (台灣本土法學雜誌) 111–122 (September 2005).

Chen, Rong-Chwan, *The Law Applicable to Torts and Maintenance Obligations*, 71 Taiwan Jurist (月旦法學教室) 24–25 (2008)

Chen, Rong-Chwan, *The Legal Foundation of Direct Renvoi*, 13 Taiwan Law Review (月旦法學雜誌) 67–68 (1996).

Chen, Rong-Chwan, *The New Way of Thinking for Codification of Private International Law: The Substantive Justice in Conflicts Rules*, 89 Taiwan Law Review (月旦法學雜誌) 50–61 (October 2002).

Chen, Rong-Chwan, *The Obligation Arisen from Clearing the Foreign Sunken Ship*, 19 Taiwan Jurist (月旦法學教室) 30–31 (May 2004).

Chen, Rong-Chwan, *The Ordre Public in a Same-Sex Marriage: A Comment on Taipei High Administrative Court's Recent Judgment*, 219 Taiwan Jurist (月旦法學教室) 27–31 (May 2021).

Chen, Rong-Chwan, *The Preliminary or Incidental Question in Private International Law*, 12 Taiwan Law Review (月旦法學雜誌) 62–63 (April 1996).

Chen, Rong-Chwan, *The Principle of Party Autonomy*, 6 Taiwan Law Review (月旦法學雜誌) 56–57 (1995).

Chen, Rong-Chwan, *The Problem of Adaptation or Adjustment in Private International Law*, 145 China Law Journal (法學叢刊) 111 (January 1992).

Chen, Rong-Chwan, *The Problem of Gambling Debt in Private International Law*, 2 Taiwan Law Review (月旦法學雜誌) 52–53 (1995).

Chen, Rong-Chwan, *The Recent Development of Private International Law in Taiwan*, in *Codification in East Asia* 235–245 (Wen-Yeu Wang ed., Springer 2014).

Chen, Rong-Chwan, *The Recognition of Hong Kong Court's Judgments*, 81 Taiwan Law Review (月旦法學雜誌) 32–33 (2001).

Chen, Rong-Chwan, *The Recovery of Stolen Cultural Objects in Private International Law*, 14-1 Soochow Law Review 67–128 (August 2002);

Chen, Rong-Chwan, *The Representatives of the US Corporations*, 1 Taiwan Jurist (月旦法學教室) 34–35 (November 2002)

Chinese Arbitration Association ed., 2 *Selected Court Decisions and Judgments on Arbitration* (仲裁事件法院裁判選輯) (Chinese Arbitration Association 1997).

de Gonzalo, Marco Lopez, *Carriage of Passengers*, in 1 *Encyclopedia of Private International Law* 269 (Jürgen Basedow et al. ed., Edward Elgar 2017).

Hague Conference of Private International Law ed., *Collection of Conventions (1951–2009)* (Intersentia 2009).

Hsu, Yao-Ming, *Property Law in Taiwan*, in *Private International Law in Mainland China, Taiwan and Europe* 119 (Jürgen Basedow & Knut B. Pissler ed., Mohr Siebeck 2014).

Ivaldi, Paola, *Carriage of Goods by Sea*, in 1 *Encyclopedia of Private International Law* 261 (Jürgen Basedow et al. eds, Edward Elgar 2017).

Judicial Yuan ed., 1 *Materials on Studying and Revising the Choice-of-law Act by the Judicial Yuan* (司法院涉外民事法律適用法研究修正資料彙編) (Judicial Yuan 2002).

Judicial Yuan ed., 2 *Materials on Studying and Revising the Choice-of-law Act by the Judicial Yuan* (司法院涉外民事法律適用法研究修正資料彙編) (Judicial Yuan 2011).

Li, Fuldien & Chen, Rong-Chwan, *Taiwan*, in *Direct Jurisdiction: Asian Perspectives* chap. 4 (Anselmo Reyes & Wilson Lui eds, Hart Publishing 2021).

Li, Fuldien & Wu, Yen-Te, *Taiwan*, in *Recognition and Enforcement of Judgments in Civil and Commercial Matters* 87 (Anselmo Reyes ed., Hart Publishing 2019).

Lin, En-Wei, *New Private International Law in Taiwan: Negotiorum Gestio, Unjust Enrichment and Tort*, in *Private International Law in Mainland China, Taiwan and Europe* 245 (Jürgen Basedow & Knut B. Pissler eds, Mohr Siebeck 2014).

Liu, Tieh-Cheng & Chen, Rong-Chwan, *Liu and Chen on Private International Law* (國際私法論) (6th ed., San-Min 2018).

Ma, Herbert H.P., *General Part of Private International Law* (國際私法總論) (11th ed., Taipei 1983).

Ma, Herbert H.P., *Private International Law of the Republic of China: Past, Present and Future*, in *Private Law in the International Arena - Liber Amicorum Kurt Siehr* 413 (Jürgen Basedow et al. eds, T.M.C. Asser 2000).

Makarov, Aleksandr N., *Quellen des internationalen Privatrechts* (Mohr 3d ed. 1978)

Makarov, Aleksandr N., *Quellen des internationalen Privatrechts, Band I: Gesetzestexte* (Walter de Gruyter 2d ed. 1953).

Metzer, Alex, *Licence Contracts*, in 2 *Encyclopedia of Private International Law* 1150 (Jürgen Basedow et al. eds, Edward Elgar 2017).

Rabel, Ernst, 1 *The Conflict of Laws: A Comparative Study* (2d ed., The University of Michigan Press 1958).

Tsai, Hua-Kai, *Recent Developments in Taiwan's Private International Law on Family Matters*, in *Private International Law in Mainland China, Taiwan and Europe* 281 (Jürgen Basedow & Knut B. Pissler eds, Mohr Siebeck 2014).

Tseng, Wang-Ruu, *Private International Law in Taiwan – Company Law*, in *Private International Law in Mainland China, Taiwan and Europe* 349 (Jürgen Basedow & Knut B. Pissler eds, Mohr Siebeck 2014).

Wang, David J.W., *The Revision of Taiwan's Choice-of-Law Rules in Contracts*, in *Private International Law in Mainland China, Taiwan and Europe* 181 (Jürgen Basedow & Knut B. Pissler eds, Mohr Siebeck 2014).

Wang, Wen-Yeu ed., *Codification in East Asia* (Springer 2014).

Wu, Chen-Huan, *Recognition and Enforcement of Foreign Arbitration Awards in the Republic of China* (Chinese Arbitration Association 2005).

Yang, Chong-Shen et al., *New Theories of the Arbitration Law* (仲裁法新論) (Chinese Arbitration Association 2008).

Zheng, Henry R., *China's Civil and Commercial Law* (Lexis Pub 1988).

Selected Bibliography

Table of Cases

The numbers here refer to paragraph numbers.

Table of Cases

www.ingramcontent.com/pod-product-compliance
Lightning Source LLC
Chambersburg PA
CBHW071433230926
51846CB00001B/215
* 9 7 8 9 4 0 3 5 4 2 2 2 5 *